More Praise for *Advanced Presentations by Design*

"Whether as a manager or university lecturer, we are only as effective as the buy-in we get. This marvelous book should be required reading for all managers and educators. I was embarrassed to see my own failings written up in cold print."

—**Tim Ambler,** senior fellow, London Business School, and
author of *Marketing and the Bottom Line*

"If you could turn your typical thirty-page PowerPoint presentation into one effective page that comprehensively states your case, engages your audience, and generates the results you want, would you do it? This book shows you how."

—**Hedy Lukas,** vice president, integrated marketing
communication, Kimberly-Clark Corporation

"Dr. Abela's ten-step process leads you through a logical approach to presentation development so that your audiences hear your message with absolute clarity. It will change the way you practice!"

—**Nancy L. Losben,** R.Ph., CCP, FASCP,
chief quality officer, Omnicare, Inc.

"If even half the strategy and market intelligence functions among the Fortune 500 took Dr. Abela's advice, corporate productivity would take a huge step forward. He brings together tried and true disciplines in such a unique way that anyone who wants to stay on top of their game will welcome this playbook."

—**Craig Albright,** vice president, finance,
Xerox Global Services, Xerox Corporation

"Dr. Abela's book will give you the skills and a comprehensive and methodical approach that will be instrumental to going beyond being a mere purveyor of data to a trusted advisor."

—**J. David Phillips,** group manager, market intelligence and planning,
EMEA (Europe, Middle East and Africa), Microsoft Corporation

"Dr. Abela expertly weaves all elements together—the audience, the story, the presentation of the story—and backs it up with reams of research from all disciplines."

—**Karen L. Fuller,** former director, global brand research, Dell Inc.

"Dr. Abela's book will give you a structured approach—which our whole company now uses—to more easily prepare impressive presentations whether for important client meetings or small internal meetings. Having the Extreme Presentation method in our arsenal enables us to provide higher value to our clients."

—**Denis McFarlane,** CEO and founder, Infinitive Corporation

"What makes this book different from other books on presentation design is that it weaves the importance of telling a powerful story throughout the ten-step process of presentation development. I guarantee you will achieve success if you follow the approach outlined in this book."

—**Lori Silverman,** author and editor of *Wake Me Up When the Data Is Over:
How Organizations Use Stories to Achieve Results*, and co-author of *Stories Trainers Tell*

About This Book

Why is this topic important?

All your hard work—your ideas, your research, your plans, your effort—comes to nothing if you cannot convince others to act on it. The way we get people to act in organizations today is to make a presentation. And yet the quality—and the effectiveness—of the average presentation today is abysmal. We are all afflicted by a plague of "Death by PowerPoint™" and, seemingly, we do not know what to do about it. There is plenty of advice on how to create presentations, but *it is this very advice that caused the plague in the first place,* and so following it will not provide the cure.

What can you achieve with this book?

This book overturns much of the conventional wisdom and practice of creating presentations to provide a comprehensive and yet easy-to-use ten-step method for *designing presentations that propel your audience to action.* This method is focused *exclusively* on designing your presentations, not on delivering them, for the simple reason that if your *content* is not interesting and persuasive in itself, then most likely you have lost the game before you even begin presenting. The ten-step method shows you how to take your ideas and information and turn them into a compelling set of slides. The method is grounded in hundreds of empirical studies on different aspects relevant to presentation, and it has been field-tested among leading corporations, including Dell, Microsoft, ExxonMobil, Kimberly-Clark, Motorola, and eBay.

How is this book organized?

The book is divided into five parts, covering the five essential dimensions of an effective presentation: politics (audience analysis and persuasion), metrics (objectives and success measurement), logic (argument and evidence), rhetoric (storytelling), and graphics (visuals). Each of the parts contains an introduction to explain why that dimension is important. The individual chapters then contain material that explains how to implement each of the ten steps in the method. The first page of each chapter gives an overview of the step, so if you are in a hurry you can just read the first page of each chapter and obtain a quick overview of the method.

About Pfeiffer

Pfeiffer serves the professional development and hands-on resource needs of training and human resource practitioners and gives them products to do their jobs better. We deliver proven ideas and solutions from experts in HR development and HR management, and we offer effective and customizable tools to improve workplace performance. From novice to seasoned professional, Pfeiffer is the source you can trust to make yourself and your organization more successful.

Essential Knowledge Pfeiffer produces insightful, practical, and comprehensive materials on topics that matter the most to training and HR professionals. Our Essential Knowledge resources translate the expertise of seasoned professionals into practical, how-to guidance on critical workplace issues and problems. These resources are supported by case studies, worksheets, and job aids and are frequently supplemented with CD-ROMs, websites, and other means of making the content easier to read, understand, and use.

Essential Tools Pfeiffer's Essential Tools resources save time and expense by offering proven, ready-to-use materials—including exercises, activities, games, instruments, and assessments—for use during a training or team-learning event. These resources are frequently offered in looseleaf or CD-ROM format to facilitate copying and customization of the material.

Pfeiffer also recognizes the remarkable power of new technologies in expanding the reach and effectiveness of training. While e-hype has often created whizbang solutions in search of a problem, we are dedicated to bringing convenience and enhancements to proven training solutions. All our e-tools comply with rigorous functionality standards. The most appropriate technology wrapped around essential content yields the perfect solution for today's on-the-go trainers and human resource professionals.

Pfeiffer
www.pfeiffer.com

Essential resources for training and HR professionals

I dedicate this book to the loves of my life: my wife Kathleen and our children, Theresa, Dominic, Monica, John Paul, Lucy, and our new baby who is arriving shortly.

ADVANCED PRESENTATIONS BY DESIGN

Creating Communication That Drives Action

Andrew V. Abela, Ph.D.

Pfeiffer

A Wiley Imprint
www.pfeiffer.com

Published by Pfeiffer
A Wiley Imprint
989 Market Street, San Francisco, CA 94103-1741 www.pfeiffer.com

Library of Congress Cataloging-in-Publication Data

Abela, Andrew V.
    Advanced presentations by design : creating communication that drives action / Andrew V. Abela.
        p.   cm.
    Includes bibliographical references and index.
    ISBN 978-0-7879-9659-8 (pbk.)
        1. Business presentations.   2. Business communication.   I. Title.
    HF5718.22.A24   2008
    658.4'52—dc22
                                                                        2008021035

Acquiring Editor: Matthew Davis   Marketing Manager: Brian Grimm

Director of Development: Kathleen Dolan Davies   Editor: Rebecca Taff

Developmental Editor: Susan Rachmeler   Editorial Assistant: Lindsay Morton

Production Editor: Michael Kay   Manufacturing Supervisor: Becky Morgan

Printed in the United States of America

Printing   10 9 8 7 6 5 4 3 2 1

Contents

Foreword

We've all sat through them—stultifying corporate presentations marked by endless bullets, irrelevant detail, and plenty of not-so-discrete BlackBerry scrolling among the audience members. Poking fun at presentations is as cliché as joking about airline food.

Because of my company's business model and my specific role, I am unusually attuned to the importance of presentation quality. My company, the Corporate Executive Board (CEB), forms memberships of senior executives (e.g., Chief Finance Officers, Chief Marketing Officers, Chief Human Resources Officers), identifies their collective problems, and searches the network for innovative solutions. We then teach these insights back to the network through a variety of channels, often through live presentation. As executive director, I'm responsible for the quality of both our research and our presentation to members.

Across seventeen years in my role, I've become convinced of how crucial the "last mile" of communication is to driving organizational impact. CEB's membership for compensation executives (the Compensation Roundtable), for example, recently demonstrated quantitatively that more than a quarter of the value of compensation can be lost based on how it is communicated to employees.

Given the importance of this "last mile," I'm struck by just how much variance exists in the quality of presentation skills. I've seen high school students energize a room, and I've seen bright, insightful, practically minded heads of Communication in large companies put an audience to sleep. My point is simply that compelling presentation of complex ideas is extraordinarily difficult and that strong presentation skills cannot be assumed for any organizational level or role.

So what separates winners from losers in creating high-impact presentations? At a high level, Dr. Abela teaches us that effective presentations are grounded in deep understanding of our audience members—their needs, assumptions, and learning styles. And at the practical level, he shows us that the techniques of high-impact presentation are empirically knowable. Unlike other writers on effective communications, Dr. Abela approaches presentation impact as a research project, collecting extensive quantitative evidence about what actually works.

For many years, I worked with Dr. Abela, applying the principles of effective presentation to teach management insights to executives. He has now developed a method that applies to a full range of presentation types, from business case creation to training to data-oriented analysis to sales.

Importantly, Dr. Abela has road-tested every idea he presents here with a variety of constituencies in highly acclaimed, hands-on corporate workshops. These workshops prove that effective presentation disciplines are learnable by you and me.

While the underlying principles Dr. Abela espouses are timeless, his book is coming at an important time. The ability to influence others is in the ascendant, whether it be to coordinate solution selling, align functions to improve the brand experience, activate customer insights, or improve the effectiveness of alliances. As a result, his contribution to the field couldn't be coming at a better time. This book will be an important resource for anyone interested in boosting his or her personal effectiveness or the effectiveness of a team.

Pope Ward
Executive Director,
The Corporate Executive Board
Washington, D.C.
April 2008

Acknowledgments

There are many people to whom I owe thanks for the help they provided in the development of the Extreme Presentation method and this book. My earliest clients' willingness to take a chance on the as-yet-untested Extreme Presentation methodology was an important source of encouragement. At Microsoft, Steven Silverman's comments about presentation design after a speech I gave there triggered the initial idea to create the Extreme Presentation method, and our subsequent phone and email interactions were critical to its early development. His colleagues David Phillips and Helen Hopper provided the forum for the first-ever Extreme Presentation workshop, at the International Market Intelligence meeting they organized in Paris in early 2005, and Lee Dirks, Nicolas Façon, and particularly Kimberly Engelkes were instrumental in setting up the ongoing series of day-long Advanced Presentation Design workshops at Microsoft headquarters in Redmond, Washington.

Jeff Drake, Hedy Lukas, Rodrigo Sampera, and Janice Treanor at Kimberly-Clark, Joan Bassett and Melanie Wing at Chase Card Services, Karen Fuller at Dell, Nancy Losben at NeighborCare (now part of Omnicare), Craig Albright at Xerox, Julie Moll at Marriott, Stew McHie and Betty Hoyt at Exxon-Mobil, and Robert Colosi at the U.S. Census Bureau were the early adopters of the Extreme Presentation workshop, all of whom provided important feedback that was instrumental to the further development of the method.

Over the years Gene Zelazny's books, *Say It with Charts* and *Say It with Presentations*, have been very helpful to me, and more recently I have also found inspiration in both Cliff Atkinson's *Beyond Bullet Points* and Garr Reynolds' *Presentation Zen*.

Other people whose help I wish to acknowledge include Paul Radich for his help on every aspect of delivering the workshops; Lori Silverman for her insights into storytelling and for introducing me to her publisher Matt Davis; Mark Randall and Michelle Gallina, CEO and VP of marketing, respectively, at Serious Magic (now part of Adobe) for the initial inspiration about ballroom and conference room style presentations; Rob Headrick for creating most of the graphics used in the workshop and this book; and Mark Ryland at Mpower Media.

The true guinea pigs for the elements that would become the Extreme Presentation method were the students in my Marketing Management and Market Research courses at the Catholic University of America, and in particular those in the Spring 2005 session of MGT 546: Missy Boiseau, Tim Burke, Chris Carrelha, Ashley Chinnici, Bill Cooper, Caroline Costa, Lindsay Fleming, Erin Galterio, Tara Hewlett, Laura Kaye, Kathryn

Kennedy, Dana Losben, Jane Maybury, Kaitlin McKernan, Kirsten Nagel, Ryan Parrish, Brendan Price, Micky Sielecki, and Nick Thomas.

Gathering all the empirical research that was relevant to presentation design was a labor of love for me, but labor nonetheless, because the research was difficult to find, scattered as it is across so many different disciplines. I found invaluable help in the form of a number of outstanding bibliographies. Scott Armstrong provided me with early drafts of his forthcoming masterpiece *Persuasive Advertising*, and it was in reviewing these that I first realized that much more empirical research exists that is relevant to presentation design than most people think. I also found a number of empirical studies in the enormous bibliography in Till Voswinckel's master's thesis on presentation, and Robert Befus' Presentation Facts column in the Visual Being 'blog provided in-depth reviews of some of the seminal presentation design research.

I am also grateful to all the colleagues from whom I have learned so much about presentation design and communication throughout my career: Pete Buer, Derek van Bever, Pope Ward, Tim Pollard, Molly Maycock, Eric Braun, Katherine Evans, Michael Hubble, and Jonathan Dietrich at the Corporate Executive Board; David Court, Roger Dickhout, Nora Aufreiter, Howard Lis, John Melin, John Takerer, Stefan Wisniowski, Patrick Pichette, Tim McGuire, Steve Bear, Toni Sacconaghi, Mehrdad Baghai, MaryAnn Lowry, and Diane Nellis at McKinsey & Co.; and Colleen Jay, Jamie McClelland, Tracy Porter, Cheryl Row, and Robert Shaw at Procter & Gamble.

I would also like to thank the editorial team at Pfeiffer, and particularly acquiring editor Matt Davis, developmental editor Susan Rachmeler, production editor Michael Kay, editor Rebecca Taff, and editorial assistant Lindsay Morton.

Introduction

THE PURPOSE OF THIS BOOK is no less than a complete reinvention of the way presentations are designed. There is a general agreement that the current state of practice in presentation design is appalling. "Death by PowerPoint"—being subjected to slide after countless slide of tedious bullet points—is ubiquitous. There is no consensus on the cause of this bad situation: some blame presentation programs, others blame presentation skills. I think that it is a question of skills, but not so much that presentation design skills are *lacking*, but rather that they are hindered by the *bad presentation design advice that is commonly given*—and the numerous *bad examples* that we are all subjected to regularly.

To combat this negative situation, this book offers a practical, ten-step method for creating successful presentations, where "successful presentations" means presentations that get people to act on the information you present. By following this method you will unlearn all the harmful advice you have been subjected to, and start seeing immediate impact from your presentation efforts.

In this Introduction, we will explore exactly why we need to reinvent the way we design presentations, describe briefly the ten-step Extreme Presentation™ method for presentation design, and talk about how exactly to begin.

Why Do We Need to Reinvent the Way We Design Presentations?

The reason that we need to reinvent the way we design presentations is that, while the presentation challenge is greater than it has ever been, presenters are still being given the same—wrong—advice about how to design presentations.

The Presentation Challenge Is Greater Than Ever

The challenges facing anyone making a presentation today are greater than they have ever been, just at the time when the need to present complex information effectively has become more important than ever. In an environment of steadily increasing competitive intensity, solid quantitative analysis has become central to competitive success.[1]

And yet, all the most effective analysis is useless if it is not communicated effectively within the organization. The conclusions from the analysis have to move from the mind of the analyst to the mind of the decision-makers and those who will implement those decisions—and the most common way for this to happen today is through a presentation.

[1]Davenport (2006) argues that a strong analytical approach has become essential to competitive success.

[2] A survey of marketers found that effective *communication* is considered to be more important than the analysis of the information itself (Clark, Abela, & Ambler, 2006).

[3] A study by the Institute of Psychiatry in London found, amusingly, that participants who were interrupted with emails performed worse on IQ tests than participants who were under the influence of marijuana (Johnson, 2005).

And yet the challenge of getting your message through to your audience is greater than ever, for several reasons. Audiences are overwhelmed with information.[2] They are much busier, due to globalization and outsourcing. They are distracted by their cell phones and wireless email devices.[3] People are so easily distracted that Hollywood comedy writers now find that to hold their audience's attention they need to provide a new punch line or gag every *fourteen seconds*.

Audiences are also much more skeptical, because of their incessant exposure to "spin" in both political and corporate communication. They have learned to be critical of what they hear, so they are going to be critical of your presentation. Audiences have also become very aesthetically demanding, because their standards of visual excellence have been raised by the extraordinarily high quality in today's digital media: websites, television news, movie special effects, and video games. Every time you project a slide, you are competing, at least at a subconscious level, with every other piece of digital media that your audience has ever seen.

We are working in an age in which complex analysis is essential to success, and yet communicating the conclusions from such analysis is more difficult than ever. What do we have to help us with this challenge? Unfortunately, mostly lots of bad advice and bad examples.

Current Presentation Standards—Space Age, or Sophomoric?

Current techniques for presentation design are inadequate to the challenge. Although presentation tools such as PowerPoint™ keep getting more and more powerful with each new release, people's use of it is not necessarily getting any better. Many people blame the program for poor presentations; I think that the issue is more complex than that. (See the discussion, Should You Use PowerPoint, in the introduction to the Graphics section of this book).

Usually, the more complex a problem, the more sophisticated and powerful the tools and techniques for addressing it. This, unfortunately, does not appear to be the case with presentations. Look at the slides in Figures I.1a and I.1b. These are two typical PowerPoint slides. Figure I.1a was created by some of my undergraduate students (before they learned the method described in this book). No need to read the text; just look at the layout.

Compare this slide with the one in Figure I.1b. This second slide was created by the U.S. Department of Energy, as part of a presentation designed to convince allies that Iran was developing nuclear weapons. Again, do not bother to read the text—just compare the layouts.

The two slides are very similar. In essence, both college sophomores and nuclear scientists are using exactly the same technology in exactly the same way. That does not make sense: the complexity and consequences of each situation are vastly different. In the one case, the most that is at stake is the students' grade for that course, which, although it may seem very important to them at the time, is not that momentous. In the other case, the consequences include potential nuclear war.

FIGURE I.1A.   College Sophomore Slide   **FIGURE I.1B.   Nuclear Scientist Slide**

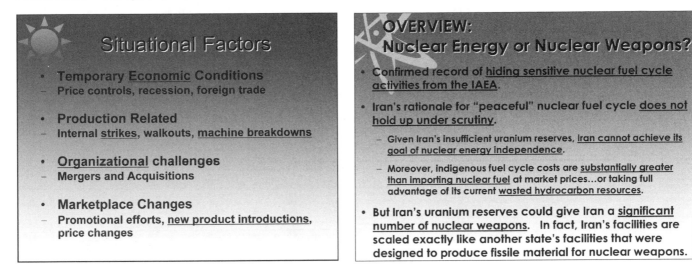

Worse yet—according to research, this kind of slide, with lots of bulleted text and no relevant visuals, is not very effective. Presenting a slide like either of these while speaking is ironically less effective than speaking *without* slides, or presenting the slides and keeping your mouth shut! This is because your audience is trying to read your slides and listen to you at the same time, and therefore they can do neither properly. The slides in Figures I.1a and b are perhaps the most typical presentation slides. They are standard practice. And this standard practice is the worst possible approach.[4]

[4]There is extensive evidence of this conflict between narration and slide text in presentations (e.g., Mayer, 2001). See Chapter 8 for a discussion of this research.

How did we get to this point? The answer to this is not clear, but it probably has a lot to do with the bad advice that is passed around, and the bad examples that we are exposed to.

Bad Advice

One example of bad advice widely propagated is the claim that only 7 percent of communication comes through words; the rest comes from non-verbal communication: 38 percent from tone of voice and 55 percent from body language. Did you ever wonder whether this was actually true? It does seem a little odd: Is a wink more effective than hard facts when you're pitching a proposal to senior executives?

The claim is false—or more precisely, its application to presentations is completely unsubstantiated. The origin of the claim is in some research done by Albert Mehrabian (1981). The thing is, Mehrabian's work was focused exclusively on personal communication about feelings of like or dislike: when people are talking to one another about how much they like/dislike each other. *It has absolutely no relevance to presentations!* In Mehrabian's own words, commenting on this abuse of his work: "This and other equations regarding relative importance of verbal and nonverbal messages were derived from experiments dealing with communications of feelings and attitudes (i.e., like-dislike). Unless a communicator is talking about . . . feelings or attitudes, *these equations are not applicable*" (Mehrabian, 2007; emphasis added).

Another example of bad advice is the recommendation that slides should contain no more than seven bullet points of no more than seven words per bullet. Ironically, it turns out that this is exactly the *wrong* amount of text to include on your slide, and again, the research that this advice is supposedly based on in fact has no relevance to presentations at all (see the introduction to Part IV for more on this).

Bad Examples

Another source of bad PowerPoint is the large amount of bad presentation examples that are delivered in conference rooms around the world every day. Worst of all, though, is the bad example set by some otherwise excellent presenters. Look at the slide in Figure I.2. This slide is from a presentation given by a very popular and dynamic business guru who is an outstanding speaker. Is this a good slide? I don't think so, for the same reasons that the slides in Figure I.1a and b are not—and yet it is typical of many of the other two hundred or so slides that this speaker delivered in the same presentation.

What is going on here? I think the situation is reminiscent of the impact that Johnny Weissmuller, an actor who played Tarzan in many early 20th century movies, had on competitive swimming. Weissmuller, in addition to being a famous actor, was also a world champion swimmer, winning five Olympic gold medals and setting sixty-seven world records in swimming. He had a style of swimming that was all his own—in fact, it was named the "Weissmuller crawl"—that involved swimming with his head fully extended out of the water. Apparently, a generation of swimmers copied this style, thinking it was the key

FIGURE I.2. Is This a Good Slide?

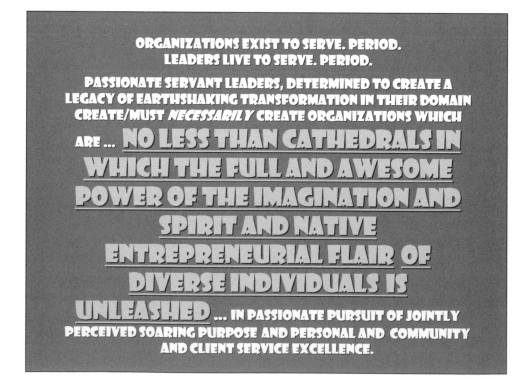

to his success. Eventually, however, it was found that the style is in fact quite suboptimal. Weissmuller, it turns out, was so powerful a swimmer that he succeeded *despite*, not because of, his unique style. Why did he swim this way? We do not know for sure, but his son thinks that it is because Weissmuller learned to swim in polluted waters and wanted to avoid swallowing any garbage. (Weismuller & Reed, 2002).

In the same way, we appear to have mindlessly followed the presentation design of great presenters, apparently never questioning whether they are great because of, or *despite*, their slides.

The Problem of Presenter-Focus and the Seven Deadly Mistakes of Presentation Design

The core problem seems to be that presentation advice and tools have been developed for the benefit of the presenter, not the audience[5]. This explains why the standard defaults in programs like PowerPoint are so popular and yet so ineffective. Bullet points that are slowly revealed one at a time, or 3D rendering of charts, may make presenters feel professional and safe, but it turns out that they actually *reduce* your audience's interest in your message and their ability to understand it.

[5]Voswinckel (2005), in a three-hundred-page dissertation on the state of presentation theory and practice, concludes that presentation programs such as PowerPoint appear to be designed for the convenience and benefit of the presenter, not the audience.

As a result of this presenter-oriented approach, several bad design habits have evolved that weaken presentation effectiveness terribly. The following are some of worst ones, with suggestions for how to avoid them, in order to start creating presentations that are designed to serve audiences, not presenters.

Mistake 1. Assuming that your audience has the same personality and communication preferences as you do. Unless you consciously consider the kinds of personalities that are likely to be in your audience, you will end up designing your presentation so that it satisfies your own personality type only. If you are a detail-oriented person, you will create a presentation with seventy-five slides full of delicious detail, and the more conceptually inclined people in your audience will be suicidal by slide number nine. If you are a conclusions- and action-oriented person, you will present your key recommendation up-front, without necessarily mentioning any of the other options you have considered, and the more cautious people in the room will think you are much too hasty, feel uncomfortable, and be unwilling to agree to your proposal. This is a big problem if they happen to be the decision-makers in the audience. (See Chapter 1 for more on how to avoid this mistake.)

Mistake 2. Setting presentation objectives in terms of what the presenter intends to do. Your objectives should not be about what you—the presenter—intend to do in your presentation. Those are not objectives; they're your *agenda*. Your *objectives* should be about *how your audience will change* as a result of your presentation: how they will think and act differently after they leave the room. If their thinking or behavior is not changed as a result of your presentation, then why are you wasting their time—or yours? (See Chapter 2.)

Mistake 3. Focusing on what you want from your audience.   Most of the time, you deliver a presentation because you want something from your audience. You are selling a product, an idea, or a new set of skills. Why else would you go through the bother of writing and delivering a presentation? But that's *your* motivation for being there. What is *their* motivation for listening to you? The only reason your audience is listening to you is that they are hoping for some information that will help them solve one of the many problems they are facing in life. If you want to capture and keep their attention, focus your *entire* presentation deliberately and undividedly on solving an important problem of *theirs*. (See Chapter 3.)

Mistake 4. Only including evidence that supports your recommendation.   It is tempting to include only facts and arguments that support the case you are making in your presentation, because you want to strengthen your case, not weaken it. However, all the empirical research confirms that audiences will find you more credible—and more convincing—if you also include the arguments against your recommendation, and then carefully rebut each one of them. Lawyers call this "stealing thunder": if you bring up an objection first, that objection has far less force than if someone in your audience does. (See Chapter 4.)

Mistake 5. Presenting your information in the order that makes most sense to you.   Typically, presenters put their material into some kind of logical order, an order that makes sense—to them. You want to cover, say, the background, the opportunity, the strategic imperative, the competitive environment, the financial implications, the human resource implications, and so on. Boring. Begin your presentation with a pressing problem that your audience has (see Mistake 2 above) and then tell them your proposed solution. Here's the important part: to decide where to go next, ask yourself, "If I were to stop right here, what is the first objection that would come from the audience?" Your response to that objection is what your next point should be. Make that point, and then repeat the question. This way you will progressively design a presentation sequenced in the way your audience wants to hear it, not in some arbitrary order that seems to make sense to you. (See Chapter 6.)

Mistake 6. Using color, sound, and clip art to make your presentation look professional.   Adding all the embellishment that PowerPoint allows you to may make you *feel* more professional, but it harms your communication. The research is unambiguous here also: any added color, sound, or image that does not directly reinforce the specific message on your slide will distract your audience from that message. Animated slide transitions, in particular, are almost universally destructive. (See Chapter 7.)

Mistake 7. Using your slides as prompts.   Perhaps the very worst example of developing a presentation for the benefit of the presenter rather than for the audience is the use of slides to prompt the speaker. You've seen this kind of presentation: slide after slide of bullet points, so that the poor presenter won't forget what he intended to say. Yet, as we noted above, when you project slides filled with bullet points while speaking at the same time, your bullets and your voice compete with each other, with the result that your communication effectiveness is worse than either if you projected your slides and asked your audience to read them (while you keep quiet) or if you spoke without any slides at all. If you are going to use visuals, make sure that they support, rather that vie with, your spoken comments. One way to do this is to use more graphics and less text (several research studies conclude that, while voice and text compete with each other, voice and graphics reinforce each other). Another way is to ensure that every slide you design passes the "squint test": if you squint at the slide, so that none of the text is legible, the layout of the slide alone should communicate or at least reinforce the main point of the slide. (See Chapter 8.)

Good Advice, Not Applied

Fortunately, there have been some good developments that are useful for presentation design over the past several years, in four different areas: storytelling, graphics, logical problem solving, and influence skills. Work in each of these areas can be applied to improve our presentation design efforts. (See Appendix D for references in each of these areas). *Unfortunately*, though, very little of this good work seems to be reflected in your average PowerPoint presentation. Why is this? Three possible reasons. First, while much of the work in these areas is very insightful, it can still be challenging to apply it. Second, where exactly should one begin: Storytelling? Graphics? Logic? It is not necessarily clear. Finally, how does one integrate all the theories and good advice in order to create a presentation that actually tells a good story, is logical, persuasive, and graphically engaging?

And that is what this book is all about. Creating a presentation that gets your audience to act on your information has become a very difficult challenge—in fact, an extreme challenge, because of the overwhelmed, distracted, demanding, and skeptical audiences— which is why it needs an extreme solution: the Extreme Presentation™ method.

How to Reinvent Your Presentation: The Extreme Presentation™ Method

The Extreme Presentation method takes a marketing approach to presentation design: focusing on how to "sell" your ideas to your audience. The method consists of the five essential elements of an effective presentation—which are also the five main parts of this book—and ten practical steps to put each of those elements into practice. Figure I.3 summarizes the method.

Look at Figure I.3. The circle in the center, with the word "impact" in it, indicates that the entire purpose of the message is to ensure that your presentation has an impact on your audience. Around that inner circle, the next ring contains the five essential elements of an effective presentation:

- **Logic:** to make sure that there is solid logic in your presentation and that your recommendations are robust;
- **Rhetoric:** to tell an interesting story, in a compelling way. Logic is important, but of no use to you if everyone has tuned out because they are bored;

FIGURE I.3. The Extreme Presentation Method

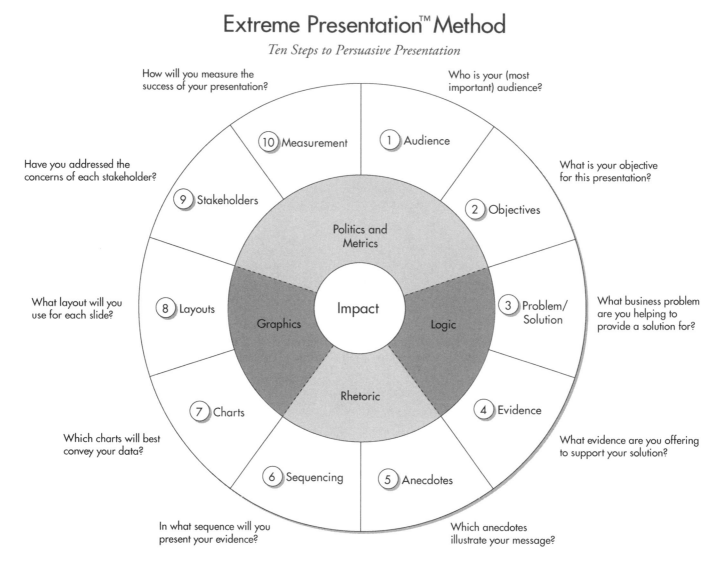

- **Graphics:** to make sure that you are using the most effective visual elements and overall layout;
- **Politics:** to apply the right influence skills to get your audience to take action; and
- **Metrics:** to be clear on what the specific objective is for the presentation, and how success will be measured.

Ten Steps for Developing an Extreme Presentation

There are two steps in each of the five elements, for a total of ten steps. These steps are:

1. *Audience:* Identify the communication preferences of the different personality types in your audience.
2. *Objectives:* Set specific objectives for what you want your audience to think and do differently after your presentation.

3. *Problem/Solution:* Identify a problem your audience has that your presentation will contribute to solving.

4. *Evidence:* List all the information that you think you may need to include in your presentation.

5. *Anecdotes:* Identify brief anecdotes that highlight your most important points.

6. *Sequencing:* Sequence your information so that it tells a compelling story.

7. *Graphics:* Identify the most effective graphical elements to use in your presentation.

8. *Layout:* Create slides that communicate your information concisely and effectively.

9. *Stakeholders:* Identify any potential roadblocks to achieving your objectives, and make a plan to deal with each.

10. *Measurement:* Decide how you will measure the success of your presentation.

One important thing to notice is that we do not draw any slides—in fact, we do not even launch PowerPoint—until Step 8, 80 percent of the way through the process. Typically, when you want to create a presentation, you open PowerPoint and start creating slides. Slide 1, slide 2 . . . slide 17 . . . what I am trying to say again? Am I making my point yet?

There are two problems with this approach. The first problem is that you can spend a lot of time creating slides that you do not end up using. You really do not have time to waste doing that. The second, and perhaps worse, problem is that you might end up including slides in your presentation that should not be there, because "Well, I spent three hours on that one, so there's no way I'm going to delete it!"

PowerPoint may be a useful design tool, but it is not a good thinking tool. The Extreme Presentation method encourages you to do your thinking *before* you start creating any slides, so that once you start creating them, you won't waste any time and you'll create only what you need.

The Importance of Iteration

The Extreme Presentation method in Figure I.3 is drawn in the shape of a circle to emphasize that it is an iterative process. The best presentations, like all good writing, are not *written*, they are *re-written*. So you need to become comfortable with iterating through the process—and with changing things on each iteration. In the workshop version of the Extreme Presentation method, we often use hotel desk bells to celebrate every time a participant changes something that's already been done, to signal and celebrate the fact that he or she is iterating, and therefore that the presentation is improving. Human beings tend to lock on to decisions they have already made. By iterating through the process, you try to break away from that and keep improving your presentation, rather than being tied to what you decided earlier.

The Main Insights in This Book, on One Page

This book contains three kinds of useful information: "know what," important guidelines about designing presentations that you need to know to be effective; "know why," the

TABLE I.1.   The Main Insights in This Book

KNOW WHAT (Guidelines to Follow)	KNOW WHY (Support for the Guidelines)	KNOW HOW (Tools for Applying the Guidelines)
1. Design your presentation to match the way different audience members like to receive information.	Different personality types need to be communicated to differently.	How to identify audience members' preferences for receiving information; How to modify your presentation to appeal to different preferences; How to handle multiple and apparently conflicting implications of audience preferences (particularly for a larger audience).
2. Be clear, before you begin designing your presentation, what your objectives are for the presentation in terms of how you want to change your audience's minds and actions.	Unless you have a clear idea of what you want your audience to think and do differently after your presentation, you will waste time and effort preparing it, and you may not succeed.	How to use the "from-to/think-do" matrix to clearly articulate your presentation objectives in terms of the attitudinal and behavioral changes you want from your audience
3. Position your presentation as offering a solution to an important problem that they have.	Unless you are solving an important problem for them, why are they listening to you?	How to identify the most relevant business problem for any situation; How to ensure that the solution you are offering is indeed the best alternative from your audience's point of view
4. Support your solution with a wide range of evidence.	Using evidence from multiple sources helps you solve the problem more comprehensively	How to generate your list of evidence; Sources for expanding your list of evidence; Particularly persuasive types of evidence to use.
5. Illustrate your more important points with interesting anecdotes.	Data is boring—stories are interesting.	Sources for good anecdotes; How to structure any anecdote using the Seven Basic Plots of all good stories
6. Sequence your entire presentation so that it tells a story.	You want to keep your audience's attention throughout the presentation. A story is more interesting and memorable than a list of points, no matter how logically they are organized.	How to decide what information should go into your presentation, and what you should put in the appendix or leave out entirely; How to decide in what sequence to present your information; The critical role of examples, and where to place them in your presentation; A checklist for evaluating your presentation outline.
7. Use lots of detail in your charts and diagrams.	Detail makes for more interesting presentations and engaging discussions, and improves your credibility.	How to select which type of chart to use, based on what you want to demonstrate with your data; How to incorporate large amounts of detail without overwhelming your slide; How to avoid "chart junk"; How to select the correct presentation idiom.
8. Ensure that the layout of each slide reinforces the main message of that slide.	A well-laid-out page organizes your detail so that your audience is engaged by it, not overwhelmed	Using the "squint test" to test your page layout; Thirty-six examples of effective page layouts; checklists for preparing and evaluating your slides.
9. Identify any other stakeholders (not in your audience) who could affect the success of your proposal.	The most effective presentation could be derailed afterwards by someone who wasn't present.	How to analyze stakeholders and their needs, and decide what proactive action to take.
10. Measure the effectiveness of your presentation.	You cannot improve if you don't know what worked and what didn't.	How to measure presentation effectiveness.

reasoning and evidence behind those guidelines; and "know how," helpful tools and techniques for doing the things you need to do to design an effective presentation. Table I.1 summarizes these for each chapter.

Where to Start . . .

If You Have an Important Presentation Due Soon (e.g., Tomorrow Morning)

Ideally, you will have time to read at least part of this book while you create your presentation. If you're short on time, read the first page of each chapter—nine pages in all—and this will give you a sufficient overview of the whole method. If you are *really* short on time, then jump ahead to Figure C.1 in the Conclusion to this book, which contains ten quick questions that will help you decide whether your presentation is going to be effective or not, and if not, where you should focus your efforts to fix it.

If You Have More Time

Read this book, chapter by chapter, and follow the step-by-step method to develop your presentation while reading the book. By the end of the book, you will have a presentation that will drive your audience to act on your recommendations. Or else pick and choose among the chapters, prioritizing where you think you need the biggest improvement; the ten questions in Figure C.1 in the book's Conclusion can help you decide which of these to focus on. The Extreme Presentation method is not all-or-nothing; use any part of it and your presentation design effectiveness will improve immediately. Use *all* of it and you will see a tremendous improvement.

What is covered in this book does require work. But it is work that pays off. In general, it should take you the same or less time working with this method than it takes you right now to create a presentation, with much more successful results.

The rest of this section describes how this book is different from all other presentation books, what the book is and is not about, and the structure of the book.

How This Book Is Different from All Other Presentation Books

This book is specifically designed for achieving impact in tough presentation situations, and in particular, situations that involve communicating complex information. It is solidly based on extensive empirical research and has been field-tested with some of the largest and most demanding companies in the world. And it provides a simple, step-by-step method for communicating even the most complex information in ways that will get your audience to act on it.

It proposes an approach to presentation design that is radically different from the conventional wisdom for designing effective PowerPoint presentations. This alone should be a good thing, because we can blame the conventional wisdom for the epidemic of "Death by PowerPoint," with its fifty-slide decks, innumerable bullet points, and "chart junk."

The reason this book is different is that the conventional wisdom is contradicted by recent research on a wide range of aspects of presentation design, as we noted above. And therefore a new approach to presentation design is needed, that is *supported by*, rather than *contradicted by*, the existing research. The recommendations in this book are supported by findings from hundreds of empirical studies from the fields of communication, psychology, education, marketing, and law. (Some of the most useful research on presentation has in fact been done by studying the impact of trial lawyers' presentations on juries' decisions.)

The method presented in this book has been field-tested with some of the largest and most demanding companies in the world. I have delivered, and continue to deliver, day-long workshops on the Extreme Presentation method at major corporations, including Dell, ExxonMobil, H.J. Heinz, Kimberly-Clark (makers of Kleenex, Huggies, and other popular brands), eBay, Motorola, WW Grainger, and Xerox. I have taught the method to my undergraduate students, and to smaller organizations, such as the municipal government of booming Chesterfield County, Virginia, and the dynamic and rapidly growing change-management firm Infinitive, which has trained its entire consulting staff in the Extreme Presentation method.

Perhaps the most definitive test of the method, though, has been in Redmond, Washington, at the headquarters of Microsoft Corporation, makers of PowerPoint, where hundreds of marketing and market research staff have been, and continue to be, trained on the Extreme Presentation method.

The Extreme Presentation method is comprehensive: it covers everything needed to create a powerful presentation—logic, storytelling, graphics, and influence—in a clear, step-by-step method.

Finally, the method is all about driving action. The fundamental assumption underlying the Extreme Presentation method, and this whole book, is that if your presentation is not going to drive change in how your audience thinks and acts, then why on earth are you wasting your time—and theirs? Every step of the method is focused on driving action.

What This Book Is—and Is Not—About

The book addresses questions such as:

- How do I turn a pile of data and analysis into an interesting story?
- How do I decide what should go into my presentation and what should be excluded?
- How much detail should I put on each slide?
- Should I use clip art?
- How do I use graphics to communicate more clearly?

- How do I adapt my presentation to different audiences?
- What do I have to do to ensure that my presentation grabs and keeps my audience's attention?
- How do I communicate complex, detailed ideas in ways that they can be understood?
- And most importantly: how do I design a presentation so that my audience will act on my recommendations?

There are two things that this book is *not* about, however. First, it is not about the mechanics of using PowerPoint, or any other presentation software. There are many good books already in print on this topic. Second, this book is exclusively about presentation *design*; it is not about presentation *delivery*. This is because there are many places you can go to learn to improve the art of public speaking, but none to my knowledge that are focused exclusively on *designing* an effective presentation. And yet if your presentation design is poor, then (unless you are an unusually gifted speaker), your presentation will be doomed to mediocrity before you even begin.

The Structure of This Book

The book is divided into five parts, covering the five essential components of an effective presentation (metrics, politics, logic, rhetoric, and graphics). The introduction to each of these parts focuses on the *why* of what is covered in the subsequent chapters. The chapters themselves then give explanations of *what* to do and *how* to do it. Each chapter begins with a summary approximately one page in length; if you are in a hurry, all you have to do is read these first pages of each of the nine chapters. The book also includes a number of appendices: Appendix A provides a set of worksheets that you can photocopy and use as you develop your presentation; B is a comprehensive case example of a typical PowerPoint presentation redesigned according to the Extreme Presentation method; C provides a set of sample slide layouts that you can use; D and E provide lists of additional resources and readings.

Electronic copies of the worksheets in Appendix A, along with other useful materials, are available at www.ExtremePresentation.com.

The best way to use this book is to work through a presentation of your own while you are reading the book: a presentation that you are already working on, one that you know is coming up in the near future, or one that you have already delivered but you would like to improve because you know you will have to deliver it again.

PART I
POLITICS AND METRICS

IN THIS FIRST PART OF THE BOOK, we will cover two of the five essential elements of an effective presentation: politics—understanding and influencing your audience—and metrics—setting a clear objective for the presentation and measuring whether you have achieved that objective. In this introductory section I will discuss why you should spend the time to consider the different personality types in your audience, and why you should set specific goals about what you want your audience to think and do differently after your presentation, and then in Chapters 1 and 2 I will explain how to do each of these things.

Politics

Different people have different learning styles and preferences for receiving information. If you can adapt your communication to these different styles, then your presentations will be more effective.[1]

The problem, of course, is that most presentations are to an audience of more than one person—a group of mixed personalities—so how do you adapt your communication to different personalities? Should you even try? This section will review some of the different methods for assessing personality types and learning styles, and then answer the question of whether you should try such assessment.

There are a number of helpful taxonomies of learning styles. Two of the most popular are the Perceptual Learning Styles and the Index of Learning Styles. There are seven Perceptual Learning Styles: print (people who prefer to learn by reading), aural (listening), interactive (talking and discussing ideas), visual (viewing pictures, charts, and demonstrations), haptic (touching), kinesthetic (moving around), and olfactory (tasting and smelling—see James & Galbraith, 1985).

The Index of Learning Styles contains four dimensions: active (learn by doing) versus reflective (learn by thinking about the subject), sensing (absorb facts) versus intuitive (discover relationships and possibilities), visual (pictures) versus verbal (words), and sequential (follow logical steps) versus global (leap to insight).[2]

A third taxonomy that can be helpful is the popular Myers-Briggs Type Indicator® (MBTI). The MBTI describes personality preferences in terms of four dimensions. These are "favorite world": Introversion (focus on inner world) and Extraversion (focus on outer

[1]McFarland, Challagalla, & Shervani (2006), in researching salesperson interactions with buyers, found that the most successful ones adapt their influence tactics to suit their different customers.

[2]Felder and Spurlin's (2005) review of the research on the Index of Learning Styles concluded that it is both valid and reliable.

[3]See Myers, McCaulley, Quenk, & Hammer, 1998. For more information on the MBTI, see the website of the Myers-Briggs Foundation, www.myersbriggs.org/.

world); information: Sensing (focus on the basic information) and Intuition (focus on interpreting and adding meaning); decisions: Thinking (logic and consistency) and Feeling (people and circumstances); and structure: Judging (get things decided) and Perceiving (stay open to new information and options). One's personality type is written in terms of four letters, representing the person's preference in each dimension (e.g., ENTJ, ISTP, ISFJ, etc.—where Intuition is written as "N" so as not to confuse it with "I" of Introvert).[3]

So how do we deal with this variety of preferences? Even though people have different personality types and learning styles, it is possible to design your presentation so that it appeals to all types, and Chapter 1 will explain how to do this in some detail.

If we are going to design our presentations to appeal more or less to all types, do we even need to think about the differences? The answer is *yes*, because if you do not think explicitly about what kind of personality types or learning styles are going to be in your audience, and how best to communicate with them, then the danger is not that you will design your presentation in a generic way. The real and more likely danger is that *you will default to designing your presentation to match your own preferences*—which will work for the members of your audience who have a similar personality type to yours, but not for those who are different from you.

[4]ENTJ and ESTJ types represent 27 percent of managers, administrators, and supervisors (Macdaid, 1997). All other types, including all I's, F's, and P's, make up the other 73 percent.

Even if you have one of the two most common personality types in management (ENTJ or ESTJ in Myers-Briggs terms: that is, extraverted, judgment-oriented thinkers) and you are presenting to other managers, the odds are that you will still only be appealing to a minority of your audience. You will be routinely turning off all introverts, perceivers, and feelers, who represent almost *three-quarters of all managerial level employees*.[4]

If there is a particular person in your life with whom you always seem to have trouble communicating—who never seems to "get" what you are trying to say—then this could be the explanation: that individual has a very different personality type from yours. Therefore it is worth thinking consciously about the different personality types that are likely to be in the room each time you develop a presentation.

And sometimes you will face a situation in which you are presenting to only one person, or presenting to a group with only one decision-maker. In that case, you can emphasize the communication elements of your presentation that will most appeal to that person's type—allowing him or her to understand you better and more quickly, and be more easily persuaded.

[5]Both the reliability and the validity of the MBTI instrument have been challenged by Pittenger (2005). However, we use it here primarily to help recognize the variety of communication preferences audience members can have, and therefore this challenge is not directly relevant.

In this book we will use the MBTI because of its widespread popularity. The MBTI is a sophisticated assessment tool that should be administered by a qualified practitioner. However, its categories are also very useful for making a quick assessment of the personality types likely to be present in your audience, which you can then use to ensure that you are communicating in ways that appeal to everyone in your audience.[5] Chapter 1 will explain how to ensure that your presentation appeals to different preferences.

Metrics

At least since the 1960s, people have been aware of the importance of setting behavioral objectives for any kind of educational effort (Mager, 1962). More recently, marketing scholars and practitioners have focused on the essential role of setting objectives and measuring results as a way to demonstrate the effectiveness and efficiency of their efforts. In particular, they have identified the importance of both attitudinal and behavioral objectives: objectives for changing what the audience is thinking and doing (Ambler, 2003).

Yet people routinely develop presentations without a clear idea of the attitudinal and behavioral changes they are trying to achieve in their audiences. If you do not know what specific changes you are trying to achieve in your audience, then the chances are that you are going to waste time creating parts of your presentation that are not relevant to the specific objectives you need to achieve, or—worse—leave out important elements that you will need to achieve those objectives. In Chapter 2, I will describe how to develop attitudinal and behavioral objectives quickly and effectively.

Understanding What Types of Communication Will Be Most Effective for Your Audience

Step 1: Identify the Communication Preferences of the Different Personality Types in Your Audience

It is important to think through which personality types are likely to be in your audience, and what their communication preferences are, because it will help you consciously break out of the (unconscious) habit of designing a presentation to appeal only to those who share your own personality type. Even if you start out by deliberately designing your presentations to appeal to all types, if you routinely skip the step of thinking about the different personalities in the room, then there is a real risk that over time you will revert to accommodating only your own personality type preferences.

There are several considerations to keep in mind to avoid defaulting to a presentation design that appeals only to those who share your personality type.

If you like details, for example, keep in mind those who prefer the "big picture." If you like people to get to the point quickly, don't assume that everyone else is this way; speak also to those who want to know what other factors you have considered and rejected to get to this point. If you make your decisions based strictly on facts, expect that there will also be people in your audience for whom emotional considerations and people issues are of central importance.

For this first step of the Extreme Presentation process, you need to list the most important people in your audience (where "important" is defined as people whose minds or actions you need to change), estimate the personality type of each, and then work out the implications of each type for your presentation design. You can photocopy worksheets A.1a and A.1b in Appendix A and use them to list your most important audience members and their personality types and indicate the presentation implications of each (or you can download copies at www.ExtremePresentation.com).

This chapter will explain:

- How to estimate your audience's personality types
- How to match your presentation design to different personality types, especially when you expect to have multiple different personality types present in your audience (which is usually the case).
- What other information you could gather about your audience

How to Estimate Your Audience's Personality Types

You need to make a list of the most important people you are expecting to see in your audience, and try to estimate the personality type of each. The "most important" people in your audience are those whom you expect to have the most influence on whatever decision or action you are trying to encourage with your presentation. If you will be giving the same presentation to different audiences, then focus on whichever is the most important to you, or else design your presentation so that it will appeal to all audiences (more on this below).

In a perfect world, you would have each of your audience members fill out a formal MBTI assessment, but for most real-world conditions this is completely unrealistic. In firms that have made a significant investment in MBTI, different executives' types are known in the organization, and so you may already have the information you need if any of these particular executives happen to be your audience. For every other situation, though, you will need to make an informal assessment. I find the following questions helpful:

- Does the person seem to become energized from being alone (Introvert) or from being with people (Extravert)?
- Does the person respond to concepts (Intuition) or facts (Sensing)?
- Does the person seem more concerned with principles and things (Thinking) or with people (Feeling)?
- Does the person seem driven to closure (Judging) or to opening up further possibilities (Perceiving)?

As you go through and try to estimate the different personality types of your audience members, if you are unsure in any way about any dimension of any personality, then leave that part blank. *This is very important.* For example, if you know that Joseph in your audience is definitely an Extravert, but you are not sure how you would classify the rest of his personality, then write down an "E" and leave the rest blank. The meaning of a blank is that you will need to appeal to both sides of that dimension—because you do not know Joseph's preference. Therefore, a blank instead of a J or P means that you need to appeal to both J's and P's, so that whether Joseph is a J or a P, you will still be communicating properly to him. But if you guess that he is a J when in fact he is more of a P, then you will be presenting to him in a way that turns him off. It is always better to leave a blank than to make a wrong guess.

How to Match Your Presentation Design to Different Personality Types in the Same Audience

Once you have estimated the personality type of your most important audience members, then you can work out the presentation design implications for each of them and note these on Worksheet 1a from Appendix A.

Different personality types like to receive information in different ways, and are influenced accordingly. These ways are summarized in Table 1.1 and explained in detail below.[1]

As we noted above, in many cases, you are likely to have a mixture of personality types in your audience. In these cases you will need to design your presentation to appeal to all the types that could be present. There will probably also be some people whose personality types you do not know. The implication here is similar: with an unknown type, you need to design your presentation to appeal to *all* possible types, so that whichever one the person turns out to have, you'll be covered. In what follows, we describe how to design a presentation to appeal to each side of the four different MBTI dimensions, and also talk about how to address situations in which both sides are present or that personality dimension is unknown.

[1]For example, richer (multimedia) communication significantly increased online purchases of a complex product for iNtuitors and Feelers, but not for Sensors and Thinkers (Jahng, Jain, & Ramamurthy, 2002).

TABLE 1.1.   Communication Preferences of Different Personality Types

Personality Type	Typical Needs	Presentation Implications
Introvert vs. Extravert	• Time to reflect on information • Interactive discussion	• Provide all or part of presentation in advance • Plan for lots of discussion and Q&A
Sensor vs. iNtuitor	• The facts and (all) the details • The big picture	• Make sure to include all relevant facts and details in presentation or appendix • Provide overview up-front
Thinker vs. Feeler	• Principles involved, costs, benefits • Whom this is valuable for, and why	• Identify principles, costs, and benefits • State implications for each person or group of stakeholders involved
Judger vs. Perceiver	• Conclusions • Alternatives	• Present conclusions up front • List all alternatives considered

Based on Bacon (1996).

Introverts vs. Extraverts

The first consideration is your audience's "favorite world"—whether they are outer- or inner-focused, extraverted or introverted.

Introverts   Introverts need time to reflect on information that they receive. The implication is that you should try to provide all or part of your presentation material—or some other relevant pre-reading—to introverts in advance of the presentation, so that they have time to think about your material prior to your presentation, especially if you expect them to make a decision by the end of your presentation. If you do not give them information in advance, they will probably be less comfortable with your presentation and less likely to agree to your recommendations.

There are times when you may not feel comfortable providing your whole presentation in advance (because it is highly confidential, perhaps, or because setting the context correctly is critically important). In such cases, try to send at least part of your presentation, or even some other relevant pre-reading, so that your audience will be more prepared for your presentation. The goal in this step—as in every other step in the Extreme Presentation method—is not slavish adherence to a process. The idea is to improve the persuasiveness of your presentations. We're not striving for some theoretical ideal of perfection; we're just looking for an improvement over what you are doing right now. With introverts, *any* amount of pre-reading is going to be better than what you are sending them right now, which is probably nothing.

Extraverts   Extraverts, by contrast, need interactive discussion, so plan for lots of question-and-answer time during your presentation. If your presentation is scheduled to last one hour, do not expect to present more than thirty minutes' worth of material, because the rest of the time will be spent answering questions and engaging in discussion. Extraverts process information by talking about it. If you expect the extraverts in your audience to make a decision during your presentation, you will have to allow them time to "digest" your material by discussing it.

Some time ago I was sharing the Extreme Presentation method with an admiral of the U.S. Navy. His staff consists mainly of JAGs (judge advocate generals), who are all trained lawyers and mostly extraverts. His concern was that if he ever opened up his presentation to questions, the questioning would take over and he would lose control of his presentation. As I took him through this material, he came to see how such questioning is a sign that his people are absorbing the information that he is presenting to them, because extraverts process information by talking about it. (For more information on the "illusion of control" that presentation slides can give you, and why you are better giving that up, see Chapter 8 on layouts).

Both Introverts and Extraverts Together   If you expect to have both introverts and extraverts in your audience, then you need to get pre-reading material to the introverts and allow discussion time for the extraverts. How do you get pre-reading to the introverts only? Don't worry about that—send it to everyone in your audience; the extraverts will most likely ignore it.

You will also allow discussion time, which the extraverts will be sure to take advantage of. However, if you also want the input of the introverts, make sure to allow the discussion to go on long enough. Initially, while the extraverts jump in and start talking, the introverts will be listening to the discussion and processing it. Introverts will not speak up until they have had enough time to think, so be sure to allow the discussion to go long enough if you want their input. One way to do this is to allow silent pauses in the discussion to go on beyond the point that you would normally consider to be comfortable, because it can take that long for an introvert to decide to speak up. Other ways to draw introverts into the discussion include taking a "straw poll" and asking people to vote their preferences on a particular question (because once people have "expressed" their opinions by holding their hands up to vote, they are more likely to speak up), announcing a brief (two- to five-minute) exercise during which you will ask each audience member to write down their thoughts on the question and then share them, or breaking up the audience into small groups and asking them to discuss a particular point and then report back to the whole group.

Sensors vs. Intuitors

The second dimension is information: do audience members prefer to focus on the basic information they take in or do they prefer interpretation and added meaning? The former are called Sensors and the latter, Intuitors.

Sensors   Sensors need to see all the facts and all the details. These should be included on the presentation page or slide, or at least in an appendix.

Intuitors   Intuitors need the "big picture." To satisfy the intuitors in your audience, you need to provide an overview at the beginning of your presentation.

Both Sensors and Intuitors Together   This is one of the more challenging dimensions to address both sides simultaneously, and this is also where most people will stumble if they do not think explicitly about audience personality type and default to their own. If you are an intuitor, you tend to focus on the big picture, and the sensors in your audience may think you are a smooth-talking flake. If you are a sensor, you will present seventy-five slides of delicious (to you) detail, and the intuitors in the audience will want to shoot themselves (or you) before you reach slide 9.

The way to satisfy both sensors and intuitors is to provide both the concept and the details, ideally on the same page. For example, let's say that you are trying to communicate that your team has just assessed nineteen different new product concepts along three different criteria, and concluded that two of the ideas pass all the criteria. The sensors in your group will want to see what all of the nineteen ideas are, and what the criteria are, while the intuitors will really only be interested in the criteria and the two ideas that stood out. If you present all the details to satisfy the sensors, such as in the sample slide

FIGURE 1.1.   Poor Design: Overwhelming Detail

Assessment of New Product Concepts

- **19 Ideas Tested (Code Names)**
  1. Alpha: low-cost version
  2. Bravo: long-life version
  3. Charlie: extra strength
  4. Delta: durability positioning
  5. Echo: double strength
  6. Foxtrot: extreme positioning
  7. Golf: leisure version
  8. Hotel: vacation positioning
  9. India: high-growth aspect
  10. Juliet: high-risk option
  11. Kilo: lightweight option
  12. Lima: small-size option
  13. Mike: high-volume option
  14. November: longer-term option
  15. Oscar: luxury positioning
  16. Papa: reliability positioning
  17. Quebec: exotic positioning
  18. Romeo: higher-risk option
  19. Sierra: environmental option

- **Criteria for Testing**
  - Feasibility: Can the service be developed with the resources available?
  - Growth: Will the new service drive top-line growth for our firm?
  - Profitability: Will the new service deliver net incremental profit?

- **Winning Ideas**
  - 6: Foxtrot
  - 18: Romeo

in Figure 1.1, you are likely to overwhelm the intuitors in your audience. Alternatively, if you present only the big picture in something like Figure 1.2, to please the intuitors, then the sensors are going to be highly dissatisfied. What should you do?

In principle, the way to satisfy both those who are detail-oriented (sensors) and conceptually oriented (intuitors) is to ensure that the layout of your page reflects the idea or main message of the page, while the details are then placed around the page in appropriate locations. This way the intuitors are happy because they see the concept and ignore the details, while the sensors focus mostly on the details. For our example, we have drawn the three criteria as screens across the slide, shown which of the nineteen ideas are screened out at each point, and placed the two winning ideas on the right, as you can see in Figure 1.3. (For a lot more information on how to do this, see Chapter 8, on layout.)

Thinkers vs. Feelers

The third dimension is about making decisions. The two sides of this dimension are called Thinkers, who prefer first to look at logic and consistency when making decisions, and Feelers, who prefer first to look at the people and special circumstances involved.

Thinkers   To satisfy the thinkers in your audience, be sure to identify the principles, costs, and benefits involved with your recommendation.

Feelers   The feelers in your audience will want to know what the implications of your recommendations are for the different people and stakeholder groups involved in your project.

FIGURE 1.2.   Poor Design: Insufficient Detail

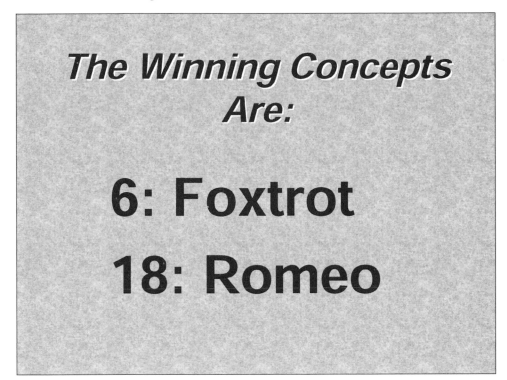

Both Thinkers and Feelers Together   At one level, satisfying both thinkers and feelers is easy. The two different groups are looking for different kinds of data (data about principles, costs, and benefits for the thinkers and data about people for the feelers), and so all you need to do is provide both kinds, and both groups will be happy.

Where it can become difficult, however, is when thinkers are presenting to feelers. Some thinkers have great difficulty addressing "people issues"; it is almost a matter of principle for them not to allow people considerations to interfere with the logic of the recommendation. Anything else, for them, would indicate bias and lack of professionalism.

If you are one of these thinkers, it may help you to keep in mind that people implications are just another form of data—you are merely describing those implications, which does not bias your recommendation in any way. For example, you may be recommending a change to a new, more efficient system for—say—expense reporting. You know that staff are going to resist the change, even though ultimately they will benefit by saving time and avoiding errors. While a thinker might be inclined to dismiss such resistance as irrational, to a feeler this would appear to be a serious flaw in your recommendation. To satisfy the feelers in your audience, you should recognize this potential for resistance as additional data, and show how you are planning to deal with it.

Judgers vs. Perceivers

The final dimension is about structure: in dealing with the outside world, do your audience members prefer to decide things right away, or do they prefer to stay open to new

FIGURE 1.3.   Good Design: Communicating Both Big Picture and Details Simultaneously

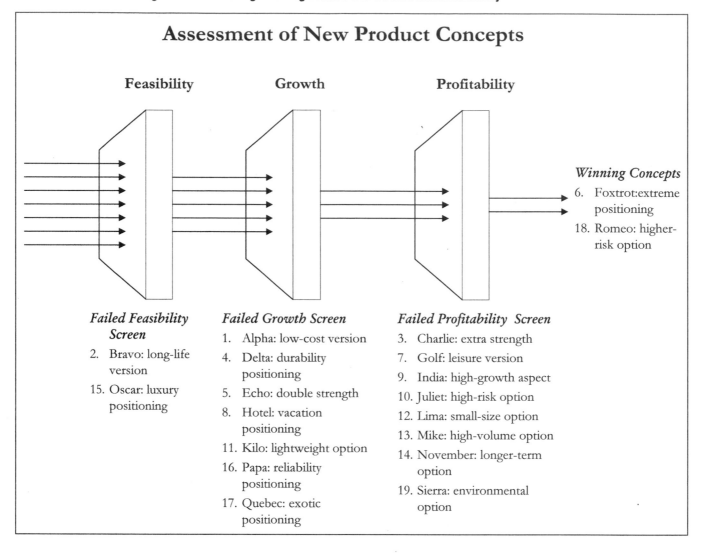

Assessment of New Product Concepts

Feasibility   Growth   Profitability

Winning Concepts

6. Foxtrot:extreme positioning

18. Romeo: higher-risk option

Failed Feasibility Screen

2. Bravo: long-life version

15. Oscar: luxury positioning

Failed Growth Screen

1. Alpha: low-cost version

4. Delta: durability positioning

5. Echo: double strength

8. Hotel: vacation positioning

11. Kilo: lightweight option

16. Papa: reliability positioning

17. Quebec: exotic positioning

Failed Profitability Screen

3. Charlie: extra strength

7. Golf: leisure version

9. India: high-growth aspect

10. Juliet: high-risk option

12. Lima: small-size option

13. Mike: high-volume option

14. November: longer-term option

19. Sierra: environmental option

information and options? The two sides of this dimension are referred to as Judgers and Perceivers, respectively.

Judgers   Judgers desperately need to know your conclusions up-front. They will not sit happily through any kind of inductive argument, no matter how carefully crafted. They need to know what your main point is, instantly. If you have a boss who is always pushing you to include an executive summary of your presentations or memos up-front, that boss is very likely a judger.

Perceivers   Perceivers, on the other hand, want to know that you have considered all available options, and they would like to know what those options are. They want to be sure that you are not being too hasty in your recommendations and jumping to conclusions.

Both Judgers and Perceivers Together   It is possible to satisfy both. The way to do this is to present your conclusions *and* the alternatives you considered, right up-front, on the first page.

All of this attempt to satisfy the various personality types may seem like a lot of effort. The main point of it, as we mentioned at the beginning of the chapter, is to avoid defaulting to your own preferences. If you can ensure this without going through this exercise, perhaps just by quickly considering who will be in the room and which personality types are most different from your own, that will probably be sufficient. If you care about communicating effectively with people who do not have the same personality type as you do, then you do need to go through this first step at some level.

Additional Information About Your Audience

Before you move on, there is some further information about your audience that, if you can find it, you will find useful in the subsequent steps of the Extreme Presentation process. For Step 2, it will be helpful to know what your audience knows or believes about the issue that you are presenting. For Step 4 you would also like to know where your audience tends to find their information (e.g., which magazines they read, which blogs they follow) and which authorities they respect, so that you can incorporate information in your presentation that will be credible to them.

Now we know who we're presenting to, and how they need to be presented to, but we don't necessarily know yet exactly what we're trying to do. We will figure this out next, in Chapter 2.

Setting a Measurable Objective for Your Presentation

Step 2: Set Specific Objectives for What You Want Your Audience to Think and Do Differently After Your Presentation

In order to be clear about the objectives for your presentation, ask yourself: "How will the world be different for my audience after I make my presentation?" This question is important, because if the answer is "It won't be," then you really need to think hard about whether you should be giving this presentation at all. *If nothing will change for your audience as a result of your presentation, then why should they even be there?*

The way to do this, with clarity, is to use the "From-To/Think-Do" matrix. (See Figure 2.1; there is also a copy of this matrix in Appendix A, Worksheet A2.) In this matrix, you specify your presentation objective by defining precisely the changes you are seeking in your audience's attitudes and behaviors: their thoughts and actions. You want to be very clear as to what you want your audience to think and do differently as a result of your presentation.

Fill in the From-To/Think-Do Matrix to clarify your objectives. You should think of this exercise as external scaffolding—something to help you construct your presentation, not something that you will include *during* the presentation. In this chapter we will cover:

- Why the typical approach to setting presentation objectives is flawed
- How to develop an effective presentation objective, with some examples
- Why an "update" presentation is generally a bad idea
- How to check if you've set the right objectives for your presentation

The Typical—and Wrong—Way to Set Presentation Objectives

Common advice for presentation objectives is that they should be "action oriented": they should have lots of verbs. Consider the example in Figure 2.2. This is a disguised version of a real slide. It is very action oriented; each bullet begins with a verb: review,

FIGURE 2.1.   The From-To/Think-Do Matrix for Specifying Presentation Objectives

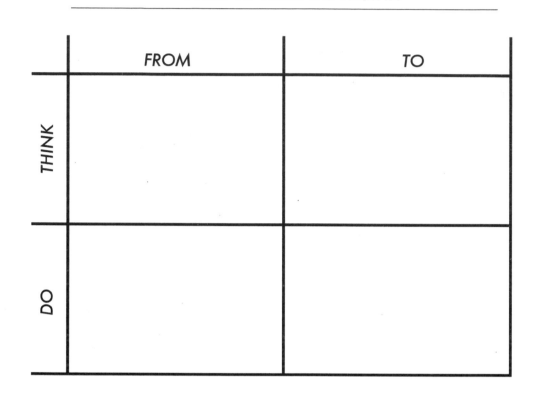

FIGURE 2.2.   What Is Wrong with This Objectives Slide?

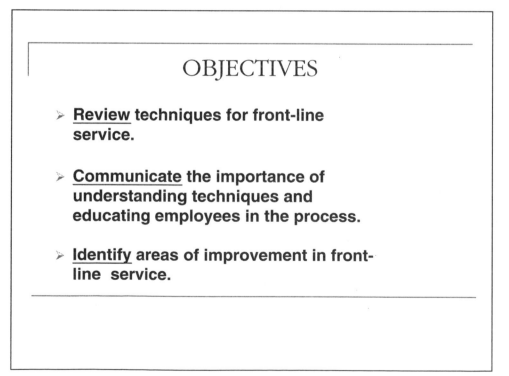

communicate, identify. But there is something *fundamentally wrong* about this slide. What is wrong with it?

Look at it again. The objectives are all about *me*, the presenter; what *I* am going to do: *I* am going to review, communicate, identify. How useful is such a set of objectives, in terms of knowing whether your presentation has been a success? Not very useful, because even before the presentation begins, you know that, barring something extraordinary such as the roof falling in, you will indeed review, communicate, and identify what you were intending to. But what we need is a way to set objectives that are all about the audience, not the presenter. Only if we measure against this kind of objective can we really know whether our presentation has had an effect.

Developing Effective Presentation Objectives

The way to do this is to use the "From-To/Think-Do" Matrix (Figure 2.1) to set your objective in terms of what you want your audience to think and do differently. In marketing terms, we call this attitudinal and behavioral change. You can't change their actions unless you first change their minds, and in general there is not much point changing their minds unless you also change their actions. And this is what the From-To/Think-Do matrix is for. Figure 2.3 contains an example of this matrix in use.

FIGURE 2.3.   From-To/Think-Do Matrix Example

From-To Think-Do Matrix

	FROM	TO
THINK	What are they thinking now? *Investing in the brand is a waste of money because it can't be measured*	What should they think after your presentation? *There are actually some very sophisticated and effective techniques for measuring changes in brand equity*
DO	What are they doing—or not doing—today? *Not investing in the brand*	What should they start doing—or stop doing—after your presentation? *Set up a brand investment test and agree on measurement goals and approach*

In this case, the presenter is delivering some market research about brand strength and wants to convince the audience to invest in a brand advertising test. The top left box, the "From/Think" box, describes what the audience is probably thinking now about brand advertising: a waste of money, because we can't measure its effectiveness. Below that, the "From/Do" box, this contains what the audience is—or is not—doing right now. In this case it's the latter: they are not investing in brand advertising. At the top right is the "To/Think" box. This is what we want the audience to be thinking once the presentation is over: "Hey, there are actually some very sophisticated ways to measure the value and effect of brands on our business." But don't stop there. Below that, the "To/Do" box: "Let's try to convince them to invest in a brand advertising test."

Figure 2.4 contains five examples of good presentation objectives developed using the From-To/Think-Do Matrix. Each of these examples is relevant to business, government, academia, and military use: one of them may fit your own situation either as is or with some modification.

FIGURE 2.4.   Examples of Good Presentation Objectives

1. *[Thinking] From* thinking that investment in proposed project X would be a waste of money *to* thinking that it could be very valuable, and *[Doing] from* not investing in project X to agreeing *to* make an initial investment

2. *[Thinking] From* thinking that current staff underperformance is due to inadequate tools *to* thinking that lack of required skills is the real problem, and *[Doing] from* planning to invest in new support technology *to* investing instead in improved staff training

3. *[Thinking] From* staff being unfamiliar with sexual harassment guidelines and implications of violating them *to* being familiar with them and their implications, and *[Doing] from* occasional violations of guidelines *to* no violations of guidelines

4. *[Thinking] From* thinking that the current procurement approach has its problems but trying to fix it will cause even bigger problems *to* believing that there may be a way to streamline it without causing undue disruption, and *[Doing] from* not making any changes to the procurement process *to* agreeing to a small scale pilot of the new approach

5. *[Thinking] From* front-line staff lacking knowledge and understanding of procedures *to* having a good grasp of procedures, and *[Doing] from* making mistakes, with heavy call volume to central office for help *to* fewer mistakes and calls for help

The Curse of the "Update" Presentation

Try to push your objectives to include *both* attitudinal (thinking) and behavioral (doing) components whenever possible, keeping in mind, on your audience's behalf, the old saying that "to think but not to do is to never have thought at all." For example, some organizations have developed a convention of stating whether a particular presentation is an information presentation or a decision presentation. I think there are two problems with this convention. First, announcing that this is an informational presentation is almost a cue to the audience that it can ignore you. (If it's just informational, how important could it be?) Second, and of more consequence, a presentation that is billed as purely informational takes the presenter off the hook from having to think though what the *implications* of that information might be for the audience.

A common type of informational presentation is the "update" presentation: "I'm just here to update you on the project/tracking study/progress to date/etc." If you begin designing your presentation with this as your goal, you are going to find it difficult to hold your audience's attention. I am not saying that you cannot or should not have an "update" presentation, only that update presentations are almost guaranteed to be boring and devoid of impact.

The way to get out of this trap is to *force* yourself to complete the "From-To/Think-Do" Matrix. What does the information that you want to update your audience about imply about what they need to think and do differently? For example: Where in your project have conditions changed so that some new thinking is needed? What parts of your project have fallen behind schedule and need corrective action? This way you will focus only on the areas that need thought and action, and move very quickly through the rest, or even skip parts of it and refer the audience to an appendix if they need the detail. This makes for a much more interesting presentation, and one that is more likely to have impact. (For more details on how to turn an informational or update presentation compelling, see Figure 3.3 and its associated text in Chapter 3.

The "From-To/Think-Do" discipline is also important for training and educational presentations. Again, ask yourself what your training session will allow participants to think and do differently once they've completed it. This will help you focus on what really matters and avoid bogging it down with superfluous information. The approach works even if you are teaching some liberal arts subject, such as art history. How are the students thinking and acting differently after the class than they were before it? Before the class, they could not tell a Rembrandt from a Rauschenberg; afterward, they can.

If you want your audience to welcome your presentations, then you need to make certain that you are giving them value for the time they are investing listening to you. A critical prerequisite for doing this is to have a clear understanding of how their thoughts and behavior will change as a result of this presentation. This will allow you to ask yourself: Are those changes worth the time they will spend with me?

How Do You Know Whether You Have Set the Right Objectives?

Once you've filled out the matrix, take a look at what you've written. If it is written in terms of what *you* are going to do, then you haven't completed it correctly. You need to rewrite it in terms of what you want your *audience* to think and do.

But what if you are just trying to reinforce something they already know? In this case, try very hard to identify what they will do differently after your presentation; if nothing, maybe you don't need to give the presentation.

What if you just have to give them more details that they can use? The answer is the same here: focus on what will be different for them once you give them those details.

How will their thoughts or actions change as a result of receiving these new details from you? If neither their thoughts nor their actions will change because of your presentation, then really, why are you bothering? *The answer to the question of "How will my audience think or act differently as a result of receiving the information I want to present to them?" is your presentation objective.*

What if you don't know what they think right now? Try to find out. There is usually no need—and no time—to do an all-out needs assessment. A simple email with one or two questions to a member of your prospective audience should usually do the trick. For example: "I am preparing next week's presentation on project X. What do you and your colleagues think about project X—are you in favor of implementing it right now?"

You don't want to waste your time and theirs trying to persuade them of something they are already convinced about. If you really can't find out, you might want to consider creating two versions of your presentation. In the first few minutes of your presentation, you will quickly find out what they think, and then you can switch accordingly.

Now that we know the objective of your presentation, the next question is what is actually going to be *in* your presentation? We will begin to answer this in Part II of this book, next.

PART II
LOGIC

IN THE NEXT TWO CHAPTERS we will cover the logic dimension of designing a presentation. This includes the business problem that your presentation is going to help your audience solve and the information you will provide to support that solution.

Before we begin those two chapters, in this section we will:

- Clarify why you should *always* focus your presentation on a serious problem that your audience has
- Argue against the common belief that style is more important than substance, and demonstrate how important the quality of your evidence is to the success of your presentation
- Introduce and explain the *Reality Principle*, which states that you should always prefer to present evidence that is concrete and particular rather than conceptual and general

Why You Should *Always* Focus Your Presentation on an Audience Problem

Focusing your presentation on a serious problem that your audience has is essential—this is the way that you get their attention. Unless you are solving a problem for your audience, why should they listen to you? You're just another waste of time for them. If you follow just this one idea—of focusing your presentation on solving a problem that your audience has—then you will see a substantive improvement in the success of your presentations. The reason that drawing your audience's attention to a threatening problem works, in part, is that *fear* is a reliable motivator when the issue is a serious one and you are offering a helpful solution.[1]

[1]Witte and Allen's (2000) meta-analysis of fifty years of research into fear appeals attests to their effectiveness when they present a significant and relevant threat and when they offer achievable and effective responses.

Think about the problems that your audience has, and then ask yourself: "Which of those problems will the information that I want to present to them help them solve?" For example, you might be providing a project update or details from an ongoing research study. Instead of just saying, "I'm going to give you an update on the construction project" or "I'm going to tell you the findings from this quarter's tracking study," think about what *new information* you have learned since the last update. What will this new information allow your audience to do? What problem of theirs will it contribute to solving? You'll then organize your entire presentation around this new information. You can still cover the rest of the update, but it will be in the context of something very helpful to them. The goal here is, instead of having them say, "Oh great, here comes Dr. Abela with another boring update," you want them to think, "Every time this person presents to us, we learn something useful."

President John F. Kennedy apparently once said "The only reason to give a speech is to change the world." We will paraphrase that and say that the only reason to give a presentation is to solve a problem.

This is crucially important. If you don't know what problems your audience has and how your presentation could help solve them, find out before you do anything else. Phone or email one of your audience members, or someone who knows them, and ask. "I'm just presenting a project update" is not good enough anymore—everyone is too busy. Your presentation has to help to solve an important problem for your audience if you want to get their attention. Chapter 3 will go into more details about how to identify your audience's problems.

You Do Need Evidence!

[2] A study of engineering students found that presentation professionalism training tended to focus on "how to gesture appropriately, to project their voice, or to eliminate the 'ums' and 'uhs' from their speech" (Dannels 2003, pp. 165–166).

There is a common assumption that style trumps substance in presentations—that communication is mostly about sizzle, not steak.[2] Research in the late 1960s provided some support for this assumption, showing that under certain conditions, the inclusion of good evidence in a communication did not have much immediate effect on changing people's minds. James McCroskey's (1969) summary of several studies found that when either the credibility of the presenter was high or delivery of the communication was poor, then including good evidence did not make much difference on immediate attitude change in the audience. There is also research that has been badly misapplied, such as the "conclusion" that only 7 percent of communication comes from words, with the other 93 percent supposedly coming from non-verbal signals—the implication of this being that your evidence counts at most for 7 percent of your communication. (But as we have seen, this is false; see the Introduction to this book for a debunking of this myth.) Because of these assumptions, there is a temptation to spend time trying to embellish your slides.

[3] Reinard (1988), reviewing fifty years of research on the use of evidence in persuasive communication, found a consistent positive effect (see also Reinard, 1998).

Yet in general, the empirical research *contradicts* the assumption that style is more important than substance. Although McCroskey found that, under the conditions mentioned above, including good evidence does not increase *immediate* attitude change, he also found that, regardless of those conditions, the inclusion of evidence is likely to increase *sustained* attitude change. So if you want to persuade your audience, and keep them persuaded, then one of the most important things you can do is include strong evidence.[3]

The Reality Principle: Show Concrete and Specific Data Whenever Possible

The *reality principle* states that you should always prefer to present evidence that is concrete and particular rather than conceptual and general. Real things, real people, and specific details are more interesting, memorable, and persuasive. Good copywriters know this:

"Specific claims increase believability. Do NOT write in your advertising, 'This car gets great gas mileage.' DO write, 'This car gets 41 mpg in the city and 52 mpg on road trips'."[4]

When summarizing customer research, for example, show a picture of an actual subject and provide specific, real details about the person (to the extent that this is possible without violating the confidentiality of your research). Show photographs of the things or people you are talking about, maps of locations, and diagrams or plans.[5]

Don't be afraid to provide lots of detail; it increases credibility. This is true regardless of audience personality type. Certainly, detail-oriented people have a strong need to see all the details. But even people who are more conceptually oriented will find your presentation more credible if you include details—*even if they do not read any of the details*, which they probably won't, anyway.[6]

In every case, be sure to explain where your details come from. When you make it clear that your facts could be easily verified, people become more confident in them, even if they don't ever bother to check them.[7]

There is also a broader—and equally important—application of the reality principle, which concerns how your recommendations fit with your audiences' lives. In addition to trying always to present concrete and particular information, you should also try always to ensure that the problems and recommendations you discuss in your presentations fit in with the concrete and particular realities in your audiences' lives. It is easy to slip into a habit of blaming your audience for their lack of attention to you or respect for your ideas. It is useful to remember that, although it may sometimes seem to be the case, this apparent indifference is not typically based on malice toward you or a desire to spoil your day. More likely, it arises because *there are constraints in their own situations that inhibit them from embracing your presentation fully.*

And often enough it is not a question of trying to find out what these constraints are, because usually you already know what they are. In most cases you already know, for example, that this department is under extreme cost-cutting pressure, or that that person has been putting in fourteen-hour days for several weeks now. It is therefore usually more a matter of trying to adjust your presentation to address these realities. Informing your audience up-front that you know what cost constraints they are under, and therefore that you are about to propose a very slimmed-down solution, for example, will help overcome their initial skepticism and avoid their writing you off before your presentation begins. In doing so you improve the chances of your proposal being accepted.

There is a danger, particularly in larger organizations where bureaucracy is more widespread, that the practice of presentation becomes part of a larger game in which we go through the motions of saying what we are expected to say, while the audience goes through the motions of listening to us. And then nothing happens. Making a deliberate effort to incorporate a clear understanding of the realities in your audience's lives into the details of your recommendations goes a long way toward breaking out of this game, because they will quickly become aware that you are speaking to them personally and

[4]Gary Bencivenga, http://bencivengabullets.com/bullets.asp?id=23; accessed 6/20/07.

[5]Eye-tracking research found that pictures of real people and things draw more attention and are remembered more (Glick, 2004). Research on print advertising found that photographs gain more attention than artwork (Finn, 1988, p. 172).

[6]These findings are based on experiments reported in Artz and Tybout (1999) and Rossiter and Percy (1980). See Chapter 8 for more on these experiments.

[7]Ford, Smith, and Swasy's (1990) research on advertising claims found that people are less skeptical of claims that could be verified.

that what you are saying has real relevance for their own work, and therefore they will be more likely to consider it. In this way you will actually be getting something useful done—and this is a much more fulfilling way to go through ones career and life, isn't it?

The two chapters in this part will show you the "how" of using evidence persuasively in your presentation. Chapter 3 will show you how to choose the right problem and compose a persuasive solution. Chapter 4 contains a discussion on what kinds of evidence to include in your presentation—and some of it is quite counter-intuitive and surprising.

Articulating the Audience's Business Problem and Your Proposed Solution to It

Step 3: Identify a Problem Your Audience Has That Your Presentation Will Contribute to Solving

If you want to capture and keep your audience's attention every time, then make sure that every presentation you make focuses on helping them to solve an important problem of theirs. This is critically important: if you're not helping to solve a problem for your audience, then *why are they listening to you?*

The problem that you choose to focus on must be a real one, one that is likely going to cause pain for your audience, professionally and perhaps personally, if it is not solved. Ideally, there should be clear risks and real dollars at stake; for example, their business profits are going to suffer, so their bonuses will be reduced or eliminated, and their career prospects will be hurt. Or they are not going to complete their project on time, and therefore they will not be able to request the additional resources they are hoping for. Or, at minimum, they are going to be stressed while they struggle with the problem. They do not have to already be aware that they have this problem, if you are able to convince them that it is important.

The important thing is that the problem must be your *audience's* problem, not *your* problem. For example, if you are a researcher and your internal clients are not taking advantage of the insights that you have identified for them, that is *your* problem, not theirs, because it is making you look ineffective. On the other hand, the fact that they are missing out on new business opportunities identified by your research, for example, and therefore they are less successful because they are not acting on your insights: now that's *their* problem. Notice the subtlety here—these are really two aspects of the same issue. The important thing is to be able to highlight why your *audience* is likely to suffer if they do not listen to you. If you refocus your presentation on the problem that *they* have, then your audience will be more willing to listen to you. The substance of your presentation may be much the same either way, but by focusing on a problem that they have, you are much more likely to win their interest and attention.

If you already understand the importance of concentrating your entire presentation on addressing a problem facing your audience, and you know the problem you wish to focus on, then write it down, along with a one-sentence summary of the solution.

The rest of this chapter will answer the following questions about articulating problems and solutions:

- Why discuss problem solving in a book about presentation design?
- How to choose the right problem, including:
  — How to find the right problem—the Five Why's
  — How do I find the right level of analysis?
  — What if the problem is so big that I cannot help my audience solve it?
  — What if all I can come up with are a bunch of small problems rather than one big one?
  — What if I'm just presenting information or providing an update?
  — What if I'm creating a training or educational presentation?
  — What if there is clearly a problem, but the audience I am trying to engage just does not seem to be interested?
  — Isn't focusing on "problems" rather negative?
- How to craft a solution, including:
  — What if I only have a solution to part of the problem?
  — How do I know if I have chosen the right solution?
  — Should I include rival solutions to the one I'm offering?
  — How do I handle really controversial solutions?
  — What if I just can't get my thoughts straight on what solution to recommend?
  — What to do if there really *isn't* a clear solution to the problem?

Why Discuss Problem Solving in a Book About Presentation Design?

One of the most common causes of a failed presentation occurs even before you begin designing the presentation: inadequate problem solving. As a result, many people develop presentations with substandard content and then try to improve the presentation by adding fancy ornamentation, such as animations or transitions.

Ironically, almost all presentation approaches *assume* that your thinking is already complete and solid before you begin to design your presentation. Yet, in my experience, this assumption is usually false. People are very busy, and will often start writing their presentations before their thinking is complete. This is why the problem-solution step is built right into the beginning of the Extreme Presentation process. It ensures that you push your thinking as far as you can *before* you start drawing any slides.

By focusing your presentation on helping to solve a problem that your audience has, you ensure that you capture their attention. Henry Boettinger wrote, "Rule 1: The *only* reason for the existence of a presentation of an idea is that it be an *answer to a problem*. . . . If you think you can break this rule, you are better than the best essayists, novelists, and dramatists in history. So far, none of them has ever done so successfully."[1]

Effective salespeople know this. In fact focusing on an important problem that prospective clients have, and helping them solve it, is a core tenet of the empirically validated and highly successful SPIN Selling® technique. If you are trying to persuade your audience to take action on your recommendations—if you want to "sell" your ideas—then it makes sense to do what successful salespeople do, and focus on solving your audience's problem.[2]

Choosing the Right Problem

You need to focus your presentation on a problem that your audience has and that you will provide some contribution towards solving. The problem needs to be big enough to be worth their attention, and yet small enough that your presentation makes a meaningful contribution to solving it.

How to Find the Right Problem—The Five Why's

To find out whether you are focusing on the real problem, you can use the six-sigma technique of the "Five Why's." Ask "Why is this a problem?" When you get the answer, ask again, "And why is *this* a problem?" Five times is usually enough to get you to the core problem. For example: the problem is that our project is delayed. Why is this a problem (number 1)? Because we can't seem to be able to decide which new supplier to go with. Why can't you decide (number 2)? Because the different suppliers have different, incompatible technologies. Why is this a problem (number 3)? Because we are afraid to commit to a particular technology. Why are you afraid to commit (number 4)? Because we don't know, longer term, which technology is going to help us get the most productivity from our staff. And why is *this* a problem (number 5)? Because we don't fully understand the drivers of productivity in our staff. Aha. Now you know the real problem, so you can focus your presentation on it and have a much greater chance of getting your audience to make some progress toward solving it.

How Do I Find the Right Level of Analysis?

Many problems can be defined at different levels, and the challenge then is figuring out which level to choose. For example, at the highest level, the problem could be that the company is not making enough money. At a level below that, this could be because it is not bringing in enough new customers. More specifically, this in turn could be because there are not enough customers from a particularly important segment (e.g., teenage girls, for the clothing department of a department store). And the problem at the heart of this could be that the current advertising does not appeal to teenage girls.

The way to decide what level of problem to address is to ask, "What is the *highest* level of the problem toward which I can make a significant contribution to solving in my presentation?"

[1] Henry Boettinger, *Moving Mountains* (1969, p. 41), one of the best books on presentations ever written.

[2] See Rackham (1988) for details on the SPIN method. A study of thousands of sales transactions found that price premiums are usually earned because the salesperson was able to help the buyer identify a problem and/or help solve it (Snyder, 2007).

[3]Gigerenzer (2004) notes that, although following the 9/11/2001 terrorist attacks many people avoided flying, more people died in the resulting increase in traffic accidents in the first three months after the attacks than actually died in the hijacked aircraft.

[4]Witte and Allen (2000), in their meta-analysis of fear appeals cited in the introduction to this Part, noted that, to be effective, fear appeals need to be accompanied by solutions that are perceived to be credible.

You want to address as big a problem as possible, because that makes your presentation more interesting for your audience. Interestingly, people appear to be more afraid of—and hence more captivated by—something that is catastrophic but rare, than they are of something that is less dramatic but more common.[3]

At the same time, you want to make sure that the problem you raise is one that can in fact be addressed. You do not want to use a sensational problem to attract people's attention and then have to admit that there is nothing credible that can be done to solve it.[4]

So you want to locate the problem at a high enough level to capture your audience's attention, but not any higher than you can actually deliver some value on. One way to identify the right business problem to address is to use the Hierarchy of Business Problems (Figure 3.1). The way this works is that you begin at the top of the hierarchy and work your way down, until you find the most relevant problem. (If you work in a different type of environment, such as in a not-for-profit organization or in the military, see the other hierarchies in Figures 3.2a and b.)

At the top of the business hierarchy is the most general problem that businesses face: they are not making enough money. Their ROI (return on investment) is inadequate; it's not where they want it to be. Then you work your way down the hierarchy to find the specific business problem. For example, if ROI is inadequate, this could be either

FIGURE 3.1.   Business Problem-Solving Hierarchy

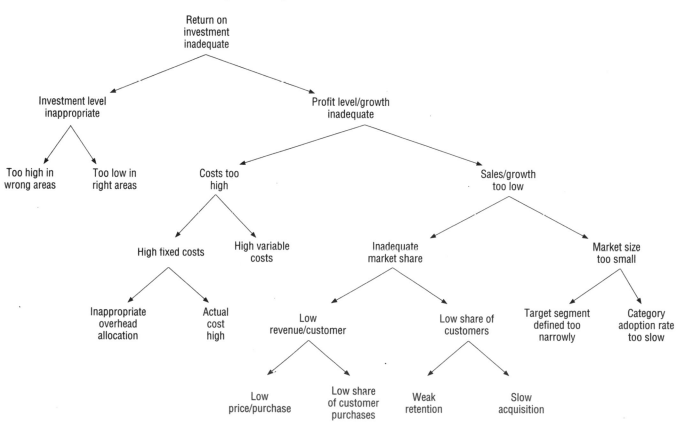

because the returns—profits—are inadequate, or it could be that investment levels are inappropriate: too high for the given profits or too low. For the sake of our example, assume that the problem is with profit levels. If these are too low, then—continuing down the hierarchy—this could be either because sales (in absolute levels or in terms of growth rates) are too low or because costs are too high. If sales are too low, this could be because your market is too small or because your share of that market is too small. If the latter, this is either because you have a low share of the total number of customers or because you have low revenue per customer. If you have low revenue per customer, this is because you have either a low share of each customer's purchases or you are getting too low of a price per customer.

Work your way through this hierarchy, and find the most likely business problem that you are facing. When you have identified the problem, write it in Worksheet A3 (Appendix A). Phrase it as a statement, not as a question, beginning something like, "The problem that my audience has is . . ."

The government/not-for-profit problem-solving hierarchy (see Figure 3.2a) starts at the top with the broadest problem typically faced in such organizations, namely, that the

FIGURE 3.2A.   Government/Not-for-Profit Problem-Solving Hierarchy

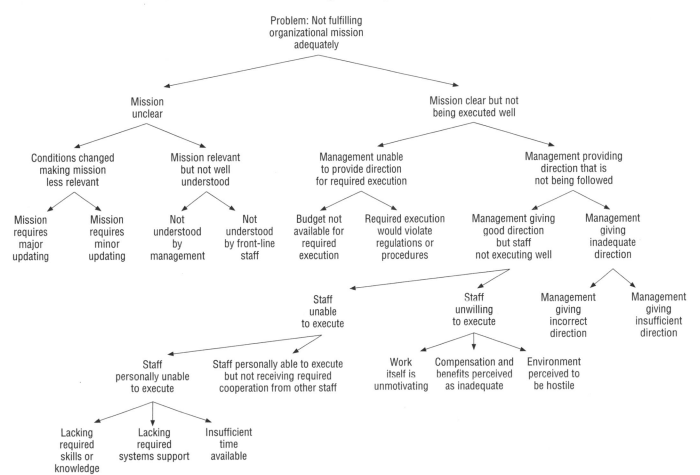

FIGURE 3.2B.   Military Problem-Solving Hierarchy

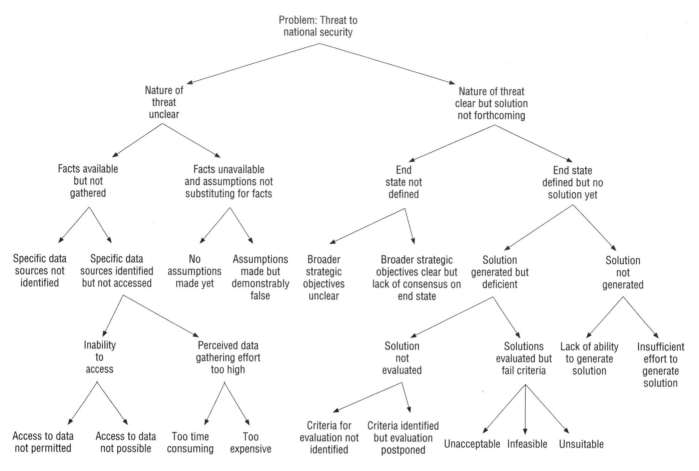

organization is not fulfilling its mission. Below that, this is either because the mission itself is unclear, or else because the mission is clear but it is not being executed well. Each of these possibilities is then disaggregated further.

The military problem solving hierarchy (see Figure 3.2b) begins with a threat to national security. It is true that the military, like other not-for-profit institutions, is also mission-based, but when looking for a specific problem to which to anchor a presentation, it seems to be more productive to focus on a threat. The nature of the problem-solving approach is going to depend first on whether the threat is clear or not. If the threat is not clear, then the problem will likely be about the availability of facts or useful assumptions. If the threat is clear, then the issue is more likely to be about whether the desired end state has been defined or not. In each of these cases, the possibilities are again disaggregated further.

What If the Problem Is So Big That I Cannot Help Them Solve It?

What if the problem that you have identified is so big that you can make very little contribution to solving it? First, recognize that simply making your audience aware that they have a serious problem, which they were not aware of before, could still be a valuable contribution to them, even if you do not offer a solution.[5]

Next, try to outline some preliminary steps for beginning to address the problem. Let's say that the problem your audience is facing is declining enrollment in a school. You could suggest some additional research to help define the problem further, such as digging into the data to understand whether the declines are broad-based or concentrated in one or a few areas, and to where departing students are transferring. Or you could provide a few case examples of organizations that have faced similar problems and how they addressed them. If these preliminary steps do not seem like they will satisfy your audience, then consider using a facilitated discussion approach instead. This is described below in the reply to the question, "What do I do if there really isn't a clear solution to the problem?"

What If All I Can Come Up With Are a Bunch of Small Problems Rather Than One Big One?

Sometimes it appears that your material is relevant to several small issues rather than one big problem. There are a number of ways to deal with this. If any one of them looks like it could grow into much larger problem if it is not addressed, then concentrate on that one. Alternatively, if you can combine all the smaller issues conceptually into a larger problem, then do so. If all of the smaller issues are related to plant maintenance, for example, you might offer your presentation as addressing a serious problem with maintenance. If you can also quantify the impact of each of the smaller problems and sum them up, then this will allow you to have even more impact, saying something like "I would like to talk to you about how maintenance problems are costing us $5 million annually." Even if the smaller issues are completely unrelated—one is about staff, another about insurance, another about vacation planning, for example—if you can quantify each and then add them all together, you can still present them as $X million in unnecessary expenditure, for example.

What if—after all your best efforts—it appears that there is just *one small problem* that you are focusing on? In this case, think about downgrading from a full-blown presentation to some less time- and resource-consuming form of communication. Consider instead a shorter presentation to fewer people, a conference call, or a brief memo or email. People will thank you for saving their time and the organization's resources.

Presentations are time-consuming, both for the person developing the presentation and for the audience. Twenty people attending a forty-five-minute presentation spend the equivalent of two full days of work for one person. A forty-slide presentation that takes thirty minutes per slide to create is almost three days' work on the part of the presenter, for a total of one person-week of work. Can your organization really afford to waste the equivalent of a week's work on a small issue?

Create presentations only when you have something particularly new or challenging to communicate. The rest of the time, deliver your material in a way that your audience will

[5]Buyers tend to reward salespeople who bring their attention to a problem they were unaware of (Snyder, 2007).

find it easy to consume: in a well-organized memo or reference document, or a simple email. Many of the techniques in this book apply also to memos and reference documents. Later in this chapter we will cover how to write a one-page memo.

What If I'm Just Presenting Information or Providing an Update?

What if you are a researcher giving an update on the latest wave of an ongoing study, for example—do you still have to focus your presentation on an audience problem? If you begin working on your presentation convinced that you are designing a "purely informational" presentation, then you are going to have a very difficult time capturing and keeping your audience's attention. If you want their attention, then you *must* help them solve a problem. Everyone is very busy, and dedicating forty-five minutes to receiving some information (which they suspect—perhaps rightly—they could have received in five minutes by skimming a memo or an email) does not feel like an attractive prospect.

As we discussed in Chapter 2, the solution to this is to find the problem that is implied in a purely "informational" presentation. The way to find the problem is to ask yourself: *Why* does my audience need this information? (If they don't need your information, then you really shouldn't be giving this presentation). If they do need your information, it is probably because they are going to use it for something, and that something is usually some kind of a problem to be solved (or an opportunity to be pursued). What is it that they need or want to do and cannot do or do well without your information? Whatever that is, *that* is the problem that you are addressing. Refocus your presentation on *that* problem, and it will be much more interesting and compelling for your audience. (Figure 3.3 summarizes this approach.)

This is particularly true if you are asked to develop a presentation to "just provide an update." In this case, don't just bombard your audience with say, all the numbers from this quarter and how they have changed from last quarter. Instead, focus on the few most newsworthy changes in this quarter's data, and ask yourself the kinds of questions included in Figure 3.3 below: *Why would my audience want this newsworthy information?*

FIGURE 3.3.   Making an "Update" Presentation More Interesting

How to turn an informational or "update" presentation into a more interesting problem-solving presentation.
Ask yourself:

1. Why does the audience need the information or update that I am going to present to them?
2. What does the information I will provide allow them to do?
3. Could they do it without my information? If so, would my information allow them to do it better? Faster? Cheaper?

Whatever it is that your information allows your audience to do that they could not have done otherwise—or do better than they could have—is a *problem* that your presentation is solving for your audience.

What does it allow them to start doing, stop doing, or continue doing that would be difficult or impossible without this information? Whatever that is, that is the problem you should be focusing on in this presentation. For example, let's say that you are asked to present an update on the Alpha project, and your main message is that everything is currently on track, but that there is one area that might slip behind in the next month. What is the problem that you are solving for your audience with this presentation? Work through the questions in Figure 3.3:

1. *Why does the audience need the information or update that I am going to present to them?* They need to know whether things are on track, and where things are or might be falling behind.

2. *What does this information allow them to do?* It allows them to take action to prevent the project from falling behind.

3. *Could they do it without my information? If so, would my information allow them to do it better, faster, cheaper?* They would eventually find out that the project was falling behind, but that won't be until later, by which time it will be more expensive to fix the problem. My presentation will allow them to fix the problem earlier and hence more cheaply.

What this exercise has allowed you to see is that the audience has a problem that project Alpha is about to be delayed and they do not even know it yet. You can now focus the presentation on this threatened delay and what can be done about it. As a result of this shift of focus, you will now have a much more interesting presentation than if you were merely giving them this month's update on project Alpha. (The "before and after" Extreme Presentation makeover example in Appendix B is also an informational update that was turned into a powerful problem-solving presentation.)

Finally, if you do not think that it is worth your effort to think through this, then perhaps you should cancel the presentation and just email them the findings instead. They can always email you back with any questions.

What If I Am Creating a Training Presentation?

Should you still focus on a problem if you are creating a training presentation? Certainly. The reason people are being trained is that they have some kind of problem, which your training session will help them solve. Ask yourself what they will be able to do *differently* once they have taken your training. Not being able to do this thing is then the problem that you are addressing for them. If it is not a big problem, then you should also ask yourself whether the effort you and they are putting into the training is worthwhile.

For example, the problem that the Extreme Presentation workshop addresses is that participants have not been obtaining the impact from their presentations that they think they should. The workshop, by teaching them the ten-step process described in this book, solves that problem. After the workshop, the participants are able to design presentations that get their audiences to act on the information they receive.

What If There Is Clearly a Problem, But the Audience I Am Trying to Engage Just Does Not Seem to Want to Hear About It?

When the problem is clear to you, but you know that your audience is not interested in hearing about it—perhaps because you've already tried to engage them about it in preliminary conversations—the common reaction is to conclude that your audience are just burying their heads in the sand, pretending that what they don't know can't hurt them.

This may indeed be the case, but before concluding so, it is a good idea to think about *why* they do not seem to be interested. Often, the real reason that they do not appear to be interested is that you have not found the aspect of the problem that is most relevant to them right now, given their particular goals and constraints. This is another application of the reality principle outlined in the introduction to the Logic section: to always ensure that the problems and recommendations that you discuss in your presentations are relevant to the concrete and particular realities of your audiences' lives.

For example, a market research manager in one of my workshops at a very large organization was struggling with getting her clients to be interested in an important business problem that she was working on. The business problem, as she first expressed it, was that the client she was serving—an advertising team—was not taking advantage of the lessons learned from research on the previous advertising campaign, and therefore they were in danger of repeating some of the same mistakes. This is clearly an important business problem—those mistakes are going to be quite costly, and yet they could be avoided.

As we discussed her challenge, the reasons why it was not very motivating to her clients became clear. First, the advertising team had moved on from the previous project on which the research was based to something quite different, so they did not think that the research from that project would be relevant to the new one. Second, they were already so far advanced into the new project that it was too late to incorporate the lessons from the previous project. What to do?

The manager decided instead to focus on the larger problem of avoiding mistakes in *future* campaigns, and decided instead to address the *next* campaign coming up, beyond the current one. It was the reality principle at work: by recognizing the specific realities of the pressures her clients were facing, she was able to modify the problem that her presentation focused on into something that was more compelling to those clients. The content is still the same—the lessons learned from previous advertising research—but the probability that the client would actually act on those lessons had now increased tremendously.

Isn't Focusing on "Problems" Rather Negative?

In an attempt to promote positive thinking, some companies have forbidden the use of the word "problem," insisting instead that staff use the word "opportunity." In one organization, this rule died a quick death when one manager addressed a meeting using the words of Pogo, Walt Kelly's famous cartoon character: "Ladies and gentlemen, we are surrounded by insurmountable opportunities."

Focusing on problems does not mean that you have to be negative and pessimistic throughout your presentation. It *does* mean that you will unmistakably attach your presentation to a problem that your audience has. But the bulk of your presentation will typically be focused on the solution.

Does it make a difference if you are offering an opportunity instead of a problem? In general, problems are more motivating than opportunities, because—all other things being equal—people tend to be more concerned about losing something than gaining something.[6] If you ignore an opportunity, people may not notice, but if you ignore a problem, it could explode in your face. Most opportunities can be redefined as a solution to another problem. For example, a growth opportunity in a new business segment can be recast as a solution to the problem of how to meet company growth goals. In the end, though, whether you call what you are presenting a "problem" or an "opportunity" will depend on your own judgment about what you think will be most motivating to your audience.

[6]Daniel Kahneman's (2003) Nobel-Prizewinning Prospect Theory states, among other things, that when amounts are identical, human beings weigh losses more heavily than gains.

Crafting Your Solution

In this section we will discuss how to define the scope of the solution you are offering and how to generate and test your solution ideas.

What If I Only Have a Solution to Part of the Problem?

Often the problems you are addressing are very large, so it is unreasonable to expect that you will resolve them in a single presentation. And that is okay; the solution you offer does not have to completely resolve your audience's problem. Solving only part of a problem can still be very helpful; even merely informing your audience that they *have* a problem can be a contribution, as we noted earlier.

What is critically important is that you define clearly what kind of solution contribution you are offering. Partial solutions will be seen as helpful contributions, so long as you set your audience's expectations correctly; if your audience is expecting you to solve the problem completely, a partial solution will seem inadequate. Figure 3.4 lays out a cumulative spectrum of possible solution contributions.

Read the spectrum in Figure 3.4 from right to left. If you are indeed able to solve the whole problem in this presentation, then you will be at the far right end of the spectrum. If you intend to solve only part of the problem, then move one step to the left of that. This is still very helpful, so long as you set expectations correctly. One step back from that, you could help them define the solution space—the range of possible options. If they are aware of the problem, but have no idea what to do about it, then explaining to them what the possible options are, even if you cannot yet tell them which one would be best for them, is a welcome contribution. Sometimes though, all you can offer are the

FIGURE 3.4. Spectrum of Solution Contributions

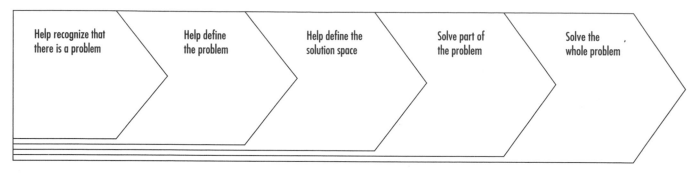

| Help recognize that there is a problem | Help define the problem | Help define the solution space | Solve part of the problem | Solve the whole problem |

two options to the left of Figure 3.4: defining their problem more clearly or helping them to recognize that they do have a problem. (A blank version of this figure is available in Worksheet A4, Appendix A.)

How Do I Know Whether I Have Chosen the Right Solution?

[7]Extensive empirical research on brainstorming concludes that group-only brainstorming is less effective than the same individuals thinking separately, which is why the modified method of individual, then group, brainstorming is recommended (Sutton & Hargadon 1996).

The question of how to create and assess solutions to problems could fill its own book. (In fact see Appendix D for a list of good books on this topic.) Very briefly, though, the surest way to find an effective solution to a problem is to try to find several, and then pick the best one. To do this, follow the principles of brainstorming. Spend some time alone listing all the possible solutions to the problem you can think of, without evaluating them in any way, and ask other members of your team to do the same. Then get together and share your ideas and come up with new ones. During this time, forbid anyone from commenting on any of the ideas. At the end of this session, evaluate the ideas using criteria that you agreed on beforehand.[7]

To be as sure as you can be that you are proposing the right solution, screen the alternatives you have generated using the criteria that your audience would use and do so as objectively as possible. Costs, time to implementation, number of people involved, expected revenues, incremental profits: these are all examples of criteria that could be used to assess alternative solutions.

As you choose your criteria, keep in mind the reality principle: What criteria will your audience use given the current realities they are operating under? There is not much point evaluating the alternatives on the basis of which one is likely to give the highest return on investment if your organization is currently facing a severe cash crunch. In that case, the primary criterion for evaluation options would most likely be initial cash outlay, and a project that provides a lower overall return might be preferable if it did not require as much money up-front.

You may believe that the members of your audience are fixating on the wrong criteria, in which case perhaps part of your presentation should be devoted to educating them on the right criteria. If that is the case, first consider whether the battle is worth fighting. If acceptance of your recommendation is going to depend on them using the right criteria, then the battle probably *is* worth fighting. If not, though, perhaps you should let them have their criteria, even though you think they are not ideal, and work within those criteria.

FIGURE 3.5. Solution Evaluation Example

Evaluation Criteria	Option 1 *Run brand advertising test* [Proposed Solution]	Option 2 *Do nothing* [Alternative 1]	Option 3 *Invest in additional sales effort* [Alternative 2]	Option 4 *Run brand advertising nationally without testing* [Alternative 3]
Revenue upside	*$800m (if test successful and advertising expanded nationally)*	—	$400m	$800m
Cost	*$150K for test $100m for national advertising*	—	$75m	$100m
Downside risk (once committed)	$150K	—	$10m	$20m

Figure 3.5 presents a framework that I have found useful for assessing solution alternatives. (A blank form for this exercise is available in Appendix A, Worksheet A5, and at www.ExtremePresentation.com.) Begin by listing your criteria in the first column on the left side of the figure. Then list the alternatives across the top of the table. Next, fill in all the cells. Each cell should be the evaluation of a particular alternative for a specific criterion. For this part of the analysis, try to be as quantifiable, and therefore as objective, as possible. Try to avoid filling in judgments such as "High" or "Low," and instead attempt to fill them with costs, expected revenues, headcount, and so on.

When you complete this exercise, you may find—I have seen this happen—that the recommendation you were planning to make is in fact not the best one, and you should propose something else instead. *Isn't it great to find this out before you make your presentation!* If you have been pushing for a particular approach for a while, and your audience (clients, superiors, staff) has been resisting you, try this analysis, taking particular care to use the criteria that they would use. At minimum, you will probably find that you understand their perspective better. You may also find that you change your own mind, once you understand where they are coming from. You might even find a way to modify your proposal so that it is acceptable to·them.

Should I Include Rival Solutions to the One I'm Offering?

Even if you believe that you have already found the best solution, be sure to consider alternative solutions. If you are proposing having your department lead a change to part of the procurement process, for example, your alternatives could include having some other department do it, piloting the change before going ahead with the full implementation, or changing the entire procurement instead of just part of it.

There is one very common alternative, which will exist for almost every recommendation you make, and that is to *do nothing*. In fact, that is the default alternative you are fighting against with almost every audience. It is your task to demonstrate that doing nothing, and every other solution they can think of, is not as effective as your own solution. Worksheet A.5 in Appendix A includes a place to list your solution alternatives.

Once you have chosen your preferred solution, do not discard the alternatives. You will want to include these in your presentation also. There are three reasons for this. First, many of the alternatives will already be present in the minds of your audience members ("Why should our department be doing this? Why not some other department?") To convince them that *your* solution is the right one, you have to address each of the alternatives. Your arguments against an alternative are far more powerful if *you* bring up the alternative first, and then dispose of it, than if one of your audience members brings it up in your presentation.[8]

Second, people who prefer to explore alternatives thoroughly before making decisions (Perceivers, in Myers-Briggs terms—see Chapter 1) are much more comfortable when you explain to them the alternatives that you have considered than when you present your recommendation without mentioning the alternatives considered. And third, if you cannot think of any reasonable alternative solutions to the problem, then perhaps the solution you are offering is rather obvious, and there is no need for a full-blown presentation. You might be able to save time for yourself and your audience by just calling or emailing them to tell them about it.

How Do I Handle Really Controversial Solutions?

Sometimes, though, your message is intrinsically controversial. You may have tried hard to find other reasonable solutions, but the only one that works is going to be a win-lose type of solution, where one stakeholder group is going to suffer. For example, funding is going to be taken from one group and given to another, or someone's pet project is going to be cancelled, or some group is going to be relocated.

How do you handle a controversial message when the "losing" parties are going to be in the room, and perhaps you need their agreement to proceed? The best solution I have found here is to widen the perspective of your presentation until the decision can be seen from a total system view, so that all parties can see all the factors at play and understand how your proposed solution is indeed the best overall solution. Present the problem, the alternative solutions, and the criteria for evaluating the alternatives. And then take your audience through the logic, as dispassionately as you can, so that they will see that, as painful as it is, your proposal is the right way forward.

For example, let's say that the problem you have identified is that the marketing department is not using their research budget very effectively, perhaps because they spend it

[8] Lawyers refer to this as "stealing thunder." Experimental research concludes that when *you* bring up a point *against* your recommendation, your audience will view your position more favorably than if it were raised by someone else (Williams, Bourgeois, & Croyle, 1993).

only on short-term, tactical issues. Your recommendation is that this budget be transferred to the market research department, so that the researchers themselves will make the decisions about what research should be done from now on. Of course, you would expect the marketing department to object vigorously to this. No one likes to have budget taken away from them, and more specifically they would have a concern that only they know what research needs to be done. In this case, your dispassionate approach would be to name the problem, list the alternatives, such as leave the budget where it is, make it a shared responsibility or educate marketers how to make better research investment decisions. Then you would share the criteria for making the decision, which would include cost-effectiveness, speed of decision making, and return on investment on the research budget. You will then show how your solution will provide better outcomes for all involved. (Chapter 6 will show how to put all this information together in the form of a compelling story.)

What If I Just Can't Get My Thoughts Straight? Using the One-Page Memo

Sometimes you will just feel completely stuck. You know you have something to say or a recommendation to make—and you know you have to give a presentation, because the date and time have been set and the audience invited—but you just cannot seem to get clear in your mind what you are trying to recommend. In a situation like this, what I have found useful is to try writing it in prose: write a brief letter or memo describing what you have in mind, either in pencil on a notepad or in a word processor.

I find Procter & Gamble's one-page memo format very useful for this. When I began my marketing career at P&G over twenty years ago, the one-page memo discipline was in full force. Every communication had to fit on one page and follow a fixed format. (It is a good example of how constraints can sometimes paradoxically be liberating. By forcing you to follow a certain format and sequence, the one-page memo frees you to think about just what you want to say.)

Here is a description of the format, with some of my own embellishments. Each one-page memo contains five parts:

1. *The Idea.* What are you proposing—what do you want your audience to do? This is typically one sentence.
2. *Background.* What conditions have arisen that led you to this recommendation? Only include information that everyone agrees on in the Background. This is the basis for discussion, so it needs to be non-debatable.
3. *How It Works.* The details of your proposal. In addition to How, also What, Who, When, Where.
4. *Key Benefits.* This is the "Why"? There are usually three benefits: your recommendation fits with the organization's strategy, it is already proven (e.g., in test market or in another organization), and will be profitable or cost-effective. You can think of these three in terms of the Total Quality mantra of "doing right things right." The first (on strategy) means you're doing the right thing. The second and third

mean you're doing things the right way, because you're being effective (proven to work) and efficient (profitable).

5. *Next Steps.* Who has to do what, by when, and to whom, for this to happen?

The P&G sales force used something called the Persuasive Selling Format (PSF) in their sales pitches. The PSF also had five steps. At some point it occurred to me that the two mapped to each other, which is why the P&G one-page memo format is so effective for making recommendations: it is a document structure that is designed to sell.

Once you've drafted this memo, you'll have a better idea of exactly what you are trying to say and what you want your audience to do. You can then go back to Chapter 2 and revise your objective if necessary and continue from there. Or else you may find that the memo alone will be sufficient and that you don't need a presentation. Finish it, send it out, and save yourself and your audience a lot of time.

What Do I Do If There Really Isn't a Clear Solution to the Problem?

Occasionally, though, even the memo will not solve the problem for you. You will see clearly that there is a problem, but you will have no idea what your audience should do about it. In this case, you should turn your presentation into a facilitated problem-solving session, with you as the facilitator. Your objective for the presentation will be to get the audience to think through an issue that they are facing that they haven't been thinking about.

Right at the beginning, tell them that you are going to present a serious problem that they have, to which you do not have an answer, and then you would like to facilitate a discussion to generate some ideas on how it could be solved. Take them through the details of the problem, and then present a few (three to five) critical questions for them to discuss. Do your best to provide at least preliminary answers to each question, and try to include more than one answer to each question, so that they can see that you truly mean to explore alternatives. As you work through these, ask them to react to the alternatives you have included, and see whether they can think of any others.

Interestingly, the results of a facilitated discussion like this can be very effective. When audiences draw their own conclusions, the effect is much stronger than if the conclusions are presented to them.[9]

Peter Norvig, author of the hilarious (and profound) PowerPoint version of Abraham Lincoln's Gettysburg Address, argues that "If everyone has set their remarks in stone ahead of time (all using the same templates) then there is little room for the comments of one to build on another, or for a new idea to arise collaboratively from the meeting. . . . Use visual aids to convey visual information: photographs, charts, or diagrams. But do not use them to give the impression that the matter is solved, wrapped up in a few bullet points."[10]

Self-persuasion is so effective that it is worth considering making every presentation interactive in this way, even when you have a clear idea about what you want your

[9] According to Armstrong's review of the literature on persuasion, this is particularly true for conditions under which you have: an intelligent audience, expected resistance, a presenter who is perceived as biased, and when the objective is to change important beliefs (Armstrong, forthcoming)

[10] See Norvig (2003). His Gettysburg PowerPoint presentation is available at http://norvig.com/Gettysburg/

audience to do. If you do this, the essential thing is not to be disingenuous: *never* pretend that you do not know the answer and that you want your audience's input if, in fact, you *do* know it and *don't* want their input. What you should do instead is state your recommendation clearly, and then ask for input. The discussion that follows, if you are open to their input and flexible enough to incorporate it, is a good opportunity for self-persuasion in the audience. *But this will only work if you are truly open to input!* You have to be as willing to allow your own ideas to be modified as you are expecting your audience to be willing to allow theirs to be modified. Otherwise, you will come across as fake and manipulative.[11]

The one place to "hide the ball" is when you have a very strong point—solidly backed up by evidence—that is counter-intuitive. In that case, first ask your audience what their opinion is. Ideally, have them write it down or at least check off some alternative. For example, you might ask them: "Which of the following options do you think would be the most costly for us? Please mark the one you think is most costly." Then present the answer and your evidence for it. This way they can see that they were wrong and have to rethink their beliefs on this. If they did not make a mark, they will likely just think "I knew that" and move on—and then forget this new information. By showing them that they need to rethink, you will increase the likelihood that they do so.

The Importance of Being Audience-Focused

It is very important in this step—as it is throughout the entire ten-step process—to be completely audience-focused. Your presentation should be all about serving your audience. You need to show them that you see everything from their perspective—their problem, in their terms, their motivations and issues. This also means that you have to be bound by their constraints. There is no point in raising an important problem and proposing new investments to solve it if your audience just does not have any money to spend this year.

Otherwise, you are just playing a game: you present an important problem and recommend the theoretically correct solution. They smile and thank you for your astute analysis. And then they do nothing. The reality is that most people *do* want to achieve something for themselves or for their organization. You need to focus on that and help them to overcome the problems that get in the way of that achievement. If you frequently present to the same audience—if you are a trainer, researcher, analyst, consultant—you want to become known as someone who helps to solve problems, not just as a provider of data. Problem-solvers are liked, respected, and rewarded. Providers of data are often looked down upon or just ignored.

Which one do you want to be? The choice is yours.

At this point, you should have a clear idea of a serious problem that your audience has and what solution you are proposing for it. But what information do we actually have to present to them to convince them of this? Turn to Chapter 4 to answer this question.

[11]Aronson (1999) has also found that self-persuasion is far more powerful than being persuaded by others.

Marshalling Your Evidence

Step 4: List All the Information That You Think You May Need to Include in Your Presentation

List all the information—all the support, reasons, evidence—that is relevant to your solution. Think of this as a brain-dump of everything that might go into your presentation. You can list everything in Worksheet A.6 in Appendix A or just on a blank piece of paper. See the example in Figure 4.1.

FIGURE 4.1. Example of an Information Brain-Dump

Evidence

1. _Brand equity study data_
2. _Quotes from customer interviews_
3. _Quote from Hyperbrand_
4. _Salesforce impact study_
5. _Other unfunded priority projects_
6. _____
7. _____
8. _____
9. _____
10. _____
11. _____
12. _____

Include all the information you can think of that supports your recommendations, and also evidence *against* your recommendations—because you are going to have to deal with this information somehow, so you cannot just ignore it.

Try to collect information broadly, from several different sources, not just the project you are working on. Don't worry about the order of your list of information, or whether it is quantitative or merely anecdotal, at this point. Just list everything that you can think of: basically all the information you can think of that is relevant to your solution.

The rest of this chapter will explain in detail:

- What kinds of evidence to include to strengthen the persuasiveness of your presentation
- What kinds of evidence are likely to weaken your presentation and therefore should be avoided
- Where to look for evidence

What Kinds of Evidence Should You Include?

What kinds of evidence should you include to strengthen the persuasiveness of your presentation? There are three things to keep in mind as you gather your evidence:

- Use real and specific (rather than abstract and general) data wherever possible.
- Include a variety of different types of evidence and arguments—including evidence *against* your proposals.
- Pay particular attention to what is new and different in your information.

Why are we so concerned about persuasiveness? Recall from Chapter 2 that if you are not trying to change your audience's thoughts or actions with your presentation, then why are you wasting your time—and theirs—delivering a presentation? Even if you are working on a training presentation, remember that *training is also a form of persuasion*: you are trying to persuade your audience to change their attitudes and behaviors to adopt the new ideas and techniques that you are teaching them.

Use Real and Specific Data

When gathering data, follow the Reality Principle: always include evidence that is concrete and particular, and not just conceptual and general. Research shows that people prefer—and are more convinced by—particular facts, information about real people, and actual photographs of things rather than illustrations. So don't just say that 75 percent of your customers prefer this new design, but also provide one or two quotes from real customers saying how much they like the new design.

If the information you are presenting is conceptual, try to support it with at least one data point, as an example. A single data point does not prove an argument, but it does prove that the thing you are talking about indeed exists. One company frequently used a conceptual chart to communicate their approach to change management. The chart showed a line of how sales would evolve through the various stages of a change management program. My recommendation to them was that the chart would be made more powerful by adding the details of one or two case studies to it. So instead of just saying, "Here, conceptually, is how a company's sales revenues will evolve through the stages of a change program," you can also say, "And here it is in practice, with the results we saw at IBM and at Microsoft," for example.

Include a Variety of Different Types of Evidence

As you gather your evidence, be sure to include different types of evidence, arguments, and support for your recommendations. Use both qualitative and quantitative data, multiple arguments, causal arguments, evidence that is inherently persuasive, evidence about the problem, and evidence against your recommendations.

Quantitative and Qualitative Data   Use both quantitative and qualitative data. While quantitative (numerical) data may seem specific and concrete, and particularly relevant for the detail-oriented members of your audience, it can actually be quite abstract. When you say that 4 percent of your products had some kind of quality defect this past month, that number "4 percent" may seem like a specific detail, but actually it is a generalization across many observations, perhaps thousands of them. To add more detail, use qualitative data also: examples, anecdotes, cases-in-point. Perhaps a diagram or— better (because more real)—a photograph of a flawed product. Or, best and most real of all, if the group is small enough and the product is portable, bring an example of a flawed product to the meeting, to serve as a three-dimensional data sample. Qualitative data reinforces your quantitative data: where the latter summarizes thousands of observations, the former zooms in on just one or two of those observations. It gives your audience comfort that your statistics are not lying, by showing them one or more of your actual observations.

Multiple Arguments   The more evidence and arguments you include in your presentation, the more likely your audience is to be persuaded. This tends to be true whether or not your audience is highly concerned about the issue being discussed. When people are more concerned about the issue at hand, using more arguments tends to increase persuasion by providing more supportive information on which to make a decision. When people are not so concerned, however, the greater number of arguments also is more effective, because it gives the *impression* (correctly) of a strong case being made.[1]

Causal Arguments   Causal arguments—when you show how one things leads to or causes another—are particularly effective. When you explain *why* or *how* your recommended actions will lead to the results they want, people find this more convincing than when you just provide evidence that your recommendations *do* lead to the desired results. People are more willing to be convinced when they understand not just that something will succeed, but also why or how it will succeed.[2]

[1]Petty & Cacioppo (1984) ran an experiment in which students were presented with different versions of a message with different numbers of arguments, and found that increasing the number of arguments increased the chance of agreement with the message.

[2]Research experiments by Slusher and Anderson (1996) indicate that causal arguments or explanations are more persuasive than statistical evidence.

For example, don't just say "our research shows that serif fonts (e.g., Times Roman) are more readable than sans serif fonts (e.g., Arial)," also say, "because the little serifs serve as cues to the brain, allowing it to process the letters more quickly."

EVIDENCE THAT IS INHERENTLY PERSUASIVE

Cialdini (2001), summarizing several decades of psychology research on persuasion, draws a number of conclusions about how people are persuaded. Based on these conclusions, we can identify additional types of evidence that should be inherently persuasive: quotes from authority figures; information about the consistency of your proposals; information about what others are doing that is similar to your proposals; and information about the scarcity of the opportunity.

- People are more likely to be persuaded by authority figures, so whenever you can, cite respected experts, such as analysts, academics, or industry experts, whose opinions support your recommendations

- There is a desire among most people "to be and look consistent within their words, beliefs, attitudes, and deeds" (Cialdini, 2001, p. 95), so if your recommendations are consistent with previous actions that your audience has taken, or aligned with a strategy that they have committed to, be sure to inform them of this.

- "[O]ne important means that people use to decide what to believe or how to act in a situation is to look at what other people are believing or doing there" (Cialdini, 2001, p. 140), so if other organizations are also doing what you are recommending, be sure to include this fact in your list of evidence.

- "People assign more value to opportunities when they are less available" (Cialdini, 2001, p. 231), so if the opportunity that you are proposing is scarce or limited in any way, mention this also.

Evidence About the Problem   Include evidence about the existence and magnitude of the problem that you are addressing, not just about the solution you are offering. The less likely that your audience is to believe in the existence of, or be concerned by, the problem you are focusing on, the more evidence about the problem you should include.

Evidence Against Your Recommendations   As counter-intuitive as this may seem, you should also include evidence that supports competing, alternative solutions and evidence against your own solution. Research consistently shows that presenting a "two-sided" message (where arguments from both sides, in favor and against, are included) is more persuasive than a "one-sided" message (where only arguments on one side are included).[3]

[3]See Allen's (1998) meta-analysis of research on one- versus two-sided messages. Pechmann's (1992) research indicates that advertising that admits a serious negative feature is associated with stronger credibility.

In addition to mentioning the opposing arguments, you should also refute them convincingly; mentioning them without refuting them can be worse than not mentioning them at all, in terms of persuasion. But even merely mentioning the opposing arguments, so long as they are serious, not trivial, arguments will increase your credibility with the audience because they see that you are trying to provide them with a comprehensive view of the issue, rather than just selecting the information that supports your case.

In refuting the opposing arguments, be careful about disparaging or trying to get your audience to disregard the contrary information, because doing so can *increase* their interest in it. People tend to be more attracted to what they are told to avoid. For example, when some counties in Florida banned phosphate detergents in the 1970s, consumers in those counties rated the same phosphate detergents more highly than consumers in counties where they were not banned.[4]

[4]See Mazis (1975). But legal research is mixed on this point. Research by Broeder (1959) and Wolf and Montgomery (1977) found that judges' instructions to ignore certain evidence can lead jurors to give that evidence *more* consideration, but other studies contradict these findings.

What we have here is another instance of the tactic of "stealing thunder," which we discussed in Chapter 3. When you are the first to bring up negative information about your argument, your argument is viewed more favorably than if someone else first brought up the negative information. Remember that if you do not bring up the contrary arguments, you run the risk that someone in your audience will, and this can be quite damaging to your presentation.

New and Different Information

Wherever possible, be sure to include information that is new and different. This is particularly true for presentations that are providing an update on a project or reporting on an ongoing research study (such as a market tracking study). In such cases, you will often have too much information. Focus on information that is new or unusual; if this quarter's tracking study finds an increased interest in organic foods among youth, for example, make that the center of your presentation.[5]

[5]In a study of several different advertising executions, Stanton and Burke (1998) found that commercials that claimed "new product" were more persuasive.

Try to avoid repeating the same, tired old "facts" that everyone else quotes. For example, anyone giving a presentation about interpersonal communication usually quotes the same old "fact" that 93 percent of all communication is non-verbal. Sometimes it is worth doing some digging. You may find that the established "fact" is in fact false—we noted in the Introduction that this is indeed the case with the "93 percent non-verbal" statistic. The information that the well-known "fact" is in fact false is then itself a newsworthy piece of information that you can include that will help your presentation stand out.

Is There Any Kind of Evidence That You Should Exclude?

We have covered several types of evidence to *include* in your presentation. Is there anything you should make sure to *exclude*? Yes—you should try to avoid evidence that is irrelevant, annoying, or induces guilt in your audience, because these kinds of evidence tend to weaken presentation effectiveness.

Irrelevant evidence does more harm than just cluttering up your presentation and taking away attention from your good evidence, because you can't assume that the irrelevant information will just be ignored by your audience. We know from advertising research that the inclusion of irrelevant evidence can actually reduce the perceived value of the *relevant* information being communicated.[6]

[6]When consumers evaluate product information, irrelevant information *weakens* their beliefs in the product's ability to deliver on the benefit (Meyvis & Janiszewski, 2002).

What about arguments or evidence that are relevant but weak? If you have strong evidence as well as weak, will the weak evidence dilute the stronger evidence? This depends on how involved your audience is with your presentation topic. For a highly involved audience, adding weak arguments to strong ones will actually weaken overall persuasion, but for a less involved audience, more is better: adding weak arguments to strong arguments improves overall believability.[7]

[7]Both Meyvis and Janiszewski's (2002) research in advertising and Friedrich, Fetherstonhaugh, Casey, and Gallagher's (1996) research in psychology conclude that adding weak arguments to strong ones weakens overall persuasion.

Try to avoid including any information that is just going to annoy your audience and make them dislike you. Anything that makes people like you less will weaken your ability to persuade them.[8]

[8]People are more easily persuaded by people they like (Cialdini, 2001).

[9]See O'Keefe (2000). The discomfort caused by guilt leads the audience to either ignore the evidence or examine it more critically (Bohner & Weinerth, 2001).

More specifically, be careful about including information that is going to make your audience feel guilty. It is tempting to think that you can motivate your audience by making them feel guilty if they do not do what you are recommending to them. However, research suggests that, instead, guilt appeals tend to *weaken* persuasion.[9]

For example, let's say that you are in human resources and you are presenting some information on how to avoid mistakes in the hiring process. Let's also say that you presented similar information last year to the same audience, who, if they had listened to you, could have avoided a number of costly and embarrassing hiring mistakes in the past year. You would be justified into wanting to begin your presentation by saying, "If only you had listened to me last year, these things would not have happened. So this year pay attention, okay!" But don't do it. Instead restate the points you made last year, as clearly as you can. You can also add the failure cases as examples of what can go wrong—so long as you do not use them to suggest guilt. You could even position them as "what we have learned in the past year" to make your presentation more current and newsworthy. And finally, rest assured that this year they *will* act on your advice, because now you are using the ten-step Extreme Presentation method!

Where Do You Find All This Evidence?

As we saw above, in general, more evidence is better. It also helps to give your audience the comfort that you have covered the issue comprehensively. To do this, you want to draw your evidence from a wide range of sources. Don't just include evidence from your current project. Use information from other projects, studies, and from secondary research. Sometimes we exclude material that is very relevant because our audience has already seen it. Do not assume that they will remember everything that you have shown them in the past; if something is very relevant, include it again.

Internal Sources to Consider
- Data from your current study or project
- Other research you've done
- Financial data

External Sources
- Syndicated research
- Analyst reports
- News articles
- Academic research
- Consultant reports
- Government statistics
- Public policy advocates' data

At this point, you should have a long, rich, comprehensive list of persuasive evidence. The next challenge is how to put it together in a sequence that will keep your audience interested, because the most logical, persuasive evidence will do you no good *if your audience sleeps through your presentation.* Turn to Part III on Rhetoric to see how to use stories to capture and keep your audience's attention throughout your presentation.

PART III
RHETORIC

HOW DO YOU TAKE a stack of evidence and turn it into a captivating, engaging presentation? The next two chapters will answer this question.

You may be wondering, however, why evidence alone is not enough. If you have worked hard to gather comprehensive, convincing evidence, why can't you just go ahead and use that evidence to convince your audience? The answer is that factual evidence and logic alone are not sufficient to persuade most people. And even those who are more open to logic are more easily persuaded if you also engage their emotions. Human beings are both rational and emotional creatures, and both of these faculties have to be engaged if you truly what to keep their attention.[1]

If you want to communicate effectively, you have to engage your audience's emotions as well as their reason. If you engage only their reason, you are less convincing than you could be. (If you engage only their emotions, however, you may be manipulating them, violating the ethical responsibilities of a communicator—more on this below).

An effective way to make information appeal to the emotions is to present it in the form of a story. Chapter 5 will explain how to illustrate your most important data points with brief stories or anecdotes. Chapter 6 will then show you how to turn your entire stack of information into one comprehensive and compelling story. What these chapters will show you is how—even if you think that your data is inherently boring, or that you are the dullest, most uninspiring presenter around—you can take however large a stack of information you have gathered and turn it into a story that grabs and holds your audience's attention from start to finish.

Before we turn to these chapters, we will first discuss the following essential points:

- The importance of stirring your audience's emotions;
- The crucial role of storytelling for doing this; and
- The ethical responsibility of presenters

Logic Alone Is Not Enough

Logic is important for persuasion, but is not sufficient alone. If you only use logic, you are restricting your appeal to people who are primarily "thinkers," and likely excluding people who are primarily "feelers." And you will not be doing as effective a job as you could with

[1] For example, both rational and emotional factors influence consumers' evaluation of the risks of purchasing different products (Chaudhuri, 2002).

people who are primarily thinkers, because they are more effectively persuaded when you also engage them with something beyond mere logic.

In Myers-Briggs terms, "Feelers," or "F's," represent well over half of the total U.S. population. They are significantly underrepresented in managerial and administrator roles—which is perhaps why many presenters default to using logic alone—but they still make up more than a quarter of this group. What this means is that if you focus on logic alone, you could be losing more than a quarter of your audience if you are presenting to managers and almost two-thirds if you are presenting to a general audience.[2]

More generally, advertising research indicates that logical arguments only play a small role in changing people's attitudes. People find it very hard to change their beliefs, even when faced with clear logic. They tend to focus on information that supports their existing beliefs and ignore or discount evidence that challenges them.[3]

This is even true for supposedly objective, fact-based people such as scientists. In an interesting experiment some years ago researchers compared the problem-solving approaches of scientists and conservative Protestant ministers. The two groups were chosen because the former were supposedly purely objective and the latter, supposedly biased by their religious convictions. The study found no significant difference between the two groups in terms of belief change, with both groups having a tendency to bias themselves in favor of supporting their ingoing hypothesis.[4]

When people hold strong, opposing attitudes, logical argument can actually cause them to "dig their heels in" on their current beliefs: the stronger the contrary evidence, the more effort they put into their counter-arguments. So if people tend to cling to their beliefs, and the more you provide logical argument, the more they cling, what should you do? One solution is to involve people in your presentations, to draw them in so that they can see the relevance of your material to their lives.[5]

Another solution to audiences' reluctance to change their beliefs is referred to as the "disrupt then reframe" technique. This is when you surprise your audience with something unusual, and then use the moment of surprise to introduce the new idea you want them to consider. The disruption temporarily "disables" the audience's instinctive negative reactions and opens them to the new information. While this method could be used to trick or manipulate, it is included here only as a method for overcoming unreasonable resistance: to give your audience an opportunity to consider new evidence rather than writing it off without considering it.[6]

For example, in one of his presentations, branding guru Tom Asacker effectively overcomes his audience's existing and strongly held beliefs that the fact that consumers are overwhelmed with marketing messages is a *new* challenge. He does this by showing a slide with a quote about how people are overwhelmed with marketing messages. Then he points out that this quote is from . . . *1918*. This surprise disrupts the audience's thought patterns, and so they are now open to his reframing, where he reframes for them what the real problems are—nothing, in this case, to do with being overwhelmed by messages.[7]

[2]Feelers, which include half of all the sixteen MBTI types, represent 59.9 percent of the U.S. population (Myers & Briggs Foundation, 2006), yet only 27.6 percent of all managers, administrators, and supervisors (Macdaid, 1997).

[3]In a meta-analysis of research on the role of product information in advertising, Stiff (1986) found that logical arguments are correlated with attitude change, but only very weakly.

[4]This experiment is described in Mahoney and DeMonbreun (1977), who found that the protestant ministers were actually slower to jump to conclusions than the scientists.

[5]See Armstrong (2008). The correlation between logical arguments and attitude change improves when the audience is highly involved with the message (Stiff, 1986); even strong arguments can be made more powerful through greater audience involvement (Petty, Cacioppo, & Schumann, 1983).

[6]Davis & Knowles (1999) describe four studies that demonstrate how the "disrupt then reframe" technique was used to persuade householders to contribute to a charity.

[7]See Tom Asacker, "On Branding: A Visual Presentation" www.acleareye.com/thoughts.

The Importance of Storytelling

An effective way to reframe your evidence *and* involve your audience is to present your information in the form of a story. There is something very powerful and elemental about stories. Alan Kay, the personal computer visionary, once said, "Why was Solomon recognized as the wisest man in the world? Because he knew more stories (proverbs) than anyone else. Scratch the surface in a typical boardroom, and we're all just cavemen with briefcases, hungry for a wise person to tell us stories " (McLellan, 2006).

Some people may hold a suspicion that storytelling is just the latest presentation fad and that presentations that begin with "Once upon a time . . ." have no place in serious communication. This is quite false. There is mounting evidence that the use of storytelling in organizations drives business results.[8]

Stories are fundamental to how we think, learn, and make sense of the world around us. Storytelling has been present in every age of human history and in every civilization and culture. Stories appear to enable understanding and memory, and much of both child and adult learning appears to be acquired through a story format. One important reason that stories are so powerful is that information delivered through stories is more memorable. Memory is strengthened by linking information together, and stories link information in multiple ways. Also, stories engage the emotions, and this too aids memory.[9]

Audiences remember stories better than they remember lists of bullet points. This is of particular relevance to presentations, because of the popularity of the bullet list slide. Lists suffer from what are called the primacy and recency effects: we remember the first and the last items on the list, but not the middle. By contrast, stories are a coherent whole, where one thing flows to the next, so we tend to remember the whole thing ("The Science of Stories," 1998).

In many cases, people tend to put information they receive into a story form; if your audience is going to put the information that you give them into a story form anyway, why not give them the information in a story in the first place–so that *you* choose the story, not them?[10]

Storytelling is therefore a very effective persuasion method. But persuasion implies responsibility. How does one use a powerful persuasion technique responsibly?

Ethical Persuasion

As presenters, we need techniques to overcome the resistance, described above, that most people have to new information. Storytelling is one such powerful persuasion technique. But with power comes responsibility. What does responsible—ethical—persuasion look like?

Much of unethical behavior is in the form of cheating: trying to achieve a goal in an unfair way, unfair in the sense that if others knew you were taking that approach, it would

[8]Silverman (2006) presents several case studies; additional case studies appear in Jackson & Esse (2006), Kahan (2006), Simmons (2006), Smart (1999), and Smith & Keyton (2001). Gold and Holman (2001) used storytelling effectively in management education.

[9]See, for example, Branigan (1992), Mallon and Webb (2000), and Turner (1996.) Cahill, Babinsky, Markowitsch, and McGaugh's (1995) experiments with stories suggest that memory storage of events that involve high emotions is qualitatively different from other memory storage. Kazui, Mori, Hashimoto, and Hirono (2000; 2003) found in studies of healthy people and Alzheimer's patients that stories that engage the emotions are more memorable than ones that do not.

[10]Research suggests that juries in criminal trials use a story approach to make sense of the data they receive. When lawyers help them with this, by organizing the evidence in story form, jurors are more likely to be influenced by it and find it credible (Pennington & Hastie, 1991, 1992).

not work, because they would not let you get away with it. One problem with cheating, for the cheater, is that you do not get any better at achieving your goals; each time you cheat, the only thing you get better at is cheating. As a result, you increase the likelihood that the next time you will have to cheat again, and therefore that eventually you will be caught. If you use persuasion to get people to do things against their own good, sooner or later they will realize this, and you will no longer be welcome as a presenter.

It's not worth it; don't do it.

A useful guiding principle to decide whether you are using persuasion ethically and responsibly is to ask yourself: Are you trying to get your audience to do something that is not in their or their company's best interests? If so, you are being manipulative and unethical. If instead you are indeed trying to get them to do what they should, for their own good and the good of the company, then your persuasion is ethical: you are helping them overcome their own inertia, so that they will do the right thing.

The underlying assumption throughout this book is that the recommendations you are making in your presentations are good for your audience, and so by getting them to act on these recommendations you are serving them, not taking advantage of them. The techniques taught in this book are highly effective at getting your audience to do what you are telling them to do. Using these techniques for anything other than the good of your audience is an abuse of the techniques, and is directly opposed to the audience-centered theme of this book.

Assembling the Anecdotes That Will Illustrate Your Evidence

Step 5: Identify Brief Anecdotes That Highlight Your Most Important Points

The next step is to identify any useful anecdotes or stories that can be used to illustrate your most important points. The idea here is not to replace the evidence you have gathered, but to emphasize it. A story is not proof; it is just illustration. A story doesn't prove anything, but it does get your audience's attention and can sometimes drive a point home much more than reams of data. From a scientific perspective, this can seem frustrating: people appear to be more persuaded by a story about a single incident (i.e. a sample size of one) than by a survey with a sample size of five hundred. But a story is not qualitative research as a weak substitute for quantitative research; it is qualitative research as a more powerful illustration—or an enrichment of—results from quantitative research.

In Step 4 you gathered your proof—your evidence—and in Step 5 you will find ways to emphasize that proof. Take the list of evidence that you developed in Step 4, and circle anything on the list that is not quantitative, anything on the list that is "anecdotal" in any way. Each of these anecdotal items can serve you as an anecdote or story (these two words are used interchangeably in this book). It could be a story told to you by a salesperson in your organization, a verbatim customer quote from a survey, a video clip from a customer interview or focus group, and so on.

Now we will explore:

- What kinds of stories should I use in my presentation?
- How do I prepare an anecdote so that it can be "told" well?
- Where do I find useful stories?

What Kinds of Stories Should You Use in Your Presentation?

You can use three kinds of stories, and all are effective. The first kind is one that is *directly related to your organization or issue*. A story that you gathered from an employee about the trouble she had using your company's online benefits portal when one of her children was sick would be one example of this kind. A story that you heard from one of your company's salespeople, about a corporate customer who would routinely stand on the top of her desk and scream at him because she didn't like your company's pricing policies, would be another example.

The second kind of story is a *hypothetical* one. This is a story about your business that is not "real" in the sense that it has ever happened, necessarily, but it is certainly "realistic" in that it *could* happen. (This is very important; for your hypothetical stories to be effective, they must be immediately credible to your audience—*and* they must be clearly identified as hypothetical.) The details of the story are what bring out its reality. A "day in the life" of one of your customers is one example, where we see in detail what she is doing at different moments. Another example would be a run-through of how an employee would use a new system that you are proposing. Again, what makes it real is the specificity—the concreteness—of the details that you provide.

[1]McCroskey (1969)'s meta-analysis of numerous studies showed that metaphors are more persuasive than literal statements. This is likely because a metaphor "helps to structure and organize the arguments of a message better than literal language" (Sopory & Dillard, 2002, p. 387).

The third type of story is one that takes *a more metaphorical approach*—which is not in itself about your situation or company specifically, but which is symbolic or illustrative of the point that you want to make. While metaphorical stories might seem less valuable because they are not specifically about your particular situation, research indicates that they are also very effective. If possible, apply the same metaphor at different points in your presentation, and try to stick to a single metaphor for the same point, rather than using several different metaphors.[1]

Here is a great example of a very powerful metaphorical story, in which the author tells a great lesson he learned about advertising (du Plessis, 2005, pp. 109–110; quotation reproduced with permission).

> "When I am asked where I learnt most about advertising theories, the answer is not a book about the brain, or a book about advertising, or any journal paper, or a specific professor. I learnt the most about advertising from a miner.
>
> In 1994 South Africa had its first democratic election, which effectively moved power from the mainly Afrikaans white government to a black government. Obviously emotions were running high, especially because (since there were many more black than white voters) the outcome was a forgone conclusion. Afrikaners felt threatened by what the future might hold for them, and blacks felt liberated and able to make aggressive statements in public showing their new-found 'power.' Afrikaners in rural areas felt especially threatened. During this time I was asked to do research among the black miners in a rural coal mine, to establish what they saw as their major problems. I did this under the condition that the results would be shown to representatives of their management (white) and trade union (black) at the same time.
>
> To my dismay the black miners rated as their third biggest problem the fact that 'White managers insist on giving their instructions in Afrikans.' I was dismayed because I knew, from my experience with focus groups, that the black miners spoke better Afrikans than English. They preferred to speak Afrikans rather than English, and to listen to Afrikans programs on television. So why would they want the

management to give them instructions in English? It seemed obvious to me that the only reason for their giving this problem such a priority was that they were making a political statement. This was not an unlikely explanation at that time.

Because mining is such a physically demanding job, both managers and face workers tend to be big, strong people. As an Afrikaner, I felt rather uneasy at the prospect of presenting this politically sensitive result in a meeting of these big people in a small room. I tried to gloss over the point in my presentation. The leader of the trade union asked me to go over it again more slowly. I tried to gloss over it again, and he again called on me to spend more time discussing it. I told him outright that I believed it was a political point-scoring exercise, and best left out of the meeting.

He then proceeded to give me a lesson in communication, which I still rate as the most valuable I have ever had. His words went something like this:

'It is true that most of us Zulus are more proficient in Afrikans than in English. However, Afrikans is our third language and English is our fourth. Most of us speak two native African languages better than we speak either Afrikans or English.

Afrikans is the managers' first language. When a manager gives an instruction in Afrikans, he will give a concise instruction, believing he has expressed himself clearly, and then be upset when we do the wrong thing.

When a manager gives an instruction in his second language he feels more insecure. He will probably repeat the instruction a few times, using different words, and will use a lot of body language to demonstrate what he means. Then he will ask us whether we understand – and patiently re-explain if we don't.

The difference is that when he instructs in his first language he believes he has done a good job of communicating, but when he does it in a language we are both less proficient in, he really does a good job of communicating!'

We all tend to forget that the people who create advertising, the agencies and marketers, are doing this in their first language (so to speak). They have been trained in the language of advertising, they have a lot of experience in the language of advertising, and they know the product very well. The people they are creating the communication for are not steeped in either the language of the product or the language of advertising. In fact, they mostly cannot be bothered to learn either."

The story is about miners. On the face of it, it has nothing to do with advertising. But du Plessis uses it to make a very powerful point about advertising, and about communication in general.

You can use stories—actual or metaphorical—to illustrate any aspect of your presentation, including the business problem that the audience has, the solution you are offering, and any of the evidence that you are including. This means that stories will have a big role to play in your presentations. Some people are natural storytellers, and they instinctively incorporate stories into their communication and do it well. The rest of us need some help in telling a story: how to get the plot right—how to identify the essential elements of the story and tell them in the right order.

How to Tell a Story Using the Seven Basic Plots

Have you ever had the suspicion that there are really only a few basic stories in the world? If you have, you are not alone. Christopher Booker had that thought back in the early 1970s, and worked on it for almost thirty-five years, reading thousands of books and watching numerous plays and movies. The result of all that effort is a book he wrote that claims that there are really only seven basic plots in all of Western literature, and he does a very convincing job of proving the claim with examples from the books, movies, and plays he studied (Booker, 2005; quotations reproduced by kind permission of Continuum Publishing Group).

Booker identifies the seven plots as (1) overcoming the monster; (2) the quest; (3) voyage and return; (4) comedy; (5) tragedy; (6) rebirth; and (7) rags to riches. He provides

TABLE 5.1.   The Seven Basic Plots

Basic Plot	Story Example	Business Example	Main Stages
1. Overcoming the monster—"seemingly all-powerful monster whom the hero must confront in a fight to the death"	Star Wars	Facing a major threat to our business	1. The Call. 2. Initial Success. 3. Confrontation. 4. Final Ordeal. 5. Miraculous Escape.
2. The Quest—"Far away . . . there is some priceless goal . . . [the hero sets out on a] long hazardous journey . . ."	The Lord of the Rings	Embarking on a major new product initiative	1. The Call. 2. The journey. 3. Arrival and Frustration. 4. The Final Ordeals. 5. The Goal.
3. Voyage and Return—"hero or heroine . . . travel out of their familiar [world] . . . into another world completely cut off from the first"	Wizard of Oz	Shared an important experience	1. Fall into Another World. 2. Initial Fascination. 3. Frustration. 4. Nightmare. 5. Thrilling Escape and Return.
4. Comedy—"general chaos of misunderstanding . . . [finally] sorted out" (not necessarily humorous)	War and Peace	Resolving misunderstanding among different work groups	1. Confusion. 2. Nightmare. 3. New Information Transforms the Situation.
5. Tragedy—"tempted or impelled into a course of action . . . in some way dark or forbidden . . . [eventually] culminating in the hero's violent destruction"	Hamlet	Business about to go bankrupt due to mismanagement	1. Anticipation. 2. Dream. 3. Frustration. 4. Nightmare. 5. Destruction.
6. Rebirth—"hero or heroine falls under a dark spell which eventually traps them in some wintry state . . . [until] from the depths of darkness they are brought up into glorious light"	Sleeping Beauty	Recovery after long period	1. Hero Falls Under Dark Power. 2. All Seems Well for a While. 3. Living Death. 4. Apparent Triumph of Dark Power. 5. Miraculous Redemption.
7. Rags to Riches—"an ordinary, insignificant person . . . who suddenly steps to the center of the stage, revealed to be someone quite exceptional"	Cinderella	Sudden success	1. Initial Wretchedness. 2. Initial Success. 3. Central Crisis. 4. Independence and Final Ordeal. 5. Final Union.

numerous examples of each plot and then describes the unique sequence of essential stages that each plot has. Table 5.1 summarizes each of the plots and the stages in each and gives a story and a business example of each plot.

This plot structure is useful if you're trying to structure an anecdote. You can figure out what type of story plot the anecdote represents, and then make sure you've got the right pieces from the column on the right-hand side.

Once you know what the main elements of your story are, you can tell it, without any visual accompaniment, or else you can support it with one or more graphics or photographs in your presentation or with some artifact, such as a product sample, a faulty part, etc. If you have a very good story that someone else has written, and you don't think you can do it justice without reading it word-for-word, then do so, if it's not too long. Tell your audience that you have something you think they will find interesting and relevant, and you would like to read it to them. It is helpful to let them know how long it will take, since most people expect to be bored if they are being read to. If you say "I would like to read this extract to you—it's short, about two and a half minutes . . . " they will be less likely to *expect* to be bored, and therefore less likely to *be* bored.

Where to Find Useful Stories

It is hard to find a good story to fit a particular point in your presentation "on demand." I suggest that you start to collect good stories as you come across them, and file them away. Once you start looking for good stories, you will quickly become good at identifying them. And then when you happen need a story, you can look into your story file.

You can find stories within your organization and outside. Within your organization, some useful sources are customer interview notes or video; focus groups notes or video; any kind of qualitative or ethnographic research; anecdotes told by sales representatives or any other employees; or verbatim quotes from survey research.

Outside your organization, useful places to look for good stories include the front page of *The Wall Street Journal*, which often contains "human interest" stories. Mary Wacker and Lori Silverman's (2003) book *Stories Trainers Tell* contains more than seventy "ready to use" stories, categorized by topics such as "problem solving," "customer service," and "living our values." Silverman's website, Say It With a Story (www.sayitwithastory.com), features three stories from the book each month, along with numerous free articles on story use and has a story shop where additional stories are available for sale. Websites such as the Smoking Gun (www.thesmokinggun.com) contain amusing and sometimes shocking information from legal documents, arrest records, and other manuscripts acquired through Freedom of Information Act requests and public records, which can form the basis of engaging stories. Another source is the work of great storytellers such as Malcolm Gladwell. His bestselling books *The Tipping Point* and *Blink* are packed with mesmerizing stories, as are his *New Yorker* columns—which are archived on his website (www.gladwell.com).

Still another source of good stories is your own life. Grady Jim Robinson, one of the pioneers of the recent revival of interest in the use of stories in business communication, advises that some of the best stories come from your own experience, where you learned useful lessons that you can then share with your audience. Stories that allow you to admit some vulnerability, or share an embarrassing moment, can be endearing to audiences. Nevertheless, do be careful with these, and avoid any story that could in any way put your authority in the area of your presentation topic into question. ("You see, I don't know as much as you think I do about depreciation schedules, folks!" *Then why are we listening to you?*)

Outright humor is a bit more delicate. If you are not comfortable with yourself as a humorist, then avoid it. It's not necessary for a successful presentation. It should go without saying (but it doesn't, so I will say it) that you should never use any kind of potentially offensive humor in a formal gathering. I once organized a dinner meeting in New York City for a group of chief marketing officers of large corporations. The invited speaker was an authority on branding. He began his talk by describing a Harley-Davidson billboard ad that he saw on his way to the gathering that evening, and how much he liked it. "It showed a motorcycle rider from behind," he said, "and on the back of his black leather jacket it said, 'If You Can Read This, The Bitch Fell Off.'" The shock and horror from some members of the audience (which was only exacerbated by the uproarious laughter coming from other members of the audience) was just not worth it.

The safest way I know to use humor is to make sure that your joke has an important point to make. In effect, use the joke as a metaphorical story. That way, if nobody laughs, it's not a failed joke—it's just a story. This gives you a safety net, taking away your fear of telling a joke, and paradoxically—because you'll be less nervous without the pressure of getting it right—makes it more likely that you will deliver your story well and therefore that your audience will laugh.

FIGURE 5.1A   PowerPoint Humor

"Sure beats hassling with PowerPoint."

Another easy way to use humor safely is to include a good cartoon in your presentation. CartoonResource (www.CartoonResource.com) and *The New Yorker*'s Cartoon Bank (www.CartoonBank.com) both have large collections, searchable by topic. Figures 5.1a and b are examples of cartoons about PowerPoint, from CartoonResource (reproduced with permission).

FIGURE 5.1B   More PowerPoint Humor

Finally, if you want to improve your storytelling ability, there is nothing better that you can do than to read more stories. Not just any stories, though. Newer fiction doesn't work as well. Since contemporary fiction competes with video entertainment—television and the movies— it tends to rely more on the inherent interest of the content—the violence, sexual interest, or other highly emotional content—and so the burden on the actual story plot is not so great. Older fiction tends to be more restrained, and so the plot—the structure of the story itself—had to work hard to keep the reader interested. To really improve your storytelling ability, then, be sure to read some of the classics of Western fiction. Appendix E contains a selection from the "1000 Good Books," books that have been popular and in print for at least three generations.

The next challenge is to decide how to sequence all the evidence that you have gathered so that your entire presentation is in the form of a story. It turns out that the seven basic plots are not as helpful here. Fortunately, there is a fundamental principle that underlies *all* good stories, which we will uncover in the next chapter.

Sequencing Your Evidence

6

Step 6: Sequence Your Information So That It Tells a Compelling Story

At this point, you should know who your audience members are and what the communication implications for each of their personalities are; what the specific objectives are for your presentation in terms of how you will change your audience's minds and actions; and what business problem they face and what solution you are offering them. You should also have a stack of facts, analysis, and anecdotes, which embody the content of your presentation. Step 6 is all about taking this stack and ordering it into a compelling story that will capture your audience's attention while you deliver your message.

While the Seven Basic Plots described in the previous chapter are useful for structuring individual anecdotes, they are not so helpful for sequencing your entire presentation into the form of a story. This is because you do not want to lock yourself into a specific plot type while you are still working on your presentation. You want to allow yourself flexibility as you iterate through the process to change the plot. You may start out thinking that you have a Tragedy on your hands, and as you work through your presentation you might find a solution that turns it into a Rags to Riches story.

Fortunately, there is a fundamental insight about all good stories, no matter which type of plot: **they proceed by creating and resolving tensions.** The way to take advantage of this insight is as follows. First, introduce your presentation with a "situation"—Why are we here? Write this down on an index card. Then write down a "complication" and a "resolution"—typically the problem and solution that you identified in Step 3. Write these down on two separate index cards. Then follow the resolution with a specific example, also on another index card. I call this the S.Co.R.E. method (Situation, Complication, Resolution, Example).[1]

Then ask yourself: At this point, what is the most likely objection the audience would raise? Write that as the next complication. How would you respond to it? That's your next resolution. Then add an example. Each of these is on its own index card. (The point of using index cards is so that you can easily move things around or substitute others as you work on the sequence.)

[1]The S.Co.R.E. method is based on the Method of Opposites, outlined in detail by Henry Boettinger in his *Moving Mountains* (1969, pp. 82–96).

FIGURE 6.1.   Sample S.Co.R.E. Story Outline on Index Cards

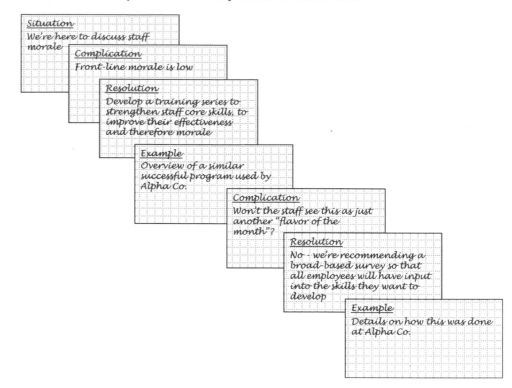

Keep on going in this way until you've covered all reasonable objections. You will most likely have included all the information you need. Whatever remains probably should not be in your presentation—put it in an appendix instead. Figure 6.1 contains an example of what this could look like for a presentation proposing a new training program.

Why does this approach work? It works because you are not giving any information to your audience without first creating the need for that information. That's the role of the complication in this process: it raises a question, which creates the need for the answer, which you then provide—the resolution.

This chapter is the most important one in the book. It will provide:

- More detail and examples of the structure of all effective stories
- How exactly to use the S.Co.R.E. (Situation, Complication, Resolution, Example) method to sequence your evidence in a way that captures and keeps your audience's attention
- What to do with information that does not fit into your new outline

The Structure of All Effective Stories

The order that you deliver your information in is of critical importance. The exact same information delivered in different sequences can achieve wildly different results in terms of audience persuasion.[2]

So how do we sequence our information for maximum impact? We sequence it so that it tells a story. How do we do that? By following a fundamental truth about storytelling. This fundamental truth about all good stories is that they repeatedly create tensions and resolve them. This is what makes them so interesting.

This structure of tension-resolution is also true about all great art. Great drama, painting, and music all create or highlight and then resolve tension.

Once tension is created or uncovered, the desire to resolve it can be so strong that we sometimes feel it as a physical need. Have you ever sat in the car after you arrived home to hear the end of a song? Or stayed up at night later than you wanted to watch the end of a movie or to finish a novel? In the Extreme Presentation workshop, we demonstrate this compulsion by singing a popular song together and pausing part-way through. Everyone in the audience can feel it: the desire to finish the song is felt as a physical desire. You can try this yourself. Play a good piece of music, and pause it right at the point at which the music reaches a climax. Don't you *feel* the desire to have it completed?

By presenting your information in the form of a story, by setting up a tension and resolving it, and repeating as necessary, you can create this physical desire in your audience for your message. You will have gone from fighting for your audience's attention to *them* fighting to hear *you*! That is a nice shift. But how do we do it, exactly? According to Henry Boettinger:

> Present your idea in this structure and sequence: statement of the problem, development of its relevant aspects, and resolution of the problem and its development. Use this structure and you send your idea rolling down the well-worn grooves of the human mind. Ignore it and you sent it into rocky, unknown canyons from which is may never return. (Boettinger, 1969, p. 37)

Every interesting story goes through this structure. It begins with a situation: "Once upon a time . . ." Then it hits you with a problem or something that creates tension. We'll call that the complication. Then it offers a solution to the problem—the problem is resolved, so we'll call it the resolution. The story could end there. Or else you could have another complication, and then another resolution, and so on.[3]

To explain this, let's look at a couple of fairytales. Consider *Little Red Riding Hood*. Once upon a time, Little Red Riding Hood went for a walk in the forest (situation). She met a wolf (complication—this is indeed a scary thing). The wolf, after speaking to her, left her alone (resolution—the complication, or threat, has been removed). The wolf went on to Grandma's house and ate her up (next complication). The woodcutter cut the wolf open and freed Grandma (resolution).

[2]McCroskey and Mehrley (1969), in a review of empirical research on message organization, found that poorly sequenced presentations are less effective at achieving attitude change.

[3]Other storytelling experts use similar structures to this, including Robinson (2000) and Booker (2005). Minto (1996) uses the words Situation, Complication, Resolution, but very differently from the way they are used here.

Or *Goldilocks and the Three Bears*. Goldilocks goes out for a walk and enters an empty house (situation). She tries two bowls of porridge, but finds them respectively too cold and too hot (complication). The third bowl is just right, and she eats it all up (resolution). She tries to sit down, but finds the chairs too high and too low (complication). She finds a third chair that is just right (resolution). She then goes upstairs to lie down, but the first two beds are too hard or too soft (complication). The third bed is just right, so she falls asleep (resolution). She wakes up to find three bears staring at her (complication). She runs away, back to her home (resolution).

Notice three things about these stories. First, they all begin with a situation, and this situation step (unlike the complication and resolution) is never repeated. Second, every complication is resolved by an accompanying resolution. And third, you can have as many complication-resolution pairs as you need to complete the story.

There is one other important thing to add to this structure. The human mind also needs time to rest after each resolution and to clarify and absorb it. If you keep hitting your audience with one complication-resolution pair after another, they may begin to get a little on edge. To give them the rest they need, you should follow each resolution with an example. And the example will typically be one of the anecdotes or analogies you identified in Step 5. Here is Boettinger again:

> An example brings the idea down to earth. It reinforces the truth of a specific presentation, so that the next floor of development takes off from a firm base. . . . After the clash of a resolution, give them the analogy as a restful period for absorption. (Boettinger, 1969, p. 86)

So here is an example. Sometime in 2000, BWM marketing managers in the United States were thinking about what kind of advertising to run the following year, and they came up with the idea of "BMW films"—short movies presented online. Here is the kind of outline they might have used to present this idea:

Situation: We need to develop some new advertising for next year.

Complication: All luxury car advertising is alike: a car, driving through the mountains, with classical music playing. Is it a BMW, a Mercedes, a Lexus? All the ads look the same. We want something different.

Resolution: Let's use advertising that really shows off the BMW's capabilities as a performance car.

Example: Like we do with the BMW Roadshow, where we allow potential customers to see what the BMW can really do.

Complication: But the TV networks won't allow us to show the kinds of performance driving demonstrations we want to show, because of their concerns about liability (if someone copies what he sees on TV and has a car accident, the networks could be sued).

Resolution: Let's do an online campaign instead; there are no such restrictions for online advertising.

Example: We tried an online campaign last year that was very successful. (Details of this campaign would be added here.)

Complication: But performance driving situations are very expensive to shoot, much more expensive than a car driving through the mountains.

Resolution: Let's use a viral campaign, where all we have to pay for is creating the advertising, and make it so interesting that consumers will pass it on to each other themselves.

Example: Some examples of other successful viral campaigns, from other industries.

That's the way it works. And it works very well. Using this approach, you create an interesting presentation that grabs your audience right at the beginning, and keeps their attention throughout. It is radically different from the typical presentation, which follows a structure that may be logical (e.g., objectives, strategy, plan, financial implications, staff implications, measurement, etc.) but can be quite boring.

Instead of having an agenda slide up-front, which you keep returning to (". . . and now we're on point number 7, the financial implications . . ." *snooze*), you are now telling a story. When you are watching a good movie, you don't expect a message to come up every now and again reminding you of where you are ("and now we will move on to scene three, where the hero is captured"). You do not sit there wondering where you are in the movie—unless it is a really bad movie. Similarly, you will no longer have to keep reminding your audience where you are in the presentation, because they'll be so interested in the story that they won't stop to think about that. It's a very effective approach.[4]

[4]3M replaced bullet-point descriptions of strategy with stories made up of situation/complication/ resolution and found that this approach was more effective and persuasive (Shaw, Brown, & Bromiley, 1998).

The reason that this method works so well is that you don't give your audience *any* information without first creating the *need* in them for that information. The complication creates the need for the information, and the resolution and example provide the information that satisfies the need. (Figure 6.2 shows a visual overview of the S.Co.R.E. method).

FIGURE 6.2.   Visual Overview of the S.Co.R.E. Method

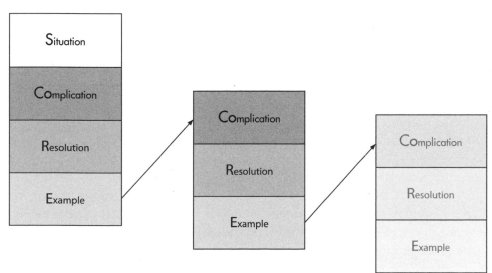

Using the S.Co.R.E.™ Method to Sequence Your Evidence

In this section we will explain in detail how to use the S.Co.R.E. method to develop a captivating outline for your presentation. We will answer the following questions:

- I need to create my outline right now—how exactly do I use the S.Co.R.E. method?
- How do I know if my outline is any good?
- Is it okay to "fork" my presentation?

How Exactly to Use the S.Co.R.E. Method

Especially when you are still starting out, it helps to use colored index cards; you'll need yellow (for situations), red (for complications), green (for resolutions), and blue (for examples). It's not strictly necessary—you could do this with just a piece of paper and a pencil—but it is useful to be able to move the pieces around as you think through your outline.

Situation   Take a yellow card. Write the word "Situation" at the top left of the card. Immediately below that, write down a one-sentence reason for your presentation: We are here today to discuss . . . This should be something that everyone in the room will agree with. Often this is the generic form of the problem that you are dealing with. So if the problem is "Our pricing is too high," then the situation could be "We're here today to talk about pricing."

Don't spend more than a few seconds on the situation. How much time should you spend covering the background that they already know? If it's clear that they already know it, then just mention it and move on quickly. If there are essential parts of the background that you're not sure people are familiar with, or if you have an original take on some aspect of the background, then include this information within a complication, resolution, or example, but not in the situation.

First Complication   Take a red card, write the word "Complication" in the top left corner, and then immediately below it, write out the first complication, which is usually the business problem you identified in Chapter 3. Be sure to phrase it as a problem, not a question. So, for example, write "Our problem is that we don't know how to increase revenues," *not* "How do we increase our revenues?" (As you fill in the cards, try to keep the bottom half of each index card empty; we will use this space later, in Chapter 7).

Your first complication should be a real attention-grabber. It should be something scary and painful – you have to catch the audience's attention here. To do this, make sure you are focusing on a *painful* business problem that they have. This is the one complication that you get to choose, so make it a really big one—choose the biggest problem they have that you will be able to contribute to solving in this presentation. After this one, the choice of each subsequent complication is driven by what you would expect the audience to be thinking.

It is very important (as we saw in Chapter 3) that the problem be one that your audience has, not that you have. "They're not acting on the information I have provided them" is still *your* problem. Rework it until it is clearly their problem—where the pain is unmistakably felt by them: perhaps "They are missing a business opportunity."

First Resolution   Take a green card, write the word "Resolution" at the top left of the card, and then immediately below that, write your response to the problem raised in the first complication: "The solution we are proposing is . . ." This is usually the solution you came up with in Chapter 3.

Example   Then take a blue card, write the word "Example" at the top left of the card, and write down an illustration of the resolution on the previous card. In Chapter 5, you identified a number of useful anecdotes; this is where you can insert one of them into your outline. As we mentioned in that chapter, you can use actual stories from your company or industry, hypothetical situations, or stories from outside your industry that are relevant by analogy. Any of the three types will do. If you are using an analogy, it will work best if you take a single analogy and carry it all the way through your presentation, showing different aspects of it at different points.[5]

[5]Meta-analysis of empirical studies on the use of metaphors in communication found that the use of one consistent metaphor increases persuasion (Sopory & Dillard, 2002).

What you are trying to offer is a specific instance of your general solution—you are trying to make the resolution concrete for your audience and bring it to life. The resolution is the generic response; the example gets specific. In Myers-Briggs terms, this helps you to speak to both N's, the conceptually oriented people (in the resolution), and S's, the detail-oriented folks (in the example). The example should allow you to say, "Let me show you what I mean."[6]

[6]An experiment conducted by LeFevre and Dixon (1986) found that people prefer examples to instructions.

The example is an absolutely critical step. Not only does it allow your audience to rest after each resolution, but it also grounds your presentation in reality. We live in an age of abstractions and generalizations. (And I recognize that the previous sentence is itself is a generalization.) If you want your audience to follow you and find you credible, you'll want to keep returning to specifics. And this is what your example does: it tells them about a specific person who did a specific thing, at a specific time and a specific place. (The example is yet another application of the Reality Principle.)

After you work through the initial S.Co.R.E., what remains is one (or more) iteration(s) of the Co.R.E. (the Situation only appears once, at the beginning of the sequence, and is never repeated); carry on repeating the Co.R.E. as long as you need to, until you've disposed of all reasonable objections.

Next Complication   This is the most important step in the entire S.Co.R.E. process. To decide what goes on your next Complication card, imagine that you presented the information in your first four cards and stopped there. What is the first "come-back," objection, or "Yah, but . . ." that you would expect to hear? ("That will never work!" "That's way too expensive!" "Senior management will never agree to *that*!" "We tried that already!") That will be your next complication: the strongest, most likely objection you would face, if you had stopped there. (Note that while the *first* complication should be phrased as a statement, not a question, the subsequent complications work equally well whether phrased as statements or as questions.)

[7]See Allen (1998), Pechmann (1992), and Williams, Bourgeois, and Croyle (1993).

But why should you bring up the arguments against your recommendation? What if no one in the room was going to bring it up—why would you bring it up yourself? As we discussed in Chapter 4, all the empirical evidence indicates that persuasion is stronger with a "two-sided" message, where you present your own arguments as well as the opposing arguments, and refute each of the opposing arguments, than with a "one-sided" message, where you just present the arguments in favor of your recommendation.[7]

It is far better that you bring up the complication yourself—even if you can't dispose of it completely—than risk someone else in your audience bringing it up. The tougher the objection and the lower your ability to address it, the *earlier* in your presentation you should bring it up. Be very straightforward about it, and lay out the facts and options.

Sometimes there might be a complication that, for good reasons, you *really* hope will not come up, and you certainly don't want to bring it up yourself. Perhaps it is a very complex issue that would derail your discussion and take up a lot of time, but is not actually relevant to the issue. In such a case, you could include a slide on it in your appendix (which you will not hand out in advance), and then if someone does bring it up, you can reveal the slide to show that you have actually thought through the issue.

Some typical complications you could expect from your audience include:

- People (don't have enough/right people available)
- Time (too soon, not enough time)
- Money (too expensive)
- Risk/uncertainty (too risky, will it work?)
- Lack of knowledge (we don't know how to do that)

Next Resolution   Your next card responds to the complication raised above.

Example   Then you have a blue example card that gives an illustration of that response.

Next Complication   The *next* most likely objection that you would face.

You will then continue working with the Co.R.E. (complication, resolution, example—because the situation is not repeated) until you have covered all reasonable objections.

The main point about the S.Co.R.E. method is that you *do not give your audience any information without first creating a need in them for that information.* The Complication creates the need, and the Resolution and Example satisfy the need. How could they ever be bored?!

The S.Co.R.E. method may seem like it takes up a lot of time. For the first few attempts, you will find that you do have to invest a bit of time. But not that much. During the

Extreme Presentation workshops, participants typically take between twenty and forty minutes to complete their first S.Co.R.E. sequence. Once you become proficient, it will take you a lot less time. And think of what you are accomplishing in this time: you are taking a stack of information, each item of which may or may not fit into your presentation, and turning it into a compelling outline for your presentation. That's a good return on your time investment.

Testing Your S.Co.R.E. Cards

Once you have completed the exercise, use the checklist in Figure 6.3 below to assess your storyline. Go through your S.Co.R.E. cards and answer each of the following questions. Make a check mark beside each question that you can answer positively. If you have a negative answer, then you need to go back and fix your storyline until you can answer the question positively.

FIGURE 6.3. S.Co.R.E. Checklist

Situation

❑ Is your situation completely non-controversial, so that no one in your audience could possibly disagree with it?

Complication

❑ Does your first complication really grab your audience? Does it address a painful problem of theirs?

❑ Is it a problem primarily that your audience has, rather than one that you have?

❑ Does your first complication represent the biggest problem that they have that you will deal with in this presentation?

❑ Does your presentation make a significant contribution to solving the problem in your first complication?

❑ Does each subsequent complication represent the most likely or most significant objection or "come-back" that you would expect from your audience at that point?

Resolution

❑ Does your first resolution lay out the overall solution to the problem raised in your first complication?

❑ Does each subsequent resolution address the concern raised in the preceding complication?

Example

❑ Is each example a specific instance/illustration/case-in-point of the preceding resolution?

❑ Could each example allow you to say "Let me show you what I mean . . ."?

Overall

❑ Have you covered all the reasonable objections that could be raised?

❑ Is every important new piece of information in your presentation preceded by a complication that creates the need for that information in your audience?

In Chapter 3 we mentioned an example of a head of market research trying to convince the product marketing groups to hand over control of their market research budgets to the market research department. As an example, let's see what that would look like after applying the S.Co.R.E. method. We'll begin by identifying some mistakes that you would catch with the checklist in Figure 6.3.

Bad Example 1   **Situation:** *We're here to discuss moving ownership of the marketing research budget away from the product marketing groups to the market research department.*

What's wrong here? The situation is itself controversial. We can imagine that the product marketing folk are not going to be too keen on this. We don't want the very first thing out of your mouth to start a disagreement. So instead try:

Situation: *We're here to discuss managing next year's market research budget.*

Bad Example 2   **Complication:** *We do not have enough funding for strategic research we want to do.*

No! This is the *presenter's* problem, not the audience's. Why should your audience (the product marketing groups) be concerned about how you manage your budget? The problem *must* be a painful problem that the audience feels. Instead:

Complication: *We're not identifying enough breakthrough growth ideas because our research is all focused on short term, tactical issues.*

Now it's clear that the problem is one that the audience cares about—they want breakthrough growth ideas, and if you can't get any for them, then that is a problem for them.

Bad Example 3   **Example:** *Here are the details of the process for making sure that the product marketing group has their needs met.*

Actually this is not so bad. Providing details can serve the role as an example. Better, though, is to use an actual or hypothetical case study to *illustrate* those details.

Example: *Here's a case study of how we managed Brand G's research using this process.*

Good Example   Now let's look at the whole example, done properly:

Situation: *We're here to discuss next year's market research budget.*

Complication: *We're not identifying enough breakthrough growth ideas because our research is all focused on short-term, tactical issues.*

Resolution: *Have market research department own the research budget.*

Example: *This is how it is done at company A, our strongest competitor.*

Complication: *Wait a minute! How would the market research department know what the research needs of the product groups are? How do we know you are going to give us the right research?*

Resolution: *We already have a process in place for understanding the research needs of each of the product groups, and we'll keep using it.*

Example: *Here's a case study of how we managed Brand G's research using this process.*

Complication: Why can't we just set aside a percentage of the total budget for strategic research?

Resolution: Because from year to year, we don't know the proportion of strategic versus tactical research we'll need to do.

Example: Chart showing the types of strategic research we should have done over the past three years, and the varying total costs.

Complication: Why don't we make it a joint responsibility and meet as a group to make the decisions?

Resolution: Right—that's just what we need, another meeting to add to our calendars! You all know that these things change very fast. We need someone to be responsible so that at all times our market research budget is being invested where it will give us the biggest return.

Example: Slice of life from last quarter, how our priorities changed dramatically three times over the course of five weeks.

Complication: But as an individual product group, aren't we going to get less for our money, since you'll be spending part of it on strategic research that may not even be relevant to us?

Resolution: First, we think your bang for your buck will go up, because if we're managing the whole research budget, that will allow us to negotiate more effectively with our vendors and get greater efficiencies. Second, we are going to make it a priority to ensure that the strategic needs of all product groups are addressed.

You'll use this method in every presentation. Even in training presentations. People sometimes think that training presentations don't need to use this persuasive story form. But, as we have mentioned before, training is an attempt to change the participants' behavior to incorporate the new skills. Here's an example of a S.Co.R.E. outline; it is from the beginning of the Extreme Presentation workshop—so it is a presentation outline for a presentation on how to design presentations!

Situation: We're here to talk about designing presentations that get people to act.

Complication: People are busier and more distracted than ever, and yet we have a lot more data that we want to present to them, and less time to prepare.

Resolution: We need a straightforward process for developing the logic, rhetoric, graphics, politics, and metrics of your presentation in an integrated, effective way.

Example: Here are the ten steps that make up the process.

Complication: But different audiences have different needs, in terms of amount of detail, amount of discussion, etc. How can one process work for them all?

Resolution: Audience analysis using the Myers-Briggs Type Indicator, and implications for presentation design.

Example: Exercise 1—Audience Analysis

Complication: I'm not sure I'm clear on what exactly my presentation is supposed to be achieving.

Resolution: Use the From-To/Think-Do Matrix,

Example: Completed SuperClean Vacuums From-To/Think-Do Matrix example and Exercise 2.

So that's it. Take your stack of evidence and anecdotes developed in Chapters 4 and 5, and then go through the S.Co.R.E. process to turn them into a story. Then use the checklist above to ensure that you have developed a good outline for your presentation. If you find that you keep working on it but you can't get your first complication and resolution to fit well together, then you probably have a problem upstream: wrong audience, wrong objective, or wrong business problem. Go back and revisit those steps, and then return to the S.Co.R.E. method.

Don't Fork Your Presentation

Don't *ever* fork your presentation: don't break it up into two, three, or seven pieces: "Today we are here to discuss Project X. There are seven things I want to tell you about it. Thing 1 . . ., thing 2 . . ., thing 3. . . ." By Thing 4, they are losing interest. You may never get to Thing 7.

In software development, to fork development of a program means to break it into two versions (as in a "fork in the road" of development); subsequent work on one version will therefore be incompatible with the other. Forking is for this reason considered to be a "bad thing" in software development.

Forking is also a bad thing in presentations. Time is linear. Your presentation, although it may appear to meander due to interruptions, will in reality be presented over time, which flows in a straight line. So design it along a straight line. If you have several complications that are all resolved with one resolution, that's fine—mention all of them and then present the resolution.

However, if you have several resolutions that are needed to solve one complication, don't present the complication and then say "and the solution to this has five parts. Let me start with Part 1. . . ." This is too boring. It is not storytelling, it is presenting a list. And, as we saw in Chapter 5, lists are less memorable than stories. Instead, what you do is present the resolution that makes the strongest contribution first, even though it only addresses part of the complication. And then the next complication will be about the part that has not been addressed (e.g., "Yes, but this doesn't cover our Western business. . . ."), and so your next resolution will address that part, and so on.

What do you do if you feel that you have just an apparent random set of points that you want to make, and you don't know where to start? First, you have to understand what the one larger problem is that they all roll up to. Then you find a S.Co.R.E. sequence that covers all your points. At all costs, avoid saying, "I have seven points I want to make." Too boring.

If you want to take them through, say, a seven-step process, you can do this by trying to get each step to generate a complication that is responded to by the next step. Think about what would happen if Step 3 did not exist. What would go wrong? Whatever that is, it is the complication that Step 3 is a resolution to. An outline for a presentation that describes a process would look something like this:

Objective: to determine whether safety procedures have been adopted correctly

Step 1: review procedures

Step 2: interview persons responsible to determine comprehension of procedures

Step 3: interview front-line staff

Etc.

The S.Co.R.E. method would give you something like this, instead:

Situation: We're here to talk about safety procedures.

Complication: We do not know whether the safety procedures are being adopted correctly, and this could lead to some serious accidents.

Resolution: We are proposing a process for reviewing safety procedures. It begins with a review of the existing procedures.

Example: Details of some of the existing procedures

Complication: But you can't know whether the procedures are being adopted if you don't speak to the people responsible.

Resolution: therefore Step 2 is to speak to those people.

Example: details about the kind of conversations that will be had

Complication: But the people responsible won't give you the full story.

Resolution: So Step 3 has us talking to front-line staff.

Etc.

In this case, the S.Co.R.E. method allows you to take what could otherwise be a dull series of steps into an interesting story.

What to Do with What Doesn't Fit into Your Storyline—The Role of the Appendix

The main thing is not to put any information into your presentation that does not have a place on your storyline. If it doesn't have a place in your storyline, it does not belong in your presentation—period. We need to be ruthless—if it doesn't fit the storyline, it shouldn't go in the presentation. If you think it *might* come up, or if you've spent so much time on it and you just want to put it in, then put it in the appendix. Typically, you will bring printed copies of your appendix to the presentation, but you will not hand them out until the end of the meeting, unless a question comes up that requires you to refer to the appendix, at which point you can choose to hand them out.

Now that we have an outline, how do we actually *show* our data?

PART IV
GRAPHICS

NO MATTER HOW CAREFULLY you think about your audience or plan your presentation, if you end up presenting fifty slides with seven bullet points of seven words each, you are almost guaranteed to numb your audience to the point of incomprehension. We have all sat through this kind of "Death by PowerPoint." It is not fun, and it does not work very well, so why do we continue to inflict it on others?

The next two chapters are about the graphical dimension of your presentation—your visual aids. For our purposes, we will define "graphics" very expansively: every two-dimensional representation that is not exclusively text. So charts are graphics, but so are photographs, sketches, diagrams, and cartoons. Graphics can contain text within them: they can be annotated, for example. Graphics can also be mostly made up of text: a table of words, for our purposes, is considered a graphic. The *location* of each word in the table carries as much information as the word itself. (Of course, the location of a word in a sentence carries as much meaning as the word itself; but in text, the words are always ordered in the same way, one after the other, while in a graphic, elements can be placed anywhere on the page).

Chapter 7 explains how to use each of the components of a slide—charts, graphics, and text—so that they strengthen your communication rather than get in the way of it. Chapter 8 is about how to put all those components together on a slide—how to lay them out on the slide so that your audience "gets" what the slide is about right away, and so that it draws them in to your message.

Before we move on to those chapters, we need to address some fundamental questions that will get to the root causes of "Death by PowerPoint." These questions are:

- Should you even use visual aids at all?
- Should you use PowerPoint?
- If you use PowerPoint, should the ideal slide have seven bullets with seven words each?

These questions might sound almost heretical, with most people's response being "Of course!" to all three. The answers are not nearly so straightforward. Research does suggest that visuals can improve presentation effectiveness, but not in all cases, and only if they are used properly. Otherwise they can distract from your message and severely inhibit its communication. There also has been a lot of criticism of PowerPoint—according to its critics, it "dumbs down" communication (e.g., Tufte, 2003a). But are there reasonable alternatives? Is there a way for PowerPoint be used constructively?

Finally—paradoxically—research shows that the standard advice of seven bullets of seven words each is about the *worst* approach to slide design. Communication improves dramatically if you either reduce the amount of text to much less than that—or increase it to much more. The next three sections will explain each of these counter-intuitive points in turn.

Should You Use Visual Aids?

This *is* a question. You should ask yourself whether your visual aids are adding anything to your presentation. Too often the first act of preparing a presentation is to launch PowerPoint. You now know better: you will go through Steps 1 to 7 out of the ten-step process before you even think about launching any kind of presentation graphics program. The word "presentation" means both to show something and to help people to imagine something in their heads. So technically, whether you use visuals or not, you are still making a presentation.

[1]See Vogel (1986) and Vogel & Morrison (1998). On visual metaphors see McQuarrie & Mick (2003) and Morgan & Reichert (1999).

Research suggests that visuals do help improve presentation effectiveness. One study found that visuals can increase your audience's understanding of your material, help convince them of your recommendations, and help them remember what you have presented. But not in every case: another study found that using slides with transitions (fades, wipes, etc.) actually gave worse results than using no slides at all, in terms of persuasion. Print advertising research experiments indicate that visual metaphors are more memorable than written ones and more easily understood.[1]

[2]In several studies, irrelevant images and details were found to hinder effective communication (Bartsch & Cobern, 2003; Edell & Staelin, 1983; Feinberg & Murphy, 2000; Mayer, 2001; Moreno, 2006; Myers-Levy & Peracchio, 1995; Slykhuis, 2005).

However, certain kinds of visual aids can actually cause harm to the effectiveness of your presentation. Projecting slides with text bullet points and/or irrelevant graphics such as clip art during your presentation will likely have worse results than speaking without any visual aids at all.[2]

[3]A study of Air Force Academy students taking a mandatory class on engineering mechanics found that the visuals used in the class were considered to be a "confusing, intimidating waste of time" (Bowe, Jensen, Feland, & Self, 2000, p. 12).

Also, if your audience is not engaged in your presentation, perhaps because they have been forced to sit through it and are just trying to get it over with, visual aids can hurt your communication efforts. In such cases, it's better to toss out the idea of slides and just talk to your audience.[3]

Should You Use PowerPoint?

The PowerPoint Debate

PowerPoint is accused of "dumbing down" communication. Graphics guru Edward Tufte, in an essay entitled "The Cognitive Style of PowerPoint," argued that PowerPoint, as well as programs like it, "reduces the analytical quality of presentations" and that PowerPoint templates "usually weaken verbal and spatial reasoning and almost always corrupt statistical analysis" (Tufte, 2003b). In a subsequent edition of this essay, Tufte concluded that "PowerPoint, compared to other common presentation tools, reduces the analytical quality of serious presentations of evidence" (Tufte, 2006).

In a *Wired* magazine article that popularized this position (titled "PowerPoint Is Evil" and subtitled "Power Corrupts: PowerPoint Corrupts Absolutely"), Tufte (2003a) claimed that "The PowerPoint style routinely disrupts, dominates, and trivializes content." Several others have also criticized PowerPoint presentations, from politicians to military personnel (Ricks, 2006).

Why should the software be blamed, rather than its users? The problem with a program like PowerPoint, according to its critics, is that it leads the user to develop presentations in a particular way, and this way may not be ideal. This criticism can be applied not just to PowerPoint, but also to other presentation programs, including Apple's Keynote and Google Docs.[4]

Other authorities on presentation have responded that it is possible to create effective slides with PowerPoint or other presentation tools, and therefore that the criticism of these tools is misplaced. While the tools may not be perfect, they assert, these tools do not deserve all the blame that is heaped on them, since there are clear guidelines that can be followed for making effective presentations using them.[5]

Most importantly, perhaps, the debate is a clash of opinions more than anything else, because neither side has provided much evidence to support its position.[6] Fortunately, though, there is some research on the effectiveness of PowerPoint as a presentation tool. This research is summarized in the box below.

[4]"Software engineers . . . necessarily implement fairly distinct ideas and concepts into any software . . . of how the final product is to be used" (Voswinckel, 2005, p. 45). Presentation software therefore provides ". . . an obvious predisposition towards a certain, default workflow" (p. 50).

[5]See Norman (2004), Holmes (2004), and Doumont (2005). The website http://sooper.org/misc/ppt/ provides an extensive list of links, in chronological order, to contributors to the debate over the past several years.

[6]Few (2006) criticizes Tufte for not providing any empirical evidence to support his argument.

POWERPOINT EFFECTIVENESS RESEARCH

Most of the PowerPoint effectiveness research described here comes from the field of education. Initial research in this area was optimistic, suggesting that PowerPoint had a positive effect on student understanding, recall, and grades. Specific conclusions included that, as a result of using PowerPoint in lectures:

- Students understood material better (Fifield & Peifer, 1994)
- Students remembered more (Pearson, Folske, Paulson, & Burggraf, 1994)
- They scored higher on tests (Jensen, Wilcox, Hatch, & Sumdahl, 1995)
- Their overall grades improved (Lowry, 1999; Mantei, 2000; Szabo & Hastings, 2000)
- They liked the lectures more and said that they helped them learn (Simpson, Pollacia, Speers, Willis, & Tarver, 2003).

Other studies, however, found mixed results, no effect, or negative results where students who had *not* been exposed to PowerPoint-based lectures scored higher on tests than those who had.

- Among students who received PowerPoint lectures, female students had improved grades, but the male students did not (Kask, 2000).
- No difference in results between lectures with and without PowerPoint (Daniels, 1999; Mines, 2001; Ranking & Hoaas, 2001).
- Kapoun (2003) taught multiple fifteen-minute instructional sessions, with and without PowerPoint, and found that students scored higher on tests afterward for the sessions *without* PowerPoint.

(Continued)

The problem with the earlier research, it turns out, was that most of the studies compared results from classes taught in years prior to the introduction of PowerPoint to those taught afterward, or classes for which the content of PowerPoint lectures was different from those of non-PowerPoint lectures.

In more recent research, when otherwise identical classes were run simultaneously, some with PowerPoint and some without, student attitudes to the class improved (as well as—not surprisingly—their ability to use PowerPoint), but no effect on their academic performance was found—either positive or negative.

So according to this research, PowerPoint is neither helpful nor harmful, at least in an educational environment.

- Susskind (2005) reports on an experiment during two sections of an Introduction to Psychology course. For the first five weeks, one section received PowerPoint lectures and the other one did not. Students were then tested, and the teaching methods were switched for the next five weeks. In each case, no differences in academic performance was found as a result of the PowerPoint lectures.

It is worth noting that in much of this research the PowerPoint presentations studied were largely text, typically lists of bullet points. As we saw above, this is *PowerPoint at its worst.* Bullet point slides are often less effective than no slides at all, so the mixed results from these studies should not be surprising.

Resolving the Debate: The Importance of Presentation Idiom

[7]An earlier draft of parts of this section and Chapter 8 were previously published in Abela (2006).

The authorities are divided, and so is the research. Where does this leave us? The authorities—and the researchers—seem to be working at cross-purposes. In a certain sense, both sides are correct, because they appear to have different approaches to presentation in mind.[7]

To understand this, it helps to understand the idea of *presentation idiom.* A presentation idiom is a form of expression and an associated set of design principles. I call the two main types of presentation idiom Ballroom style and Conference Room style. Ballroom style presentations are what most typical PowerPoint presentations are trying to be: colorful, vibrant, attention-grabbing, and (sometimes) noisy. They typically take place in a large, dark room—such as a hotel ballroom. Conference Room style presentations are more understated: they have less color, with more details on each page; they are more likely to be on printed handouts than projected slides, and they are more suited to your average corporate conference room.

The *biggest single mistake* that presenters make—and the root cause of the PowerPoint debate, it seems to me—is confusing the two idioms, and particularly, using ballroom style where conference room style is more appropriate. Almost all PowerPoint presentations are given using ballroom style—yet most of the time presentation conditions call for conference room style. Ballroom style is appropriate for when the objective is to inform, impress, and/or entertain a large audience and when the information flow is largely expected to be one-way (presenter to audience). Conference room style presentations are more suited to meetings for which the objective is to engage, persuade, come to some conclusion, and

TABLE IV.1.   Characteristics of Two Presentation Idioms

	Ballroom Style	*Conference Room Style*
Purpose	Inform, impress, or entertain a large audience	Engage, persuade, drive action in a smaller audience
Look	Colorful, vibrant, attention-grabbing, noisy	Black and white, lots of detail
Typical information flow	One-way (presenter to audience)	Two-way (interactive)
Delivery	Projected	Printed handout
Typical location	Hotel ballroom	Office or conference room

drive action. Conference room style presentations are therefore appropriate for any of the following:

- Making recommendations
- Selling
- Training
- Communicating the implications of research
- Raising funds

Information flow in this idiom is expected to be two-way—it's more interactive. Table IV.1 summarizes and compares the main characteristics of ballroom and conference room style presentations.

From this perspective, Tufte is criticizing—correctly—the use of ballroom style presentations in situations that need conference room style presentations. His critics are defending ballroom style presentations in situations in which they are appropriate. Therefore, in that sense, both are correct.

Should Each Slide Have Seven Bullets and Seven Words Per Bullet?

This advice, widely offered, is based on a faulty reading of George Miller's 1956 paper, "The Magical Number Seven, Plus or Minus Two: Some Limits on Our Capacity for Processing Information." Miller himself debunks this flawed interpretation in an email to Mike Halpern. The conclusion of his paper, summarized in this letter, was that ". . . seven was a limit for the discrimination of unidimensional stimuli (pitch, loudness, brightness, etc.) and also a limit for immediate recall, neither of which has anything to do with a person's capacity to comprehend printed text."[8]

[8]The Halpern-Miller exchange can be found at http://members.shaw.ca/philip.sharman/miller.txt. There is an interesting discussion of this faulty reading on Edward Tufte's site, at www.edwardtufte.com/bboard/q-and-a-fetch-msg?msg_id=0000U6.

Now that we understand the differences between ballroom style and conference room style presentations, we can see how slides should contain either much more, or much less, text. Ironically, therefore, seven bullets of seven words each actually gives you the *worst possible slide*, because it is too many for a good ballroom style slide and too few for a good conference room style slide. Ballroom style slides should have much less text than (seven times seven equals) forty-nine words, because they are heavily visual. Conference room style slides could have a lot more text than that; you could fill up an 8-½-by-11-inch sheet of paper with well over a thousand words in nine-point font, and—if the page is properly laid out—you will still have a very effective presentation page. (Chapter 8 will explain how to design this kind of page.)

The core problem here is that spoken and printed words can conflict with each other in a presentation. There is extensive research evidence, from multiple fields, that when you speak and present text at the same time, communication is harmed because the text and your voice compete with each other in the minds of your audience. This research is summarized here.

RESEARCH ON THE HARMS OF COMBINING VOICE AND TEXT

The "redundancy principle," that people "learn better from graphics and narration than from graphics and redundant narration and text" is well established in research (see especially Mayer, 2001, and Moreno, 2006, p. 65). Specific findings include:

- Mousavi, Low, and Sweller (1995), summarizing six experiments about teaching geometry, found that visuals combined with spoken words were more effective for student learning than either visuals combined with spoken words and text, or visuals and text without spoken words.

- Images plus narration is better than images with text and no narration, and better than images with text *and* narration (Mayer. 2001, p. 134).

- When unneeded words are eliminated, effectiveness increases (Mayer, 2001).

- "If learners are required to coordinate and simultaneously process redundant material such as written and spoken text, an excessive working memory load is generated" (Kalyuga, Chandler, & Swelling, 2004, p. 567)

- Eye-tracking research found that when web viewers received pictures, audio, and text simultaneously, they tended to ignore the text (Outing & Ruel, 2004).

Researchers explain these results by suggesting that humans have multiple short-term memories for different types of information. Visual and auditory are different types of information, and so receiving both at the same time actually improves overall short-term memory. But written and spoken words use the same short-term memory, so when both are received at the same time, the audience suffers from cognitive overload.

[9]See Outing & Ruel's (2004) website eye-tracking research.

The one exception is when you are trying to get people to remember specific facts, names, or places, in which case you should use text. Unfamiliar concepts are recalled better when presented with a multimedia graphic, while facts, names, and places are recalled better when presented with text.[9]

Not surprisingly, therefore, using graphics or a graphical layout is superior to a text slide in many ways, as the following research indicates.

RESEARCH ON THE SUPERIORITY OF GRAPHICS OVER TEXT ALONE

In several experiments, researchers have found that using graphics in visuals increases recall, persuasion, and positive attitudes toward the material being shown.

- Use of visuals in print advertising increases positive attitudes (Rossiter & Percy, 1980).
- Data communicated through graphics (rather than tables) improved both the speed and quality of decision making in a laboratory experiment simulating a product management budget allocation exercise (Benbasat & Dexter, 1985).
- Visuals and/or animation increased persuasion over text alone (King, Dent, & Miles, 1991).

Photographs, in particular, tend to be more interesting and attractive to audiences.

- In print, the eye goes to large pictures, even before the title or headline (Garcia, 1991).
- Addition of photographs made news articles more likely to be read, and made facts from the articles more memorable (Zillman, Knobloch, & Yu, 2001).

Chapter 7, on visual presentation elements, explains what kinds of graphics to use in your presentation, which charts to use and when, whether to use color and animation, and which fonts and type sizes to use. Chapter 8, on layout, explains how to take all those elements and put them together on each slide so that the result is impressive but not overwhelming. In particular, it will show you how you could put a lot of words on a page and still have a very effective slide.

Visual Presentation Elements: Graphics, Charts, Color, Animation, and Fonts

Step 7: Identify the Most Effective Graphical Elements to Use in Your Presentation

In Step 7, you will decide which charts will provide the most convincing display of your *quantitative* evidence (if you are using any), and whether to use any other graphics to emphasize or clarify your *qualitative* evidence. In Chapter 6 you created your storyline on a series of S.Co.R.E. cards. For Step 7, you will draw a thumbnail sketch of which chart or graphic you will use on each S.Co.R.E. card that represents data that you would like to present graphically. To help you do this, we will now cover:

- What kinds of graphics should you use?
- Should you use clip art?
- How do you decide which chart will best communicate your data?
- Should you use bullet-points, color, animations, or transitions?
- What type fonts and sizes should you use?

What Kinds of Graphics Should You Use?

You will want to use a variety of different graphical types to maintain the interest of your audience: use charts, diagrams, photographs and cartoons. Threatening images can be particularly eye-catching.[1]

The most important thing, though, is that each graphic you use must be *relevant*. We know from research that when interesting but irrelevant pictures (or sounds, or music)

[1] See research done on print and online magazines by Knobloch, Hastall, Zillman, & Callison (2003) and Outing & Ruel (2004). Images of victimization also draw people's attention (Zillman, Knobloch, & Yu, 2001).

[2]See Mayer (2001). Also, recall is lower, and likelihood of distraction higher (Edell & Staelin, 1983). This is known as the coherence principle: "Students learn better when extraneous material is excluded rather than included in a lesson" (Moreno, 2006, p. 65, building on Mayer, 2001).

[3]See Feinberg & Murphy (2000). In two related studies, students performed worse on quizzes and recall and recognition tasks when irrelevant pictures were used in presentations (Bartsch & Cobern, 2003). In an eye-tracking test, students eyes were drawn more to relevant photographs on PowerPoint slides than to irrelevant ones (Slykhuis, 2005).

[4]A study by Bergen, Grimes, & Potter (2005) showed that audiences recalled about 10 percent fewer facts from news stories communicated in a format in which graphical clutter is added to the video of the announcer than from news stories without the visual clutter.

are included in communication, effectiveness of that communication (measured in terms of ability to apply what's been learned) is reduced.[2]

Your audience has limited processing capacity; irrelevant information can overload this capacity and reduce the effectiveness of your communication.[3] On television, clutter reduces the amount of information conveyed; the success of MTV, which included a cluttered format, led others, particularly CNN, to emulate that clutter. But researchers now conclude that other factors—the youth of the announcers, the language used, and the music itself—contributed to the success, and that the visual clutter actually harms communication.[4]

Should you use clip art? No. Never. Clip art is an example of irrelevant graphics, and should be avoided, without exception.

How Do You Decide Which Type of Chart Will Best Communicate Your Data?

To help you select a good chart, use the chart selector guide in Figure 7.1. This diagram helps you think about which kinds of chart to consider, depending on what you want your data to demonstrate. Your choice of chart will depend first on what task you want the chart to accomplish on the slide. Each chart could accomplish any of four tasks on a slide: it can show a *relationship* (e.g., when advertising goes up, sales go up too); it can make a *comparison* (e.g., retention rates are higher among women than among men, or this year's sales are higher than last year's); it can display the *distribution* of your data (e.g., there is a broad range of prices that people are willing to pay for car warranties); and it can show the *composition* of your data—what the component parts are (e.g., final cost of the product is made up of manufacturing cost, transportation cost, and insurance).

Next, you must consider various characteristics of your data set, such as the number of observations, the number of variables per observation, and whether you are looking at static (point-in-time) data or data over time (time series). Which characteristics will drive your choice of chart depends on your initial choice of what you are intending to demonstrate.

The way to use this diagram is as follows. Start in the middle, with the question "What would you like to show?" Then decide which of the four choices you want your data to demonstrate: relationship, comparison, distribution, or composition. If you want to show more than one of these, you will probably end up drawing more than one chart.

Displaying Relationships Within Data

If you want to show that your data provides evidence of a relationship, for example, between advertising and sales revenues, then you would move to the bottom of Figure 7.1.

FIGURE 7.1.   Chart Selector Guide

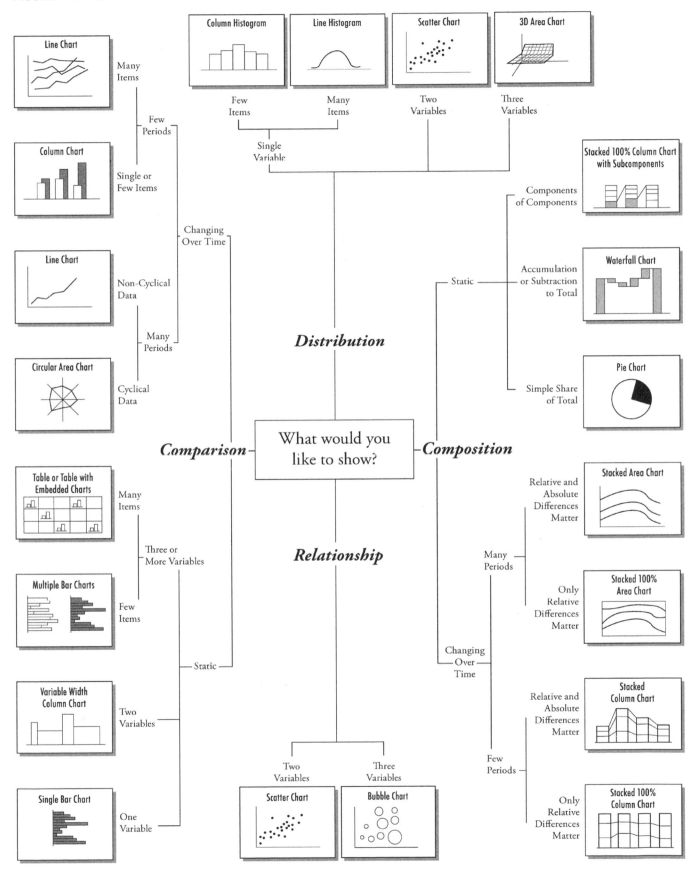

When choosing the right chart for displaying a relationship, the important characteristic is the number of variables in your data; for bivariate data, a scatter plot is appropriate, while for trivariate data, a bubble chart works well. The relationship between advertising and unit sales involves two variables (advertising and unit sales), and therefore a scatter plot would be a good choice here.

If you wanted to show the relationship of advertising, price, and unit sales (three variables), then the suggestion is a bubble chart, where the x-axis, the y-axis, and the size of the bubbles represent the three variables.

Displaying Data Distribution

If you want to show the distribution of your data, move to the top of Figure 7.1. If you have univariate data, move upward and left. If your observations are graphed into few intervals, the suggested chart is a column histogram; if many intervals, a line histogram. For example, if you are showing age breakdown of a particular sample of people in brackets of twenty years (0 to 19, 20 to 39, 40 to 59, etc., that is, few intervals), then a column histogram would be appropriate. If you are showing instead age breakdown by year (how many people are age 0, 1, 2, 3, etc., that is, many intervals) then a line histogram is suggested. To the right of that, if you have bivariate data, a scatter chart is proposed, and if trivariate data, a 3D area chart.

Displaying Comparisons

To show a comparison, move to the left of the figure. The first question is whether you want to show how your data is changing over time, in which case follow the chart to the upper left, or if it is static data, just a single period, which is at the lower left. For static data, use a bar chart for univariate data, with each bar representing one observation. Sales for five different companies would be shown on five different bars. Bar charts (bars lie horizontally) are for comparisons among things, while column charts (columns rise vertically) are for comparisons over time.

For static bivariate data, use a variable width column chart. The height of each column corresponds to one variable, and the width, the other. So if you had two variables representing sales—dollar sales and sales growth—each column would be drawn using those two variables. (Although drawing this chart in column form would seem to contradict the conclusion that columns are only for showing change over time, I have never seen it drawn in bar form.) For static multivariate data with few subjects, use multiple bar charts, lined up across the page, where each chart represents one subject and each of the bars correspond to the different variables. For example, if you wanted to compare GDP per capita, GPD growth, population size, population growth, and population density (variables) for four different countries (subjects), then each of the bar charts would represent one country, while each of the bars would represent one of the variables for that country. This way you can compare variables across subjects by reading across the page, and variables within each subject by looking at each bar chart as a whole.

Finally, where you have many items and many variables, use a trellis chart, which is a table of charts. You can either use the table as a space saver—allowing you to fit, say, twenty bar charts on a page in a four-by-five matrix—or you can use it to highlight one or two of the more important variables by using those variables to determine which cell in the table you place each chart on. (Of course, there are limits to this approach, because you cannot place more then one chart in each cell, and the intervals on each axis have to be roughly equal.)

For time-series data, if you have only a few periods of data, then you could use a column chart if you also have only a few data items (with each data item represented by a different set of columns, in different colors or shades of gray), or else a line chart if you have many data items, with several lines, one for each data item.

If you have many periods of data, then also use a line chart if you have non-cyclical data or a circular area chart (sometimes called a spider chart) for cyclical data.

Composition of Data

The last option, on the right side of Figure 7.1, is composition: this is when you want to highlight the components of your data. Your first choice here is again whether your data is static or changing over time. Time-series data is also a comparison of sorts—except that you are comparing the same items over time, rather than different items—so the options are similar to the choices for comparisons. If you have few time periods to display, then choose a stacked column chart to show both the relative and absolute differences between periods, and if only the relative differences matter, than use a stacked 100 percent column chart, where the height of each column is fixed and the components are shown as percentages rather than absolute numbers.

If you have many periods to show, then you will again use lines rather than columns. To show relative and absolute differences over time, use a stacked area chart, and to show relative differences only, use a stacked 100 percent area chart. Options for displaying static data are at the upper right. For showing a simple share of total, the pie chart is very popular, although some people have found it to be less effective than other options. If you are trying to show how components of your data add up to and subtract from a total, use a waterfall chart, and if you want to show how some of your subcomponents also have subcomponents, then a stacked 100 percent column chart with subcomponents is ideal.

The chart selector diagram is only a guide. The best way to decide which chart to use, once you have decided what you want to show with your data, is to use the diagram for suggestions and then try a few alternatives—have your colleagues take a look at the options—to see which one works best.[5]

[5]An experimental electronic version of the chart selector diagram is available at www.ChartChooser.com.

Fortunately, one factor that does not seem to be important in choosing a good chart is audience personality type, so while audience personality type is critical for several other aspects of your presentation design (see Chapter 1), it does not appear to be relevant to choosing charts.[6]

[6]Research on impact of different graph types on personality types didn't find any significant differences (So & Smith, 2003).

RESEARCH ON CHARTS

Perhaps the most thoroughly researched aspect of presentation design is the use of charts. There are several relevant findings:

- Line graphs are better than bar graphs for trends (Shah, Mayer, & Hegarty, 1999).
- Based on an extensive review of empirical work on graphs, Jarvenpaa and Dickson (1988) recommend using a horizontal (bar) chart rather than a vertical (column) chart when making comparisons among variables.
- Lewandowsky and Spence (1989) found that in scatterplots, discriminating different data series with color provided the fastest comprehension.
- Cleveland (1984) found that people make less accurate judgments about the quantities in a pie chart than in a bar or column chart.
- For multiple comparisons, divided bars are better than pies, so long as the height is kept the same (Hollands & Spence, 2001).
- Horizontal (bar) charts are more effective for showing parts of a whole than either pie charts or cumulative (stacked) column charts (Jarvenpaa & Dickson, 1988), but Spence and Lewandowsky (1991) found that pies are more effective when the reader has to mentally add two or more quantities together (likely because if the quantities are adjacent in a pie, they can be read as a single quantity—but this is also true of stacked bars).

For additional research on the use of charts, see the Graphics section of Appendix D.

As you consider which charts to use, make sure that you include lots of relevant detail: detail improves the persuasiveness of your presentation. (Chapter 8 will discuss the importance of adding lots of detail—properly organized–to each of your slides, particularly for conference room style presentations.)

Which Type Fonts and Sizes Should You Use?

The research here is inconclusive. While several studies (such as Wheildon, 2005) claimed to show that serif fonts (such as Times New Roman) are more legible than sans serif fonts (for example, Arial), many other studies have found no difference, and more recent analysis has found methodological problems with the studies that conclude that one type of font is better than the other (Lund, 1999). Therefore, do not spend any time worrying about fonts; just pick a readable one and stay with it.

Should You Use Bullet Points, Color, Animation, Transitions, or Animation?

We will deal with each of these in turn.

Should You Use Bullet Points?

[7]Bullets are superior to paragraphs in terms of audience recall (Almer, Hopper, & Kaplan, 2003; The Science of Stories, 1998).

People seem to remember information presented in bullets better than information in paragraphs[7]. But don't rely on this, because—as we saw in the introduction to the Rhetoric section of this book—*stories* are more memorable than bullet points. Use bullet points to deliver information that cannot fit into a story form, such as lists of items.

It is very important, though, that the bullet list not be the central feature of your slide, otherwise you will run into the problem of verbal redundancy described in the introduction to this part of the book (see "Should each slide have seven bullets with seven words per bullet?"). The bullet list is just one element in your overall slide—and therefore is usually only appropriate in a conference room style slide, because in ballroom style it would take up the whole page. (Chapter 8 will explain how to incorporate bullet lists, and text in general, in conference room style slides in a way that avoids verbal redundancy.)

Should You Use Color?

The results of the research on the use of color in communication is mixed on whether color adds any benefit. This suggests that there are more factors involved in deciding the answer than have been captured in any particular research study. One study indicates that the different results depend on *how involved the audience is*. For an uninvolved audience, color can be useful for attracting attention and persuading, but for a more involved audience, irrelevant color is harmful because it distracts your audience and wastes their mental effort processing material that is extraneous to your message. The most effective use of color therefore seems to be for highlighting specific items on your slide.

RESEARCH ON COLOR

Research on color from some studies is mixed:

- Vogel (1986) found that color is more persuasive than black and white; this study was done using projection of acetate slides.
- Butler and Mautz (1996) found that use of animated color graphics improved recall among those who are visually inclined, versus use of text-based visuals only. However, it is unclear from this study whether the improved recall is attributable to the color, the graphics, or the animation.
- Kelly and Hoel (1991), studying Yellow Pages advertising, found that in three out of four test ads, the addition of color had no effect, while in one case it did appear to increase the likelihood of the consumer selecting the advertised business over others.

Other research shows that color attracts attention.

- Color can attract attention and help convey specific information (Finn, 1988; Fernandez & Rosen, 2000).
- In print advertising and direct mail, color gains attention (Rossiter & Percy, 1997) and response (Woodside, Beretich, & Lauricella, 1993)
- People tend to select color ads from Yellow Pages directories over black and white (Lohse, 1997)

Irrelevant color is harmful.

- A review of the research on the role of color in speeding up identification of information, from the 1950s to the 1970s, found that irrelevant color harms both speed and accuracy of information access (Christ, 1975).

Color helps speed up both information extraction (from certain kinds of charts) and decision making.

- A laboratory experiment showed that color helped decision making when under time pressure for audiences who are "field dependent," that is, more holistic, "big picture" thinkers, who tend to have less attention to detail (Benbasat & Dexter, 1985).

(Continued)

- A laboratory experiment showed that color sped up information extraction from bar and pie charts (Hoadley, 1990), but the alternative tested was a black-and-white chart with awful cross-hatch shading—arguably anything would be better than that.
- One study found that using color symbols to discriminate among different data series in a scatter plot provided faster comprehension than any other type of symbol differences, such as shading or letters (Lewandowsky & Spence, 1989).
- Christ's (1975) meta-analysis concluded that color used for reinforcement or highlighting improved both access speed and accuracy, so long as the viewer knew what color to look for.

Perhaps the most useful guidance on the role of color is provided by a study of print advertising, which concluded that, when your audience is not very motivated, color helps persuade, likely because color leads them to make a superficial judgment that you have a higher quality presentation. When the audience is motivated, however, full color is harmful to persuasion, because the audience has to spend brain effort processing the meaning of the color, where black and white would be easier to comprehend. If the color is used only to highlight and reinforce relevant aspects of the presentation, though, (and the audience is motivated), then persuasion is improved.

- Myers-Levy and Peracchio (1995) conducted two experiments with students who viewed print advertising for bicycles. They measured the impact of color on the students' favorability ratings of the bikes in each ad; presumably, more persuasive advertising would lead the viewer to rate the bike more favorably.

Finally, there are two practical considerations, both of which suggest avoiding color. One is that a non-trivial proportion of the population is colorblind, and the other is that if people make copies of your presentation, chances are that they will be in black and white.

The question of whether to use color, therefore, along with the question of how much detail to include, which is covered in the next chapter, depends on whether you are making a ballroom style or conference room style presentation. Ballroom style presentations, which are used to inform or entertain, would seem to have less motivated audiences, and therefore would benefit from the use of color. In any case, the use of color photographs is appropriate, because all the colors in photograph are "relevant." You should avoid using color to embellish your slides, though, because it will be distracting. Conference room style presentations, which are used to engage and persuade, have more motivated audiences (and use printed presentations, which might be photocopied), and therefore should use color just for reinforcement or not at all.

Should You Use Transitions or Animation?

[8]See Vogel & Morrison (1998) on the effects of transitions. On using transitions and animations together, the study identified a directional, but not statistically significant, improvement in perceptions of the speaker, in terms of preparedness, professionalism, clarity, strength, and quality of support data.

Transitions and animation are two forms of moving content. Transitions are when one slide changes to another, while animation is any moving content *within* an individual slide. Typical examples of transitions include dissolving, shrinking, or page turning effects. Transitions alone are generally a very bad idea. Research suggests that using transitions alone, without animations within the slides, is *worse than using no visuals at all*, in terms of getting attention and agreement. This is probably because, as so much of the research has shown, irrelevant material tends to harm communication, and transitions are largely irrelevant to your message. Transitions and animation together might be better than visuals alone, but the research is not conclusive here.[8]

The research on animation is not very encouraging, either, which suggests that both transitions and animation should be avoided. The only time when animation is warranted appears to be when the animation effect communicates something more than could be shown through static images only. (And this is good news, because developing an animated sequence for a presentation takes a lot of work.)

RESEARCH ON ANIMATION

Research on the benefits of animation in communication, similar to that of color, is very mixed. Where benefits are found, they tend to be only for particular types of people (e.g., those who are visually inclined, or those who are novices in the subject matter being presented).

- No difference was found between static visuals and animation in several studies (Hegarty, Narayanan, & Freitas, 2002; King, Dent, & miles, 1991; Mayer, Mathias, & Wetzell, 2002; Narayanan & Hegarty, 2002; Ricer, Filak, & Short, 2005).

- Animation, when combined with graphics and color, did improve recall, versus text-based visuals, but only among those who are visually inclined. Recall among audience members who were not visually inclined was actually reduced with the animated version (Butler & Mautz, 1996).

- Lai (2000a; 2000b) found that animation with audio is superior to static graphics and text with narration in computer-aided instruction.

- One recent study found that animated charts were superior to printed statistics; however, this could have proven only that charts are superior to numbers, which we already know to be the case. Further, the finding held only for "novice" audience members; expert audience members were not swayed by the technology (Guadagno, Sundie, Asher, & Cialdini, 2006).

The only time that research finds animation to be consistently superior to static display is when animation provides additional information about changes in the process or system being described.

- In a review of recent empirical research on the use of animation, Tversky, Morrison, & Betrancourt (2002, p. 21) concluded that where animation is found to be superior to static visuals, it is usually because the animation contains some additional information, so it is not a fair comparison. They suggest that animation might be most useful for showing the "qualitative aspects of motion or . . . the exact sequence and timing of complex operations," but they are unable to say whether even in these cases animation would be superior to static graphics.

At this point you know what elements you are going to use on each slide or page. But how exactly do you lay them out all together to communicate them most effectively? That is what Chapter 8 is all about.

Laying Out All the Elements on Each Page

8

Step 8: Create Slides That Communicate Your Information Concisely and Effectively

The previous chapter was about how to select and create all the elements of a good presentation page or slide: the graphics, charts, color, animation, and fonts. In this chapter, we will look at how to put all those elements together—how to lay them out on each page.

Before you begin laying out your slides, you need to decide definitively whether you are going to use ballroom style or conference room style. Steps 1 to 7 of the Extreme Presentation method work equally well for both idioms. Once you start step 8, however, you have to decide on—and commit to—which idiom to use for your presentation. (If you do not know the difference between conference room style and ballroom style, then go back and read the introduction to Part IV: Graphics).

The main determinant of which style to use is whether you are trying to persuade a small audience, in which case you should use conference room style, or whether you are trying to inform or entertain a larger audience, which would instead call for ballroom style. If you recall the discussion in Chapter 3, we argued that "purely informational" presentations have a very hard time attracting and keeping audience attention (which is why they need the vibrant imagery and the emotional appeal of ballroom style). The recommendation in that chapter was that you should always try to identify a problem that your

FIGURE 8.1A. Layout Showing Two Alternatives

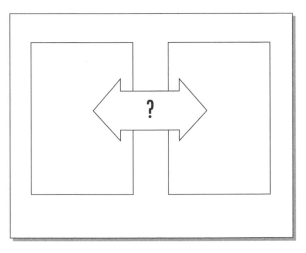

audience has, and then focus on persuading them to take action to solve it. We will assume that you have followed this advice, and therefore this chapter will focus mostly on conference room style.

A critical question in this chapter is, "How do you lay out each slide so that it grabs the audience's interest and persuasively conveys the intended message?" The answer to this question is to *design each page so that the page layout itself reinforces the main message of the page.* For example, if the slide is talking about two alternatives, then draw the alternatives on either side of the page (Figure 8.1a). If your slide is about how you had several ideas, which you put thorough a number of screens, then draw it that way (Figure 8.1b; Figure 1.3 in Chapter 1 is an example of this layout). If you're explaining how several factors are converging to create a new situation, then draw the factors around the side of the page and the new situation in the middle (Figure 8.1c).

FIGURE 8.1B.   Layout Showing Screening of Ideas

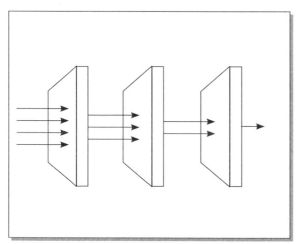

FIGURE 8.1C.   Layout Showing Factors Converging

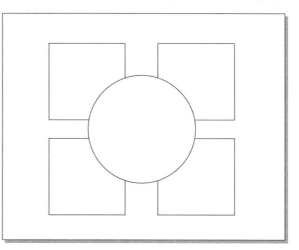

One of the advantages of the greater detail that conference style presentations allow is that you can combine what would otherwise be several slides into one, with the added benefit that the *relationships* within the content of those formerly different slides is emphasized visually. Figure 8.1c is an example of this: each of the four factors and the conclusion in the center might have been drawn as five different slides; instead, we draw them as one slide to visually reinforce the notion of the four factors coming together to create the conclusion. (Figure 8.1d is a fully drawn variation on Figure 8.1c.) Always prefer diagrams and images to text, because, as we saw in Chapter 7, pictures reinforce a spoken presentation, while text competes with it.

What you should do now is work through your S.Co.R.E. cards and see how many you think you can fit on each slide by grouping your cards. As you take each card, in order, think about how much space each will take on a slide, and then keep on adding cards until you think you will have filled your first slide. Put those cards in a pile, and then take the next card and start a new pile. Keep doing this until you have used all your cards. At this point, you should have a series of piles of cards, each pile representing a slide.

FIGURE 8.1D.   Slide Showing Factors Converging

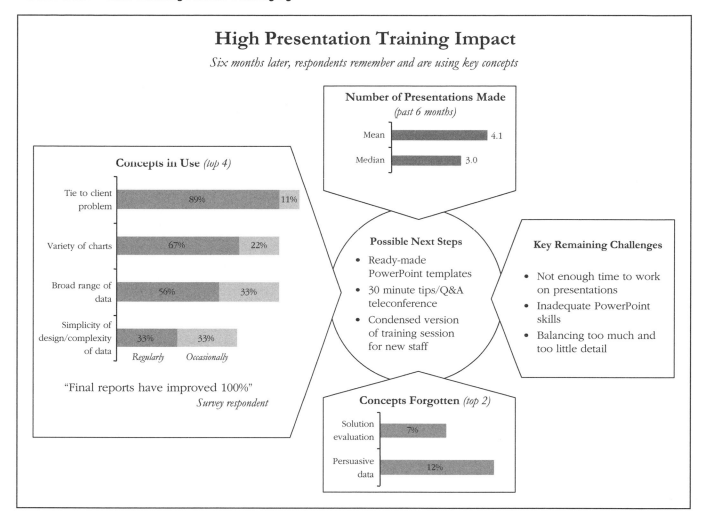

Then think about what the central message of each slide should be and make a rough sketch of the layout of each slide so that the layout of the page supports the main message of the page. Once you have a rough sketch of the layout of each page, place the sketches side-by-side across your desk, and you will have a storyboard for your presentation. Scan this storyboard to make sure that there is enough variety in page layout, from slide to slide. If there isn't, this may be an indication that your presentation is repetitive; consider combining some of the pages or changing their design. Note that you *could* create this storyboard in PowerPoint, but if so, be sure that each slide is only a very rough layout for now. You do *not* want to be spending much time on any given slide until you are sure that you have the right layout.

Once you are happy with your storyboard, you can then create your actual slides or pages, in PowerPoint or whatever your preferred layout program is. While this is still one of the most time-consuming steps in the presentation-design process, having gone through all the preceding steps you should find that you do spend a lot less time actually drawing your pages than you did before. This is because you are clear on what you want to show and how you will show it, so you will spend less time redrawing pages or drawing pages that you do not end up using. Also, you will have far fewer slides to draw because the method you have followed creates much shorter presentations.

The rest of this chapter will cover the following:

- How to make sure that your slide layout reinforces the main message of the slide
- How to design effective ballroom style presentations
- How to design effective conference room style presentations
- When you can use multiple presentation idioms in the same presentation
- How much detail to put on each slide
- How to avoid bad detail, or "chartjunk"
- How much text to put on each slide
- Whether to combine graphics and text on the same slide
- How *exactly* to decide what goes on each slide

How to Make Sure That Your Slide Layout Reinforces the Main Message of the Slide

The most important message of this chapter has already been introduced, namely, that if you want to design slides that really grab your audience's attention, you need to make sure that the layout of each page itself reinforces the point you're trying to make on the page. But how exactly do you do this? The answer is to use what designers call the "squint test."

FIGURE 8.2.   Squint Test Example

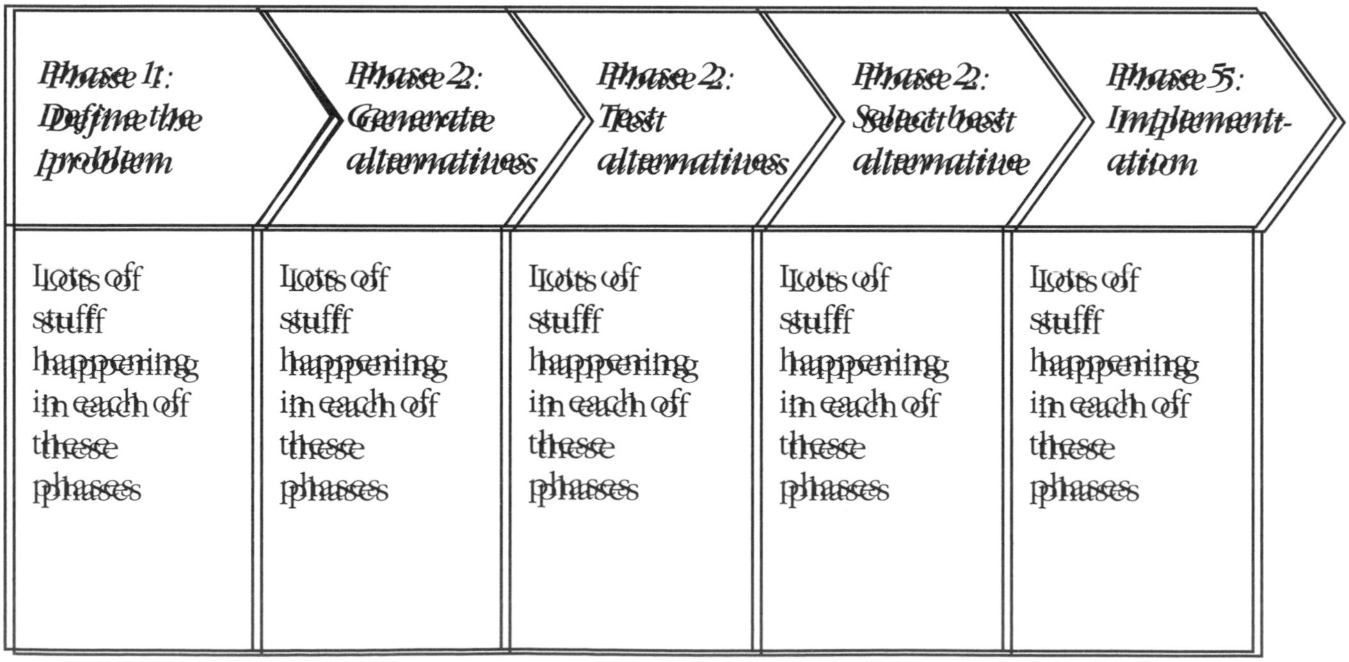

To apply the squint test, squint at the slide, so that all the text is blurred and illegible. Do you understand anything about the slide, without having to read the text? If you can see, already, what the main message of the page is—that the page is showing a process, for example—then your page passes the squint test (see Figure 8.2). The squint test seems to simulate what the brain registers in the first fraction of a second when the image from your slide hits the viewer's retina. If this introduces the main point of your page, the rest of your message from that page can be received more easily than if the brain has to spend the next few seconds trying to decipher what your point is.

Does your typical bullet point page pass the squint test? Not really. At best, this kind of page layout suggests a list. If the message of the page is a list, then this page layout may be appropriate. But if so, help the viewer understand what kind of a list it is. If it's a checklist, use checkboxes instead of bullets. If it's a series of steps, wouldn't a more effective layout be a process diagram, across the page? At worst, when the brain registers a series of bullets—perhaps for the fiftieth time that hour—it wanders off to some other more pleasing image, such as next summer's vacation.

Here are some examples of slides that fail the squint test being transformed into slides that pass the squint test. In the first example, Figure 8.3 shows a series of four slides from a real presentation, disguised. The slides describe the objective and a sequence of steps in a procedure. If you squint at them, though, all you see is a bunch of bullet points and therefore these slides fail the squint test. Consider now the slide in Figure 8.4. This is the

FIGURE 8.3.   Slides That Fail the Squint Test

Compliance Review
- Objective
  - Determine if facility has developed & operationalized polices and procedures that xxxxxx
    - Screening potential hires
    - Training employees, new & on-going
    - Prevention policies
    - Identification of possible incidents
    - Investigation of incidents, allegations
    - Reporting incidents, investigations, facility response

Procedures
1. Obtain and Review policies and procedures for key components
2. Interview individuals responsible for coordinating policies and procedures
3. Probes

   How staff is monitored to assure xxx?

   How to determine xxx?

   How do you ensure xxx?

Procedures (Cont.)
4. Request evidence of how the facility has handled alleged violations. Select 2–3 alleged violations since last survey
5. Interview several customers about xxxx
6. Interview 5 staff over 3 shifts including xxx
   - What, when, and to whom to report according to policy

Procedures (Cont.)
7. Interview at least three frontline supervisors or staff to determine how they monitor xxx
   - Xxxxxxx
   - xxxxxxx
8. Obtain a list of all employees hired within the past four months, select five and ask the facility for written evidence of pre-employment screening.
   - Xxxxxxx

FIGURE 8.4.   Slide That Passes the Squint Test

Compliance Review Process

Objective: Determine whether facility has developed and operationalized procedures that xxxx

1. Obtain and review policies and procedures	2. Interview policy and procedure coordinators	3. Probe procedures	4. Request evidence of violation handling	5. Understand customer awareness	6. Determine staff knowledgeability	7. Evaluate monitoring	8. Confirm pre-employment screening
Obtain and Review Policies and Procedures for key components	Interview individuals responsible for coordinating Policies and Procedures	Ask how staff is monitored to assure xxx	Request evidence of how the facility has handled alleged violations	Interview several customers about their awareness of reporting procedures	Interview five staff over three shifts to determine if they are knowledgeable about how to xxx, and what, when, & to whom to report according to policy	Interview at least three frontline supervisors or staff to determine how they monitor xxxx	Obtain a list of all employees hired within the past four months, select five and ask the facility for written evidence of pre-employment screening.

[1]Several designs of layouts that pass the squint test are available for download from www.ExtremePresentation.com.

same content, on one slide. If you squint at this slide, you can tell, even without reading any of the content, that it represents a process, just by the layout of the page. So it is an improvement, because it passes the squint test. And as an added benefit, page count is reduced by 75 percent, from four pages down to one.[1]

How to Design Effective Ballroom Style Presentations

It is not enough to choose the right presentation idiom. You also have to make sure that you adhere to the guidelines for your chosen idiom. If you present ballroom style slides with lots of text, or conference room style slides that do not pass the squint test then your results are likely to be *worse* than anything you have tried before. To ensure that this does not happen to you, this section covers the essential guidelines for effective ballroom style presentations, and the next one does the same for conference room style presentations.

Good ballroom style presentations should have minimal text, perhaps just a brief title, and rich, relevant visuals. The look that you are trying to achieve with ballroom style is that of the evening news: visually rich and thoroughly professional. Therefore your slides should be projected and not printed out, not least because there is little point in printing out slides with very few words on each one, but mostly so that you can make extensive, but always appropriate, use of color, animation, and sound in your ballroom style presentation. How do you know what "appropriate" means? Color, animation, and sound are "appropriate" when they are used to convey or emphasize information. As we noted in Chapter 7, they are *inappropriate* and should be *ruthlessly eliminated* when they serve only to embellish or distract. Use of relevant video segments, photographs, and diagrams are examples of appropriate additions to a presentation.

Because ballroom style presentations use very little text on each slide, you might end up with a lot of slides, perhaps one (or even more) per minute of presentation. So a thirty-minute presentation could have thirty slides, fewer if you spend time talking without visual aids. This is not a bad thing, so long as each slide has relevant content and represents a part of your story. As a rule of thumb, calculate between one and five minutes per slide, but do not plan for more than forty-five minutes of continuous ballroom style presentation, or else you risk having an audience that is dozing in the dark (because projection typically requires you to dim the lights). Therefore the maximum length of a ballroom style presentation is forty-five slides (forty-five minutes × one slide/minute).

How to Design Effective Conference Room Style Presentations

Although most presentations right now are delivered in ballroom style (but badly), relatively few occasions actually call for ballroom style, because this style of presentation is really only appropriate when you have a large audience (say one hundred or more people) whom you are trying to inform or entertain. If you are presenting to a smaller group and/or your goal is to persuade the group in some way—which would seem to be the more common occasion for a presentation—then you should use a conference room style presentation.

A conference room style presentation should look more like an architectural drawing than something you'd see on television. Good conference room style presentations should have lots of relevant detail and text, and should be handed out on paper, never projected. Paper allows a much greater density of detail on your slides, which, if projected, would be mostly incomprehensible. On paper, you can use font sizes as small as 9 point without difficulty, whereas in ballroom style 24-point is usually the minimum safe size.[2]

Conference room style therefore allows you to put much more information on each page. This facilitates more productive conversations, because all the information for the discussion of the moment is right in front of everyone on a single page; a single printed page can fit the contents of three, four, even ten projected slides. Paper delivery also allows people to write on the presentation, so that they can engage with your content better, and—as Edward Tufte says—it sends a message that you are confident in your content, because you are allowing your audience to walk away with it. Because conference room style presentations contain so much more detail on each page, they tend to have significantly fewer pages—you could spend anywhere between ten minutes to over an hour on each conference room style page.

Conference Room Style and the Problem of Control

Conference style is a very powerful presentation idiom, but it is new to most people. Since it is new, it will take some practice to become proficient in it. However, some

[2]Many people prefer illustrated paper handouts. Research on subjects with lower reading ability found that illustrated paper handouts outperformed plain text handouts, video, and self-paced PowerPoint presentations (Campbell, Goldman, Boccia, & Skinner, 2004).

people are reluctant to even try it because they do not like the idea of giving out their slides for fear of losing control of their presentation. If you hand out your slides to your audience, they can read ahead—they do not have to wait for you. But if you project your slides, you decide when to go to the next slide. So with a projector, you keep control. You decide where the audience's minds will be at any given point.

Or do you? In reality, with a projector, you only have the *illusion of control*. Certainly, you decide which slide is being projected, and when. But you have little or no control over where your audience's minds are. They could be thinking about anything—the problem they left burning on their desk, their last vacation, lunch. . . . And with many projected presentations, they probably *are* thinking about anything—anything except the presentation, that is.

At least with conference room style slides, you have some feedback as to whether your audience is keeping up with you. You can see whether a person is getting bored and reading ahead, because you can see that she's turned the pages, or if another person is having trouble keeping up and is falling behind, because he's still looking at the previous page. With conference room styles slides, you give up the illusion of control, and in return you get the *reality* of knowing whether your audience members are still with you.

I think that the concern with audiences reading ahead stems from experience handing out copies of ballroom style slides—which is something you should never ever do, as we noted above. Ballroom style slides, by their nature—with their big fat 30-point text, have very little content on each, and so it is no wonder that your audience will be reading ahead—there's so little on each slide. Properly done, each conference room style slide will be so rich that your audience will not want to be reading ahead.

One other benefit of handouts for conference room style presentations is that they avoid the apparent tension between presenter and audience that comes from one having control of the projector, while the others do not. When one person controls the projector, it appears as if he or she is trying to dominate the room. By contrast, when everyone has copies of the handouts, then control over the presentation feels as if it is shared. As an audience member, no one is forcing you to move to the next slide if you are not ready, or to stay on the current slide if you are bored. Also, perhaps most importantly, you can mark up the slides in front of you—deface them if you want—which helps maintain that sense of each audience member being in control. This reduction in tension should be helpful for presentations with emotionally charged or particularly contentious topics.

How Many Slides Should a Conference Room Style Presentation Have?

The quick answer to this question is: as few as possible. Do not assume that each of your S.Co.R.E. cards should become one slide. The goal is to fit the content of as many cards as possible onto one slide, to keep your presentation as brief as possible.

Fewer slides is always better here. Has anyone ever said to you: "I think your presentation was great . . . except that I wish that you had a few more slides"?! I ask this question in every workshop I run, and almost no one has ever had this experience. It is probably fair to generalize that almost all presentations are too long. Therefore, it is a good idea to try to shorten them for a change. When you think your presentation is too short, it will probably be just right.

Fewer slides make for better presentations because they allow for more understanding and richer, more interactive discussions. Your audience can see more steps in your logic on each page in front of them, so they can understand your argument better. People learn better when presentations follow what are called the spatial and temporal contiguity principles: where words and graphics are presented all together, on the same page—spatially—and at the same time—temporally—rather than spread out over multiple pages.[3]

When your audience has all the information relevant to a particular discussion right in front of them, that discussion can flow more freely than if they have to keep asking you "Could you back up two slides to the one about, um, cost savings—no, not that one, three slides back I guess. . . ." If you want your audience to absorb and adopt what you are presenting to them, then it is important to allow interactive discussion, which gives them the opportunity to engage with your material and reflect on it. Having everything on one page in front of them allows for this.

But isn't communication more effective when complex information is presented piece by piece rather than all at once? On the contrary, research indicates that, from an educational perspective, if you break up a complex task into too many steps, learning can be less effective.[4]

Finally, having fewer slides that you hand out is better because people are limited in how far they *can* read ahead if it turns out that you are going too slowly. If you have only five or seven pages in total (rather than the forty or so pages that make up an average PowerPoint presentation), then you can spend the time to make each one of them just right.

[3]Both principles are derived from extensive empirical research. See especially Mayer (2001) and also Moreno (2006).

[4]A multimedia learning experiment conducted on law students in Holland found that breaking up a learning task into a higher number of steps actually reduced learning efficiency (Nadolski, Kirschner, & van Merrienboer, 2005).

RESEARCH ON THE IMPORTANCE OF INTERACTIVITY

The importance of promoting interactive discussion of your presentation is underscored by the interactivity, reflection, and personalization principles:

- The *interactivity principle* states that "Interactivity encourages the processing of new information by engaging students in an active search for meaning."
- The *reflection principle* states that "Students learn better when given opportunities to reflect during the meaning-making process."
- The *personalization principle* states that "Personalized messages heighten students' attention, and learning is more likely to occur as a result of referring the instructional material to him/herself." Interactive discussion gives you an opportunity to personalize your information to individual members of your audience, as you respond to their questions.

See Moreno (2006, p. 65) for more details on each of these principles.

What Is the Ideal Length of a Conference Room Style Presentation?

The theoretical, ideal length of a conference room style presentation is *one page*—with lots of detail, well laid out. Why? Because if you can achieve the goals of your presentation in one page, why would you use two, or ten, or forty? If you are able to distill your message down to one page, your audience will get the sense that you have really captured the essence of the subject. They will also appreciate (and probably be stunned by) the brevity of your presentation.

You will work through the S.Co.R.E. method described in Chapter 6 to organize your material into a story, and then you will use only as many pages as you need to tell the story. Any extra material that does not fit into your story but might come up during the presentation can go into an appendix. You could have a one-page presentation and a fifty-page appendix. The main thing is that you are not compelling your audience to sit through fifty slides.

One page is an ideal, not a rule. The *rule* is: *use as few pages as possible to deliver your message effectively*. When we take this approach in workshops that I have run, participants routinely end up with presentations that are seven, five, or two pages long, and occasionally they do come up with a one-page presentation, where in the past they would typically present between twenty-five and fifty pages. By aiming for the ideal of a one-page presentation, you may not hit it, but you will end up with far fewer pages than you would have otherwise. This is a good thing.

What if you are given a one-hour time slot for your presentation, and you show up with a presentation that is only one page long? One slide, well designed and rich with detail, can easily absorb the interest of a group of people for an hour. It makes interaction and discussion easier: we are all poring over the same page, rather than being frog-marched through fifty slides, and so the meeting tends to be very satisfying and productive. Decisions are made, and people act on them. Finally, if you do finish early, give your audience some time back. Who could possibly be upset with that?

When to Use Multiple Presentation Idioms in the Same Presentation

Sometimes it is appropriate to switch between the two styles within a single presentation. For example, you might provide a conference room style handout at the end of a ballroom style presentation, particularly if you want your audience to walk away with some important details. Or, in the middle of a conference room style presentation, you might pause to project a brief video segment or some images—ballroom style—and then return to the handout to continue the discussion.

This works so long as you are *alternating between styles*. But don't ever try to *mix* the two styles: never, EVER project a conference room style page, or hand out a ballroom style slide. Figures 8.5 and 8.6 show two (admittedly exaggerated) examples of this bad mixing of styles. Figure 8.5 represents an attempt to project (which is only appropriate to

FIGURE 8.5.   Bad Example: Projecting a Slide with Lots of Detail

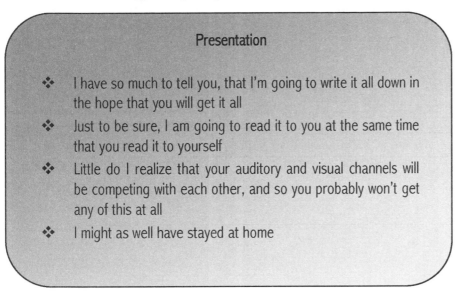

FIGURE 8.6.   Bad Example: Printing a Slide with Very Little Detail

Presentation

- Not Very
- Much to
- Say Today

ballroom style) a lot of detail (which is only appropriate to conference room style); and the slide fails the squint test, anyway. Figure 8.6 has the opposite problem: printing (conference room) a slide with very little detail (ballroom). And it also fails the squint test.

How Much Detail to Put on Each Slide

The answer to this question may be somewhat counterintuitive, because the most common advice is to "Keep It Simple." The problem with this maxim as a general guide is that most of the problems you are presenting about are *not* simple—otherwise why bother making a presentation about them? In general, more detail is better. You want to show, not hide, the details of the complexity of the issue you are addressing. If the issue you are presenting has no complexity to it, then perhaps you do not need a presentation; a simple email or phone call might be more appropriate.

The answer is therefore not "simplicity at all costs," but a creative combination of what Edward Tufte calls "simplicity of design and complexity of data" (2001, p. 177). You need to find ways to respect the inherent complexity in your data, while explaining it with a persuasive and comprehensible simplicity.

[5]Based on two experiments, Slusher and Anderson (1996) concluded that causal arguments or explanations are more persuasive than statistical evidence.

Showing more detail gives important benefits. Your audience will understand your presentation content better, and you can have more constructive discussions about it. Showing more dimensions of data allows more discussion about possible cause-and-effect relationships, which are critical for effective problem solving.[5]

Also, detail gives you more credibility, because you are showing your facts, not saying "Trust me, the facts are there." Sometimes, just the visual impression of lots of detail, well organized, is convincing, even if you audience does not actually *read* that detail. David Ogilvy, the advertising guru, once asserted: "I believe, without any research to support me, that advertisements with long copy [lots of text] convey the impression that you have something important to say, whether people read the copy or not" (1983, p. 88).

[6]Concrete words ("factory," "customer," "furniture") are more memorable than abstract words ("compromise," "coverage," "illusion"; Walker & Hulme, 1999, p. 1271). Concrete metaphors are easier to understand than abstract metaphors (Morgan & Reichert, 1999).

Genius that he was, he knew the truth without needing research evidence. Advertising research has since shown him to be correct—ads with more detail get more attention, generate more interest, are more convincing, and drive action more effectively.

Using details—particularly concrete details—is another application of the reality principle: always prefer to present evidence that is concrete and particular rather than conceptual and general. Concrete words and metaphors are easier to understand and remember; a concrete metaphor is more like a story than an abstract one because it contains details and texture, which make it more interesting.[6]

[7]A meta-analysis of sixteen empirical studies of "powerful" versus "powerless" language, mostly in legal research, found that the former is perceived as more persuasive and credible (Burrell & Koper, 1998).

Concrete details—and concrete language in general—is also more persuasive. Extensive research has found that use of abstractions in language, such as empty (non-specific) adjectives, hedges (e.g., "sort of" or "kind of"), and intensives (e.g., "very" or "really"), which researchers have labeled "powerless language," are significantly less persuasive than "powerful language," which is more straightforward, precise, and therefore concrete.[7]

RESEARCH ON THE PERSUASIVE POWER OF DETAIL

- Rossiter and Percy (1980) found that specific details of product claims in print advertising (for beer, in their study) were more persuasive than general claims.
- Both business buyers (Soley, 1986) and consumers (Lohse, 1997; Woodside, Beretich, & Lauricella, 1993) find detail more convincing.
- Ads with more specific detail are more likely to be considered by consumers (Fernandez & Rosen 2000).
- Kelly and Hoel (1991), in their study of Yellow Pages advertising, found that in the majority of cases, increasing the amount of copy in the ad was associated with an increased likelihood of the consumer selecting that company over others.
- Armstrong (2008) cites several studies that conclude that, when your message is high-involvement, ads with longer copy (more text) are more attention-getting, generate more interest, and drive action.

Two kinds of detail that can add concreteness to your presentations are illustrations and numbers. Adding several illustrations to your page can increase audience interest, while adding numeric—quantified—details is more persuasive, because this implies credibility.[8]

And finally, more detail on each page means that your overall presentation will likely be shorter, because you can put the content of what would have been several slides onto one page; the advantages of shorter presentations were discussed above.

More detail allows you to communicate more information on each slide. Consider the two charts in Figures 8.7a and b. Both present pricing data. Figure 8.7a is very straightforward. The first column shows that findings from this piece of research was that 70 percent of all sales were made at below the minimum target price, indicating poor pricing discipline, and next to it, that 12 percent were sold at below cost, which means that the company is losing money on each of those sales. Clearly, these are concerning findings from the analysis.

Look at Figure 8.7b. It contains a scatter chart, with each dot representing a single sale. The vertical axis shows the relative sales price and the horizontal axis shows the size of the customer who bought it, in annual revenues. The zigzag line across the chart is the minimum price target, and below that, the dotted line shows the cost of each sale.

[8]Using multiple illustrations on the same page made a business advertisement more interesting to its audience (Chamblee & Sandler, 1992). Particularly when the communicator is perceived to be an expert, providing *quantified* details is more persuasive (Artz & Tybout,1999).

FIGURE 8.7a.   Pricing Chart - Low Detail

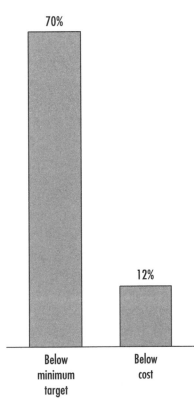

FIGURE 8.7b.   Pricing Chart - High Detail[9]

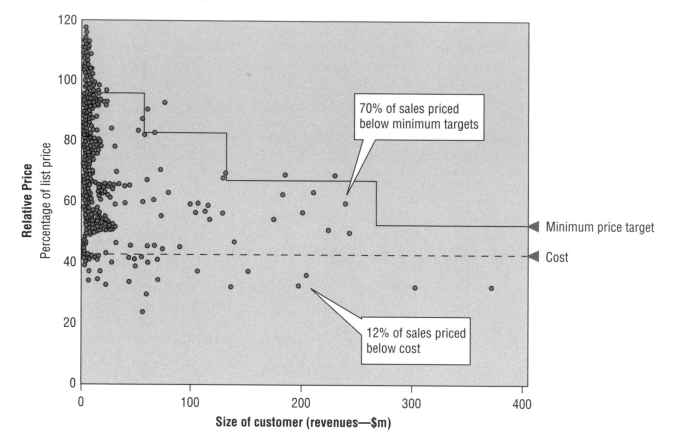

[9]Chart based on Bundschuh &
Dezvane (2003).

If you look above the zigzag line that indicates the minimum price target, you can see that very few of the sales were made above that, which we do know from the first chart. But something else shows up in this more detailed chart. To whom were most of the sales made, at or above the recommended price? To very small customers: you can see them all clustered near the top left corner of the chart. There are very few sales made to larger companies at or above the recommended price, which suggests that customers of any size except the smallest are able to bargain the company down below its targeted price. This is information that was not available in the simple version of this chart on the left.

What's the point? The point is that we are trained to simplify things. But if you are communicating complex issues, *do not be afraid of detail*. To extend and paraphrase Tufte's dictum: the goal here is *simplicity of design and complexity of detail*.

Here is another example (Figure 8.8). The occasion for this chart was the retirement of Justice Sandra Day O'Connor from the United States Supreme Court. The newspapers at the time were talking about how she was the justice closest to the center of the court, and the evidence for this was that she tended to agree to with other justices more than anyone else on the Court. Figure 8.8 is an attempt to show this. The chart portrays the percentage of times that Justice O'Connor agreed with each of the other justices; you can see their names across the bottom of the chart. She agreed 71 percent of the time with then-Chief Justice Renquist, 67 percent with Justice Anthony Kennedy, and so on.

FIGURE 8.8.   Bad Example: Supreme Court Agreement

Justice O'Connor % Agreement with Other Justices

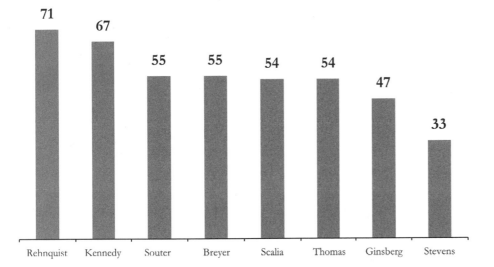

But, of course, what this chart does not show us is how much the other justices agreed with each other, so we cannot conclude, from this chart alone, that Justice O'Conner was the most "agreeable." Instead consider Figure 8.9, a chart that appeared in *The New York Times* of July 1, 2005 (reproduced with permission). Down the diagonal are the nine justices on the Court at that time. To see how much any particular justice agreed with any other you follow the row and column that connects them. So to see how much Justice Stevens agreed with Justice Breyer, look at the top left box, and the number there is 62 percent. Thomas and Scalia, 79 percent. Thomas and Stevens, 15 percent. And the size of the circle in each box is proportional to the percentage agreement. If you look at Justice O'Connor, you can see a lot of larger circles in both the row and column extending from her name.

The third example, in Figure 8.10, is of a fictitious company. Products from this company are laid out on a 2 by 2 matrix, with higher priced products at the top part of the matrix and lower priced ones at the bottom, and with lower market share products on the left, and those with a higher share on the right. At the top left, products A1, ZX80, and PDQ1, these are all higher priced, lower market share products. At the bottom left, products Z1 and S1 are lower price, lower share products. And at the bottom right of the matrix, the X150 and the R2000 are lower price, high market share products.

If you were presenting this information, you could use this chart to show a number of things. You could show that there are no high priced, high market share products, and your audience could conclude that perhaps being a higher priced product is not a good place to be. Maybe, or maybe not; the actual conclusion would depend entirely on the relative profitability of each product—which this chart does not show.

But the bigger problem with a more "impressionistic" chart like this is that it is too easy to challenge. I call this an "impressionistic" chart because, like Impressionist paintings, it intends to show only a rough representation of the data, not the actual data itself. And

FIGURE 8.9.   Good Example: Supreme Court Agreement

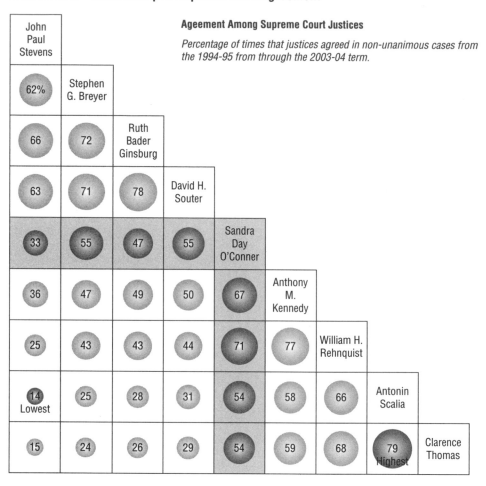

therefore your audience can disagree with its content too easily, because it is all based on judgment. They might argue that A1's 16 percent share is actually quite high for this industry. Or they may say that the R2000 is actually pretty expensive.

A better approach is to show the details. Look at Figure 8.11. Again we are using a 2 by 2 matrix. However, this time, instead of allocating the products to quadrants using human judgment, we let the data set speak for itself.

So the products are plotted on a scatter chart, with price on the vertical axis and market share on the horizontal axis. And by turning the chart into a bubble chart, we can add a third variable—the important profitability data. The size of the bubble shows the total profits generated by each product. The picture is now quite different. Instead of favoring lower priced products, your audience is now likely to see that the higher priced products, even though they have lower market shares, overall are generating a lot more profit.

Detail is not only important for quantitative data; it's also really important for qualitative data. The detail in qualitative data is the richness—or "texture"—that it has. Look at the example in Figure 8.12. This is from the Government Accountability Office (GAO),

FIGURE 8.10.   Bad Example: Segmentation

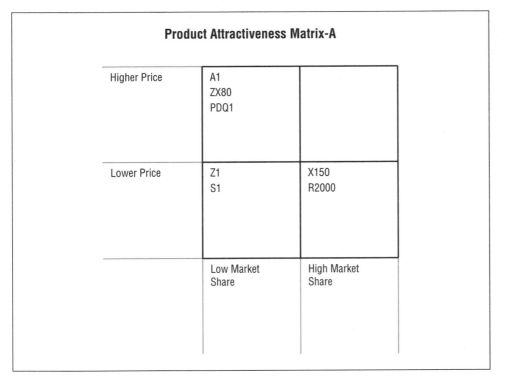

FIGURE 8.11.   Good Example: Segmentation

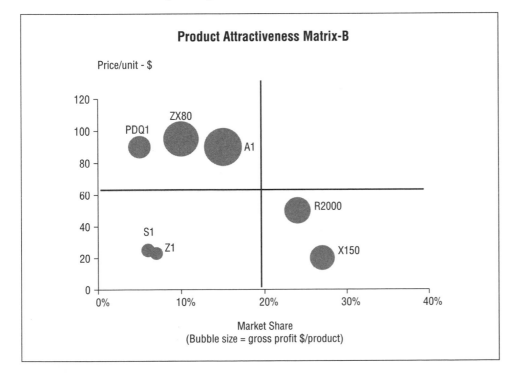

FIGURE 8.12.   Good Example: Qualitative Details

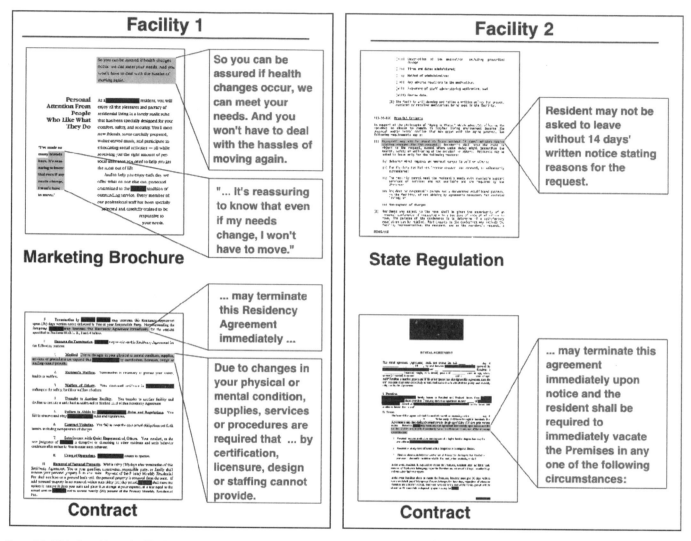

Source: United States General Accounting Office Report on ALF: 1999

which is the U.S. Government's private consulting firm. It is taken from a report investigating assisted living facilities, and its purpose is to show how contracts in this business tend to contradict what is advertised and also sometimes the law.

The graphic on the left in Figure 8.12 shows an image of a page from a marketing brochure of a long-term-care facility. Some of the text from that page is magnified, to highlight the claim that the facility can handle a wide range of care, so that if the resident's health conditions should change, he or she would not have to move to another facility. The image below it is from a contract from the same facility, with text highlighted stating that the facility can require a resident to leave if his or her health condition should change. The contradiction is blatant, and well communicated by juxtaposing the details of the two documents. The same approach is used on the right, where text from state legislation requiring facilities to provide fourteen days' notice before asking a resident to leave is contrasted with an extract from a contract stating that the resident can be evicted with no notice at all.

The details in this example do not *prove* anything. They are examples: they merely illustrate the point. But examples hold an important place in the storytelling (S.Co.R.E.) sequence (see Chapter 6). Details in qualitative evidence are the visual equivalent of storytelling and have the same fascination for your audience.

How do you include all this detail without overwhelming your audience? By following the guidance of the squint test. If your slide passes the squint test, then the amount of detail on the slide is irrelevant, because the overall message will be immediately evident to your audience, and they will not be put off by the detail. Also, as you might have guessed, conference room style slides will carry lots of detail much more easily than ballroom style slides. Detail is still appropriate for ballroom style slides, though, particularly if it is in the form of detailed photographs or diagrams.

How to Avoid Bad Detail ("Chartjunk")

There is only one kind of bad detail, and that is what Edward Tufte calls "chartjunk" (2001, p. 107). Look at the two charts in Figure 8.13. Does the one on the right communicate anything more than the one on the left, for all the embellishment that it contains? No, it does not. Worse than that—it is somewhat harder to read. Research confirms that the addition of this kind of ornamentation hurts communication, because the viewer is distracted and wastes mental energy trying to figure out whether there is any significance to the embellishment.[10] The three-dimensional bars, in particular, have been shown in research to slow down viewers' processing of a graph.[11] The harmful effect of irrelevant details applies even beyond graphics. Advertising research has found that adding irrelevant information into an advertisement reduces its persuasiveness.[12]

[10]In several studies, irrelevant images and details were found to hinder effective communication (Bartsch & Cobern, 2003; Edell & Staelin, 1983; Feinberg & Murphy, 2000; Mayer, 2001; Moreno, 2006; Myers-Levy & Peracchio, 1995; Slykhuis, 2005).

[11]In an experiment with eight subjects, Fischer (2000) found that irrelevant depth cues were associated with slower decision times.

[12]Meyvis and Janiszewski (2002) concluded that consumers look for evidence that confirm product claims and categorize all non-supporting information—whether it be negative or just irrelevant—as non-confirming.

FIGURE 8.13. Chartjunk: Which Chart Is Easier to Read?

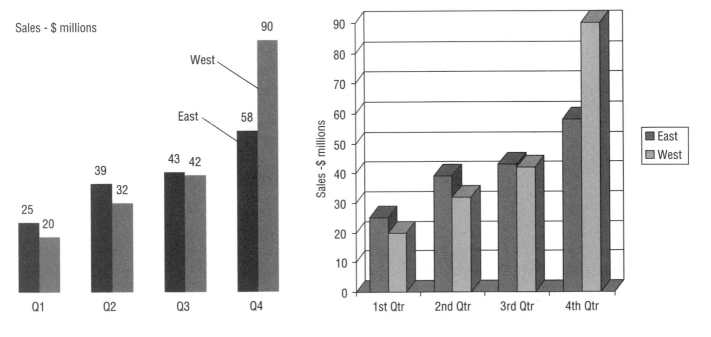

FIGURE 8.14.   Bad Example, But for Different Reasons

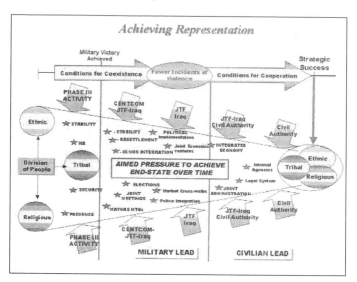

[13]Put data values on the top of each bar (Jarvenpaa & Dickson, 1988). Communication effectiveness increases when graphics and text are placed close to each other (Mayer, 2001).

[14]Ricks, (2006). See also http://armsandinfluence.typepad .com/armsandinfluence/2006/08/ death_by_powerp.html and http://blogs.chron.com/ watercoolerconfidential/2006/09/ death_by_powerpoint.html.

In order to eliminate chartjunk, any detail that is not communicating something unique, or emphasizing something important, should be eliminated from your graphics. In our example, the gridlines can be removed, and the vertical axis also, and instead each of the bars can be labeled with its specific value. This makes it easier for your audience to read the value that each represents than if they have to try to estimate the values by reading them off the vertical axis. The legend can be removed and replaced with direct labeling of the bars, which is easier to read. And the three-dimensional effect, of course, has to go.[13]

The slide in Figure 8.14 shows a different type of chartjunk. This slide, from a military briefing on the Iraq war, was featured in a book critical of the war and the planning process that led up to it. After the book's publication, the image of the slide and the accompanying criticism from the book appeared online, and the slide itself was heavily criticized. Much of the criticism centered on the apparent incomprehensibility of the slide: it is "as clear as mud."[14]

We need to be careful about criticizing slides out of context; this was the only slide we could see from a (safe to presume) very long deck, and the buzzwords and jargon on the slide that make it seem so obscure to us are presumably quite familiar to its intended audience. In fact, I do not think that the unintelligibility of the slide is its main problem. To those familiar with the situation, the slide is in fact quite intelligible. The slide passes the "squint test": flow from left to right is clearly evident, as is the compression of the forces on the outside, funneling the elements in the middle of the slide into the supposed unity on the right side of the slide. And the message is quite clear: a series of pressures will force the disparate elements within Iraq to move toward unity. So the slide does have simplicity of design, of a sort.

The real problem with this slide is that it is lacking *complexity of detail*. It *appears* to have a lot of detail—there is certainly a lot of stuff on the slide. But the problem is that all that "stuff" is not actually details. In fact, it is the opposite of details: a bunch of abstractions, such as "stability," "resettlement," and "integrated economy." Detail implies *specifics*: this is the role that detail plays in your presentation, bringing it down from the abstract into the concrete, to make it credible and useful to your audience. And this lack of detail was exactly the problem, apparently, that the subordinates who received the presentation of which this slide was a part—in lieu of actual orders—were facing. In the absence of specifics, it was unclear to them what they were actually supposed to *do* to achieve the goal expressed in the presentation.

How Much Text to Put on Each Slide

The answer to this question depends first on whether you are using ballroom or conference room style, and second on whether you are designing your presentation primarily to be presented live or to be read by others without the presenter. As we mentioned before, ballroom style slides should have very little text, while conference room style slides can have lots more. The amount of text on a conference room style slide will depend on whether your material will be presented live or not. Live presentations can have less text, because the information is conveyed through the presenter's commentary. Stand-alone presentations need a lot more text, to avoid any ambiguity (since the presenter is not there in the room to clarify things).

One way to add this text is to use callout boxes: boxes of text with arrows that point from them to the relevant graphic on the page (see Figure 8.15 for an example of a using callout boxes). If your presentation document is going to be used both for a live presentation and a stand-alone document, you should seriously consider making two versions of the document—one for the presentation and one for takeaway. The Extreme Presentation method makes your presentations shorter, so this becomes easier to do, and often it is just a case of creating the stand-alone version first, and then deleting some of the callout boxes for the live version.[15]

[15]Annotating a graphic using callouts for important conclusions increase the memorability of those conclusions (Myers-Levy & Peracchio, 1995).

FIGURE 8.15.   Callout Box Example

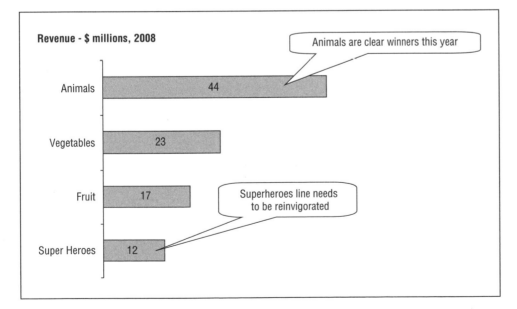

128   ADVANCED PRESENTATIONS BY DESIGN

FIGURE 8.16.   Bad Example: HR Presentation

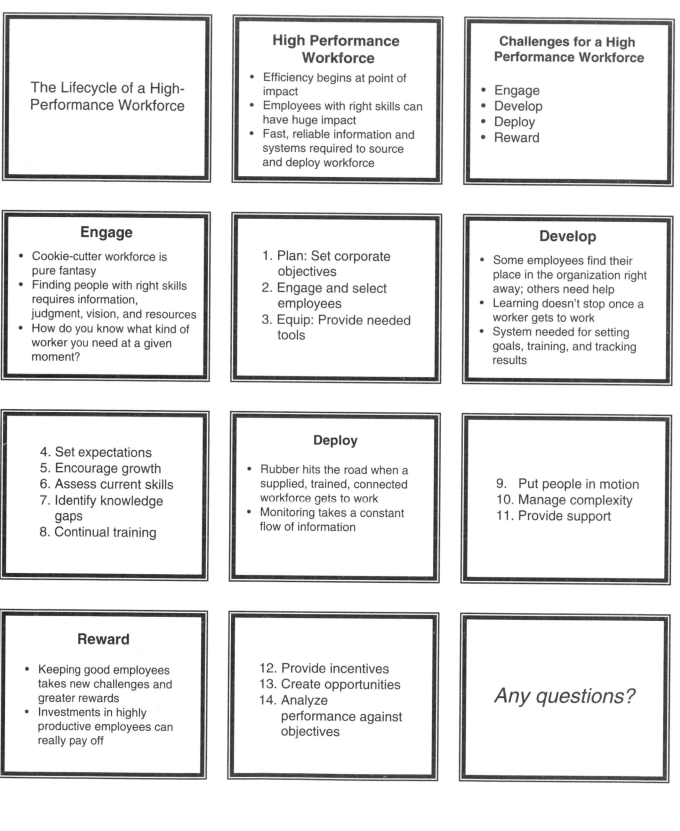

It is possible that, if you combine graphics and text well in a stand-alone presentation document, its effectiveness can be equal to that of a spoken presentation, so long as the audience takes the time to study it.[16] But, of course, that is the question—will they take the time to study it? Which is why an in-person presentation is more reliably effective: because your audience is present and therefore has already chosen to invest their time in your message.

But is there such a thing as too much text, even in a conference room style slide? In the Introduction to this book, we saw how presenting typical bullet-list slides along with a verbal explanation is worse than speaking without slides at all or presenting slides without speaking because audiences have difficulty listening to you and reading the slide at the same time. Won't this be just the same for conference room style slides, even if they pass the squint test?

I think that the answer is No—*because of* the squint test. When you present a bullet-list slide, your audience does not know what is on that slide until they read at least a few of the bullets. So they are going to start reading those bullets as soon as you show them the slide, even if you are trying to explain something to them. When you show them a well-designed slide that passes the squint test, though, as soon as they see the slide they have some idea of what it is about, and therefore they do not have to read all the details and they can focus on what you are saying.

Look at the sequence of slides in Figure 8.16. There are twelve slides in this presentation. If you squint at any of these pages, you see lots of bullets, but nothing beyond that. What this is, in fact, is a presentation on the stages in the human resources (HR) process in a typical company: hiring, developing, deploying, and rewarding.

Figure 8.17 shows a much more interesting and effective way to present the same information. The HR process is clearly evident here. It starts at the top left, with new employees being engaged by the company; you can see them walking through the door. Through several steps of on-boarding, they reach the development stage, at the top right of the page. They are then deployed into the various functions in the company, at the bottom right, and through several more steps are rewarded, on the bottom left, and promoted—you can see some of them climbing the staircase to their next position.

The point of including this graphic is not to suggest that everything you do should look this polished. This graphic was created by Xplane Inc., a company that specializes in such things, so you should not expect to meet their standards in your daily work. It does, however, show just how much detail you can put on a page and still be very comprehensible and effective. You can imagine what a rich and involved discussion you could hold, just using this one page. (If you happen to be just flipping through this book right now and noticed Figure 8.17 and think that it looks too "busy," then go back and read this chapter from the beginning. You will then understand the power of the detail in it.)

[16]Ginns' (2005) meta-analysis of forty-three different experiments found that when participants were able to study the presentation on their own, results can be equal to a live presentation.

FIGURE 8.17.   Good Example: HR Presentation

The life cycle of a high-performance workforce

Efficiency in any organization begins at the point of impact — where a worker does a job. Employees with the right skills, drives, and habits can have a huge impact on your company's bottom line. Unfortunately, good employees don't materialize on their own. It takes fast, reliable information and a system behind it to source, develop, deploy, and reward your workforce so that people can have the greatest positive impact — for themselves, for you, and for your shareholders.

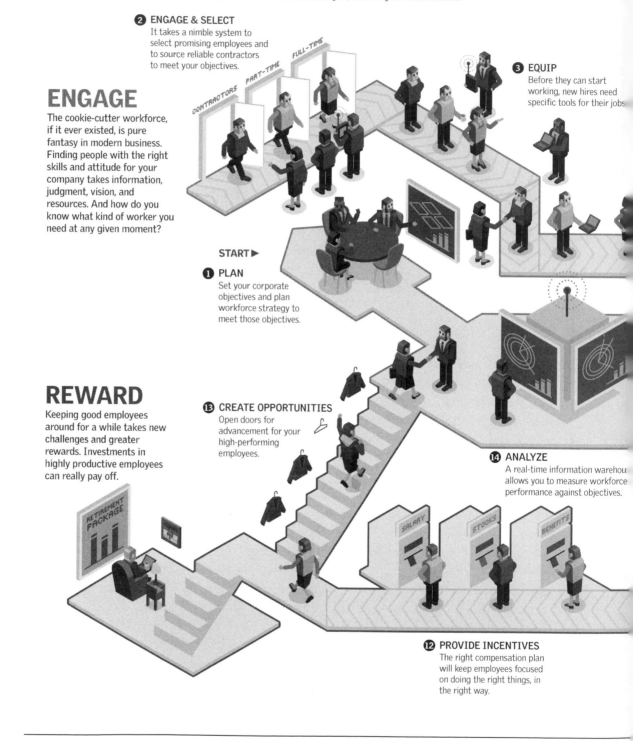

❷ ENGAGE & SELECT
It takes a nimble system to select promising employees and to source reliable contractors to meet your objectives.

ENGAGE

The cookie-cutter workforce, if it ever existed, is pure fantasy in modern business. Finding people with the right skills and attitude for your company takes information, judgment, vision, and resources. And how do you know what kind of worker you need at any given moment?

❸ EQUIP
Before they can start working, new hires need specific tools for their jobs.

START ▶

❶ PLAN
Set your corporate objectives and plan workforce strategy to meet those objectives.

REWARD

Keeping good employees around for a while takes new challenges and greater rewards. Investments in highly productive employees can really pay off.

⓭ CREATE OPPORTUNITIES
Open doors for advancement for your high-performing employees.

⓮ ANALYZE
A real-time information warehou allows you to measure workforce performance against objectives.

⓬ PROVIDE INCENTIVES
The right compensation plan will keep employees focused on doing the right things, in the right way.

PeopleSoft. PeopleSoft Human Capital Management is an enterprise-wide business strategy to manage, optimize, and leverage the workforce to drive a higher level of business performance. For more information, contact PeopleSoft at www.peoplesoft.com or 800/773-8277.

SET EXPECTATIONS
Executive vision has
to be communicated
to everyone.

5 ENCOURAGE GROWTH
Encourage individuals to set
challenging goals and to
plan for individual growth.

6 ASSESS CURRENT SKILLS
Determine people's current
skill levels so you will know
when they're improving.

DEVELOP

Some employees find their
place in an organization right
away, while others need help.
Either way, learning doesn't
stop when a worker gets to
work. A system for setting
goals, periodic training, and
tracking results helps
manage an employee's
personal growth — and the
growth of the business.

CLOSE GAPS
Give underperformers
a way to realize
their potential.

7 IDENTIFY KNOWLEDGE GAPS
Measure their current skill levels
against your performance goals,
and identify gaps.

8 CONTINUAL TRAINING
Manage a training schedule that fits
learning opportunities into the daily
activities of your workforce.

DEPLOY

The rubber really hits the
road when a supplied, trained,
and connected employee gets
to work. Monitoring their
performance without getting
in their way or losing them —
especially when operations
are spread across the globe —
takes a constant flow
of information.

9 PUT PEOPLE IN MOTION
With the right people in the right
places, even a complex global
enterprise can run smoothly.

OBJECTIVES

MY CAREER

EMPLOYEE INFO

HR HELP DESK

?

MANAGEMENT

ACCOUNTING

TIME TRACKING

LABOR RELATIONS

MARKETING

SALES

SHIPPING & RECEIVING

LOGISTICS

©2003 XPLANE.com®

PROVIDE SUPPORT
Should an issue arise that can't be
resolved through self-service, your
HR Help Desk puts employees in
contact with informed HR personnel.

10 MANAGE COMPLEXITY
Your workforce must be managed,
in all its complexity, from global
sales and logistics, to compliance,
labor relations, and time tracking.

XPLANATiONS® are simple visual maps and stories that make
complex business issues easier to understand. For more information
visit XPLANE at www.xplane.com or call 1/800/750-6467.

FIGURE 8.18.   Combining Graphics and Text

Whether to Combine Graphics and Text on the Same Slide

It is a good idea to put text and visuals close together.[17] Remember, though, that in any case, ballroom style slides should have very few words. In conference room style slides, which work well with lots of text, you will want to make sure that your text is placed close to the relevant graphics whenever possible. Figure 8.18 shows a page from a popular children's book. Note how closely integrated the text and visuals are. This is the kind of thing you are trying to create for your conference room style slides.

[17]When corresponding text and illustrations are placed near each other, effectiveness increases. It is better to show corresponding illustrations and text simultaneously than sequentially (Mayer, 2001).

How *Exactly* to Decide What Goes on Each Slide

What you should do now is work through your S.Co.R.E. cards and see how many you can fit on each slide by grouping your cards. Begin with your first card, think about how much space the information it represents would take on your slide, and then keep on adding cards until you think you will have filled your first slide. Then move on to the next slide, working through the subsequent cards, and so on, until you're finished. Your situation card will typically take up very little space—it usually represents just a spoken comment. Ditto for your complication cards: unless they represent data about the complication, or images to illustrate it, your complication is usually also just spoken; it is your transition between slides, or between different points on your slide (e.g., "You are probably thinking now that this all sounds very expensive; well, let me show you why that is not the case").

Preparing to Draw Your Slides

At this point you should have a series of piles of cards, each pile representing a slide. What you'll need next is a rough sketch of the layout of each slide—so that the layout of the page supports the main message of the page. One effective way to do this is to try to write a one-sentence version of the main point of each page. The discipline of trying to craft a one-sentence message can be a good test of your presentation: Is each message new to your audience, interesting, and important for them to know? Will it be solidly supported by the details you will put on the page?

If you can't answer yes to each of these questions, then it is probably not worth drawing a page. (See Figure 8.19 for a checklist approach to this.) You may want to go back through

FIGURE 8.19. Checklist: Before Drawing a Slide

Unless you can answer "yes" to all the following questions, you are not really ready to draw a slide.

- ❑ Can I write a one-sentence summary of the main message of the page?
- ❑ Will this message be solidly supported by the information and details on the page?
- ❑ Will this message be new to my audience?
- ❑ Will this message be interesting to my audience?
- ❑ Is this message important for my audience to know?

the Extreme Presentation process and change some things. Begin by trying the one-sentence exercise again. Can you rewrite the sentences so that they *are* newsworthy, interesting, important, and well supported by your data? Sometimes we undersell our own content, and rephrasing our messages can help avoid this. But on other occasions we may have to go back and do the S.Co.R.E. card exercise again. Or maybe you need to focus on a different business problem. You might even have to go back and revisit the objectives for the presentation, perhaps because the data you have does not support as aggressive an objective as you set initially. But this iteration is good—it just makes your presentation stronger.

Once you have a one-sentence message for each page, think about what page layout design would best communicate or support this point, and then sketch the layout for each page, using paper and pencil. We noted above that to ensure that your page passes the squint test, you need to make sure that the layout of the page reinforces the main message of the page. This is what you are doing here. Appendix C contains thirty-six examples of slide layouts that pass the squint test. (PowerPoint versions of these layouts are available at www.ExtremePresentation.com.)

Rather than drafting your layouts in PowerPoint right now, it is probably better to hold off from using any kind of presentation software a little longer, because inevitably you will spend too much time designing slides at this rough draft stage, and therefore you will be unwilling to toss out earlier versions to try again.

Once you have a rough sketch of the layout of each page, place the sketches side-by-side across your desk, and you will have a storyboard for your presentation. Scan this storyboard to make sure that there is enough variety in page layout, from slide to slide. If there isn't, this may be an indication that your presentation is repetitive; consider combining some of the pages or changing their design.

When we do this exercise in our workshops, we almost invariably come up with presentations with single-digit page counts—where the typical presentations were between twenty-five and fifty slides long, with 100+ page presentations not unheard of.

Before going any further, you may wish to review the front-to-back Extreme Presentation case study of "SuperClean Vacuums" in Appendix B.

The Importance of "Roadmapping"

When you use lots of detail on your slides, particularly conference room style slides, you will need to guide your audience's eyes across each slide. There are three things you can do to help with this. First, you can number the elements of the page in the order that you want your audience to look at them. Second, you can give them spoken guidance, to help "roadmap" the slide for them. As you present the slide, say, for example, "First look at the top left of the slide—the chart there shows the increase in employee attrition. To the right of that, you can see. . . ." And so on. Finally, you should lay your slide out so that there is a natural flow around the slide. This does not have to be always from left to right,

FIGURE 8.20.   Thomas Cole's "Voyage of Life" Series, "Youth"

Source: Thomas Cole, *The Voyage of Life: Youth,* Ailisa Mellon Bruce Fund, Image Courtesy of the Board of Trustees, National Gallery of Art, Washington, D.C.

or from top to bottom. In fact, if you can vary the flow from slide to slide, it makes for a more interesting presentation.

We can see such varied flow in good artwork. Consider the Thomas Cole painting in Figure 8.20. This beautiful painting, hanging in the National Gallery of Art in Washington, D.C., is part of a four-painting series called "The Voyage of Life," all painted in 1842. The title of this particular painting, the second in the series, is "Youth." First, look at the angel at the bottom right of the painting. Next, look at the hero of the painting, the youth to the left of the angel, who is setting off in the ship of life. The river, flowing to the back left of the picture, seems like it will take the youth toward the castle in the clouds, which represents his youthful dreams and ambitions. There is indeed a path through the fields beyond, barely visible, and seemingly heading toward this castle. But, in fact, the river itself take a sharp turn before that path and flows across the middle of the painting, behind the trees, to the right side, and appears again above the angel. The mist above the river there gives a hint of what is to come in the next painting:

a waterfall, with the now older hero cascading down helplessly in his boat, representing the turbulence and doubts of adult life.

Notice the flow we have followed. We started at the bottom right, moved across the bottom and up the left side of the painting to the upper left (the castle in the clouds), then back down across the middle and out the right side. On your own slides, any flow will do, so long as it fits the content of your page, and so long as you guide your audience clearly. Ideally, you will want to vary the flow from one slide to the next, which is more interesting than having every slide read from top to bottom or left to right.

Final Details

[18]www.Powerframeworks.com is a subscription site that offers over a thousand different layouts, many of which pass the squint test.

At this point, you are ready to create your slides. Create your own layouts, or use any from Appendix C. Incorporate all the elements you gathered in Chapter 7 into these layouts.[18]

Once you are done with this, there are certain elements that are important for every page: title, guide marks, annotations, source, and page number. These are illustrated in Figure 8.21. The title of the page should, like the layout, reinforce the main message of the page. This will be helpful in your presentation and also ensures that the point of the page will not be misunderstood when people read your handout when you are no longer around.

If you need it, you can also add a subtitle. Some people—from certain consulting firms— have a habit of putting a descriptive title at the top of the page and the conclusion or main message at the bottom. This seems to me to give the impression that you weren't really sure what the point of the page was until you finished it. Better to start out with the point, and then have everything on the page reinforce it.

The importance of "roadmapping" was mentioned above. Using numerical or alphabetical guide marks can help with this. You can direct your audience to "Look first at box 'a,'" for example. As noted above, callout boxes or annotations are helpful for drawing attention, and also for ensuring clear communication to people who read your handout without the benefit of the presentation.

Finally, make sure that each page lists the source for the data on the page—this is important for credibility—and also that each page is numbered. If you are handing out more than one page, then you need page numbers to ensure that everyone is "on the same page." (Figure 8.22 contains a post-checklist for evaluating each of your slides.)

FIGURE 8.21.   Final Details

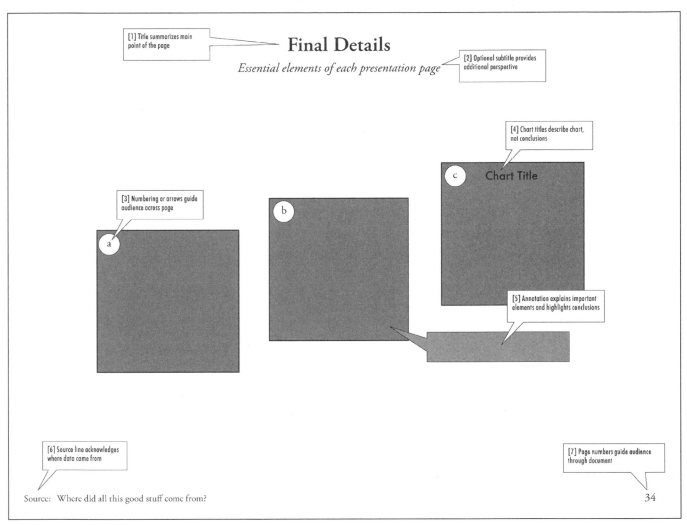

FIGURE 8.22.   Checklist: Evaluating Your Slides

Your page is not complete until you can answer "yes" to each of these questions:

❑ Does the layout of the page reinforce the main message of the page?

❑ Does the page have a title, and does the title reinforce the main message of the page?

❑ Do all the elements on the page reinforce the main message of the page, as expressed in the page title?

❑ Does the page contain lots of relevant detail?

❑ Is your page properly "roadmapped"? (Are the elements on the page numbered in the order that you want your audience to look at them?)

❑ Are the data sources identified?

❑ Is the page numbered?

FIGURE 8.23.   Frederick Church's Painting of Niagara Falls

In the Collection of The Corcoran Gallery of Art. Accession Number 76.15. Artist: Frederic Edwin Church. Title: *Niagara.* 1857. Medium: Oil on canvas. Dimensions: 42 1/2 3 90 1/2 inches. Courtesy of Corcoran Gallery of Art, Washington, DC. Credit Line: Museum Purchase, Gallery Fund.

It takes effort to create excellent visual communication—to find a good combination of simplicity of design and complexity of detail. Look at the picture in Figure 8.23. This is Frederick Church's famous painting of Niagara Falls. It represents an impressive demonstration of simplicity of design and complexity of detail. Church put a tremendous amount of effort into this painting. He made six separate visits to Niagara Falls. He drew hundreds of preliminary drawings. He painted twenty-one trial "sketches"—which were really complete oil paintings in themselves—to try to out different angles, times of day, and so on. The final version, which hangs today in the Corcoran Gallery in Washington, D.C., and is seven-and-a-half feet wide, took him six weeks to paint (Johnson, 1998).

What's the point here? If you're working on getting good detail into your presentation, you need to put a lot of effort into it. Not necessarily as much as Frederick Church put into his painting, but more than we usually do in banging out the typical PowerPoint slides. This is because we are not just putting in the detail, but we are also organizing the detail so that it makes sense to the viewer. Fortunately, since you are creating far fewer slides, and perhaps even only one, then you can spend a lot more time on each, and very likely the total amount of time you spend on your presentation will be less than you would otherwise—and yet your presentation will be far more effective.

We are almost finished. But after all this work, someone in your audience could still surprise you with some unanticipated opposition and wreck your presentation. What can you do to avoid that? The last chapter in the book will address this question, and also discuss how to measure your presentation's effectiveness.

PART V
POLITICS AND METRICS AGAIN

THE FINAL PART OF THE BOOK includes two more steps, from the politics and metrics dimensions, respectively. It is important to begin each presentation with an understanding of the audience and your specific objectives for them, and likewise it is important to end it with another look at the larger audience for your proposal, and with measurement of whether you achieved your objective. This is why Parts I and V of this book are both devoted to politics *and* metrics, rather than one being focused on each—because you want to start and end your presentation with both.

The next chapter, Chapter 9, presents the last two steps in the Extreme Presentation™ method. The ninth step, a politics question, asks who beyond your immediate audience has to play a role in your recommendations being implemented. The tenth and final step is a metrics question: How will you know whether your presentation is successful?

Satisfying Your Stakeholders and Measuring Success

9

Step 9: Identify Any Potential Roadblocks to Achieving Your Objectives, and Make a Plan to Deal with Each

Not infrequently, some of the people who are necessary for the successful adoption and implementation of your recommendations will not be in the room during your presentation. If you want to be sure of success, you need to identify these people and create a plan to get them to agree to the steps that you need them to take if your recommendations are to bear fruit.

Think through each of the critical decisions that have to be made in order for your recommendations to be implemented and who needs to make each of those decisions. Think also about whether there are any people who, if they decided that they did not like your ideas for any reason, could *block* their implementation. These are your stakeholders for this particular project. Make a list of all these people. You will need to approach those who are not going to be in your audience, preferably before your presentation. You may also want to approach some of the more important ones who are going to be in your audience to try to "pre-sell" them on your ideas.

FIGURE 9.1. Stakeholder Analysis Example

Whose help will we need for our recommendations to be implemented?	Jane	Joe
What must each of them think or do for the recommendations to be successful?	Agree that the brand investment is worth a test	Agree that he can do without the incremental funding for his salesforce
Where do they stand on this?	Currently doesn't agree	Currently doesn't agree
What do we need to do to close the gap?	Private meeting to go over the data in more detail	Work on his boss, because Joe himself will never agree to this

Once you have your list of stakeholders, the people whose buy-in you need, write down beside each name what the person needs to think or do for your recommendation to be a success, and where you think he or she stands right now. Then create a plan for how you will influence each, and schedule meetings accordingly. (See Figure 9.1 for an example; a blank form is included as Worksheet A.7 in Appendix A.) Then move on to Step 10.

Step 10: Decide How You Will Measure the Success of Your Presentation

The final step in the Extreme Presentation™ method is to measure the success of your presentation. Why should you bother to measure success? At one level, the success or failure of your presentation should be obvious rather quickly: either your audience did what you asked them to do, or they did not. Informally, another measure of success is to observe the quality of the discussion that accompanied or followed your presentation. If your audience starts to work out the implementation details of your proposal *during* your presentation, then you know you have succeeded.

In addition, you may want to be more deliberate in how you measure success. You have already taken the most important step in measuring your presentation's success, and that was back in Step 2, where you wrote clear and specific objectives for how you want your audience to change what they are thinking and doing with respect to your subject. To measure success, you want to know whether you have achieved these objectives. This is particularly important for a training presentation; for a presentation proposing an idea, recommending a course of action, or pitching a product or service, you want to know for yourself how successful your presentation was, but for a training presentation you typically also need to know to prove to others who have paid for your presentation.[1]

At the beginning of the book we mentioned that the Extreme Presentation method takes a marketing communication approach to presentation. The measurement step is just an extension of this analogy, and it suggests one additional goal beyond changing what your audience is thinking and doing. To know whether marketing is effective, we don't just measure changes in attitudes and behaviors—we also want to measure the change in brand or relationship equity. This allows us to determine whether our marketing efforts are strengthening our brand or, alternatively, whether they are just cashing in on it and therefore weakening it. Think of it in personal terms: If you try to convince people you know to do something, they may do it because you have convinced them that it would be good for them to do it, or else they may do it just as a favor to you. In the former case, your relationship may be strengthened because you have given them some useful information that allowed them to do something new; in the latter case your relationship is likely weakened. Too many such requests for favors and your friends will no longer be returning your phone calls.

It works the same way for presentations: we want each presentation to not only achieve its attitudinal and behavioral change objectives, but we also want each presentation to strengthen our personal credibility with our audience, so that the next presentation with the same audience achieves its goals more quickly and efficiently.

[1]See Brinkerhoff's Success Case Method (2003; 2006) for a detailed approach to measuring training effectiveness.

One way to gather all this information is to announce to your audience, at the end of the presentation, that you are working on an initiative to improve the impact of your work and that you would like to send them a very brief, less-than-one-minute online survey. Gain agreement from everyone in the room to respond to it, to increase the chances of receiving a good response rate. Then email them a link to a survey by the next day at the latest. The survey should have a few simple questions, which will cover these A-B-C's:

- *Attitudes:* ask them to what extent they agree/disagree with a statement or two that describes the "thinking" that you are hoping to achieve with your presentation.
- *Behaviors:* ask them to rate the probability that they will undertake a particular action or set of actions (these actions representing the "doing" that you are trying to get them to do).
- *Credibility (personal "brand equity"):* ask them to rate their willingness to attend another presentation of yours, and whether this willingness has increased, decreased, or remains the same as a result of this presentation.

In all cases, however, do not tell you audience *before* your presentation begins that you will be asking them to evaluate your presentation at the end, because it may foster an (unnecessarily) critical mindset in your audience to your whole presentation. Only announce your request for feedback at the end.[2]

For more important projects, you may also want to send a similar survey again a few weeks, or months, after your presentation, to ask whether they have actually taken the actions they said they would.

Once you have decided how you will measure your success, you have completed the tenth step. Designing a presentation is an iterative process: if you have time, go through the method, the ten steps, one more time quickly, to see whether there is anything else you need to change. The next chapter, the Conclusion to this book, has a "quick" version of the ten steps that you can use for your final review.

[2]Consumer research suggests that informing customers in advance that they will be asked to evaluate something tends to reduce satisfaction, because they tend to focus on the more negative points (Ofir & Simonson, 2001).

Conclusion

You have just completed the ten-step Extreme Presentation method. As a result of this exercise, you have created a presentation that will get people to act on your recommendations.

With practice you will get through the ten steps much more and more quickly; in all cases, the amount of effort you put in to designing your presentation should be directly proportional to the importance of the presentation.

The Scalability of the Extreme Presentation Method

You could spend five minutes or five months working through the method on a single presentation, depending on the importance of that presentation and the time you have available for it. You do not have to use all the tools in every step for every presentation. The more complex your presentation is, and the more important its success is, the more time you will want to spend working on it. Using the Extreme Presentation method is not an all-or-nothing choice: every additional effort you make will increase your presentation's effectiveness.

What if you really do not have very much time to work on your presentation? In that case, take a look at Figure 10.1. This is the quick version of the Extreme Presentation method. It contains a list of ten questions, corresponding to the ten steps in the method. Ask yourself each of the ten questions, and your answers will give you an idea about whether your presentation could benefit from some additional work, and if so, where.

Figure 10.1 is also useful for a final iteration through the method and as a way to give others feedback on their presentations. When someone asks your opinion about a presentation, you can go through the ten questions to identify any points for improvement. You can then point them to the specific tool or framework to use to achieve this improvement. Figure 10.2 repeats the Extreme Presentation method graphic from the introduction to this book and adds the key frameworks that are associated with each step.

A Language and a Framework for Providing Effective Feedback

One of the added benefits of the Extreme Presentation method is that it provides a common language and framework about presentation design. Once you and your co-workers are familiar with the method, you will be able to give each other very specific feedback. Instead of having to deal with generally vague and unhelpful comments such as

FIGURE 10.1. Extreme Presentation Quick Review

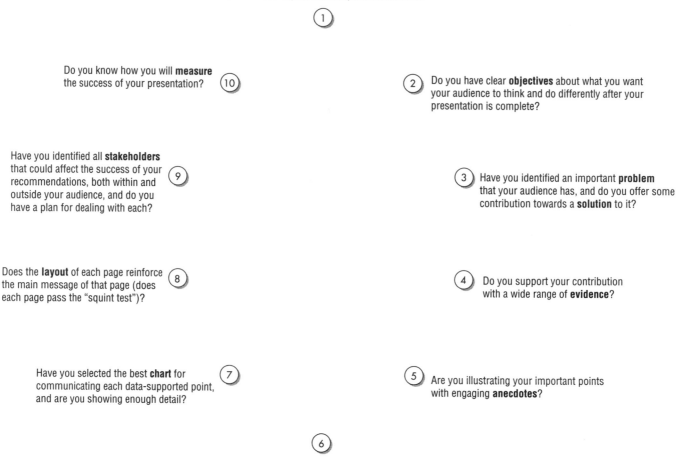

"This slide is too busy," or "That slide is not working for me" or "Could you just pretty it up a bit more," you and your colleagues can now provide more specific comments such as "This slide does not pass the squint test" or "What complication in your story sets up this point?"

Contradicting Other Approaches to Presentation Design

The advice offered in this book may have contradicted almost everything you have ever heard about how to design a good presentation. Sometimes this is because the advice you received previously is fundamentally wrong, such as the advice to limit slides to seven bullets of seven words per bullet. Other times, though, the advice is not so much wrong as redundant. For example, the advice: "Tell 'em what you're going to tell 'em; tell 'em; and then tell 'em what you told 'em." This is not in itself bad advice, but if you use the Extreme Presentation method, you will find that you no longer need to have to repeat yourself—twice—to get your message across. Advice such as this is designed for

FIGURE 10.2.   The Extreme Presentation Method on One Page

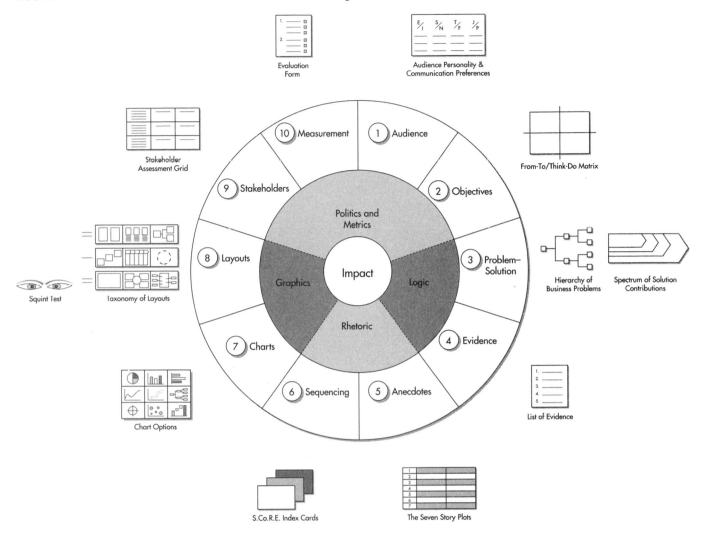

the typical, Death-by-PowerPoint presentations—which are not very effective—so they need crutches to prop them up and help them get their message across. Now that you understand the Extreme Presentation method, you no longer need such help—your presentations can shed their crutches and stand on their own. Instead of trying to tweak your presentation to improve it, we have attacked the *root causes* of presentation weakness. Your presentation is now designed from its core to grab people's attention and to drive them to action.

Let us go forward and change the world, one presentation at a time.[1]

[1]To see the latest information on the Extreme Presentation method, visit www.ExtremePresentation.com.

Worksheets

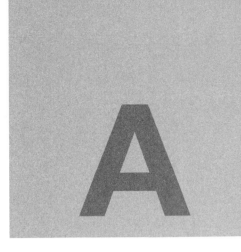

Worksheet A.1a. Audience Personality Type

Audience   Personality Type

_____   _____

_____   _____

_____   _____

_____   _____

Worksheet A.1b. Audience Personality Implications

Presentation Implications

☐ Provide all or part of presentation
  in advance
☐ Plan for lots of discussion and
  Q&A
☐ Make sure to include all relevant
  facts and details in presentation or
  appendix
☐ Provide overview up-front
☐ Identify principles, costs, and
  benefits
☐ State implications for each person
  or group of stakeholders involved
☐ Present conclusions up-front
☐ List all alternatives considered

Worksheet A.2. From-To Think-Do Matrix

From-To Think-Do Matrix

	FROM	TO
THINK		
DO		

Worksheet A.3. Audience Problem

The problem that my audience has is _____

_____

_____

Worksheet A.4. Spectrum of Solution Contributions

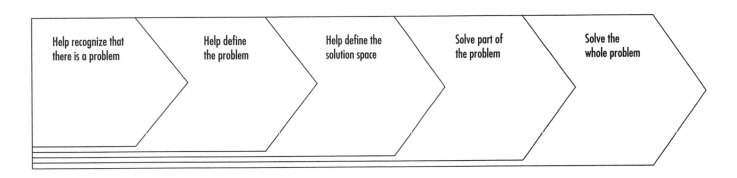

| | Help recognize that there is a problem | Help define the problem | Help define the solution space | Solve part of the problem | Solve the whole problem |

Worksheet A.5. Solution Evaluation

Evaluation Criteria	Option 1 [Proposed Solution]	Option 2 [Alternative 1]	Option 3 [Alternative 2]	Option 4 [Alternative 3]

Worksheet A.6. List of Evidence

Evidence

1. _____
2. _____
3. _____
4. _____
5. _____
6. _____
7. _____
8. _____
9. _____
10. _____
11. _____
12. _____

Worksheet A.7. Stakeholder Analysis

Whose help will we need for our recommendations to be implemented?			
What must each of them think or do for our recommendations to be successful?			
Where do they stand on this?			
What do we need to do to close the gap?			

Extreme Presentation Makeover

This appendix contains an Extreme Presentation™ makeover: a "before-and-after" example of a presentation that was redesigned according to the Extreme Presentation principles. The "before" presentation is based on a real presentation that has been heavily disguised, and is used here with permission. For the purpose of this example, we are pretending that the presentation is a brand update for a fictitious SuperClean vacuums company.

Figure B.1 in this appendix shows the first eighteen slides of this original seventy-five-slide "before" presentation. Even a quick glance will show you that this presentation would not have been much fun to watch—or to deliver.

FIGURE B.1.   First Eighteen Slides of the Original Seventy-Five-Slide Presentation

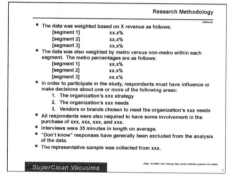

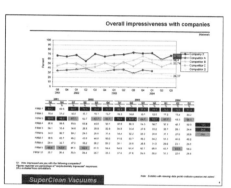

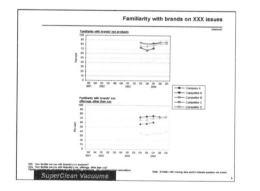

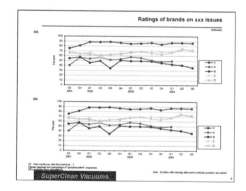

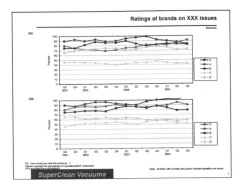

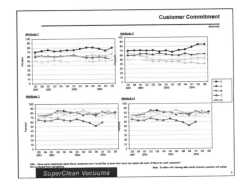

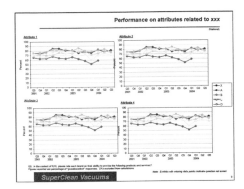

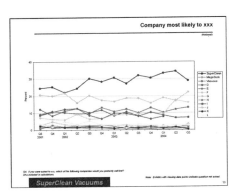

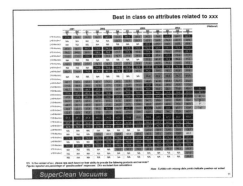

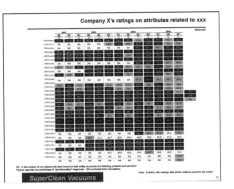

(Continued)

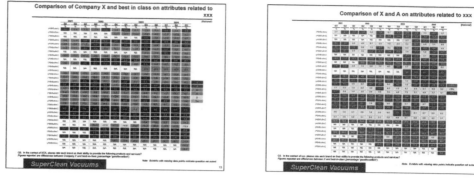

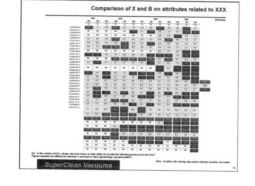

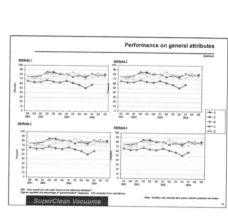

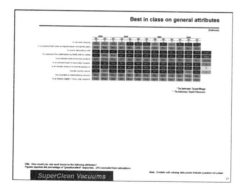

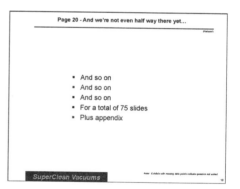

Page 20 - And we're not even half way there...

(National)

- And so on
- And so on
- And so on
- For a total of 75 slides
- Plus appendix

SuperClean Vacuums

Note: Exhibits with missing data points indicate question not asked.

Figures B.2 through B.10 show the completed exercises for the relevant steps using the Extreme Presentation method to create the "after" version. Figure B.2 shows the exercise from Step 1, listing the audience for this presentation—the CEO, CFO, and head of Sales for SuperClean Vacuums—and their respective Myers-Briggs types.

FIGURE B.2.   **Audience Personality Types**

Audience	E/I	N/S	T/F	P/J
J. Casimir — CEO	E	N	T	J
M. Wolodyjowski — CEO	I	S	T	J
J. Zagloba — EVP Sales	E	S	F	P
	—	—	—	—

As you can see from Figure B.2, the audience members' Myers-Briggs types cover the full range of dimensions, and therefore all the presentation implications in Figure B.3 are checked.

FIGURE B.3.   **Audience Personality Implications**

Presentation Implications

☑ **I**—Provide all or part of presentation in advance

☑ **E**—Plan for lots of discussion and Q&A

☑ **S**—Make sure to include all relevant facts and details in presentation or appendix

☑ **N**—Provide overview up-front

☑ **T**—Identify principles, costs, and benefits

☑ **F**—State implications for each person or group of stakeholders involved

☑ **J**—Present conclusions up-front

☑ **P**—List all alternatives considered

FIGURE B.4.   From-To Think-Do Matrix

From-To Think-Do Matrix

	FROM	TO
THINK	Brand advertising is a waste of money	Brand advertising is worth testing
DO	Not spending significantly on brand advertising	Agree to a brand advertising test

For Step 2, you can see in Figure B.4 that the objective of this presentation is to move the audience from thinking that brand advertising is a waste of money to thinking that it is worth testing, and to move them from not spending significantly on brand advertising, to agreeing to a brand advertising test.

In Step 3, we can see that the business problem that this presentation will focus on is that this company is having trouble growing their high-end, heavy-duty vacuum cleaner business (Figure B.5), and the solution being offered, to solve part of this problem, is to run brand advertising research (Figure B.6). The alternative solutions to this would be to do nothing (as always), and also to spend more money on in-store promotion, or to hire more salespeople (Figure B.7).

FIGURE B.5.   Audience Problem

Business Problem

We are having trouble growing our
high-end, heavy-duty business

FIGURE B.6.   Solutions Offered

Solution Contribution

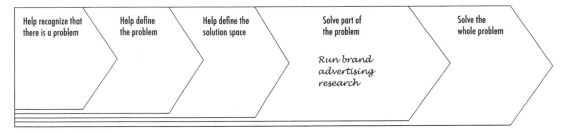

| Help recognize that there is a problem | Help define the problem | Help define the solution space | Solve part of the problem | Solve the whole problem |

Run brand advertising research

FIGURE B.7.   Alternative Solutions

Alternative Solutions

Do nothing

Spend more on high-end product in-store support

Hire more sales reps

For Step 4, Figure B.8 shows the list of evidence to be presented, containing five items: tracking study data for SuperClean products and for their competitors, a correlation between awareness change and sales change in the Southwest region, overall advertising spend versus market share change results for several previous quarters, and a quote from Hyperbrand, a brand consulting firm.

FIGURE B.8.   List of Evidence

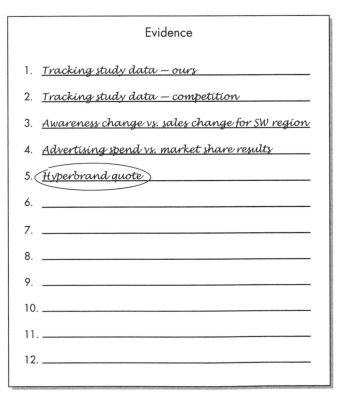

Evidence

1. *Tracking study data — ours*
2. *Tracking study data — competition*
3. *Awareness change vs. sales change for SW region*
4. *Advertising spend vs. market share results*
5. *Hyperbrand quote*
6.
7.
8.
9.
10.
11.
12.

FIGURE B.9.   S.Co.R.E. Cards for the Presentation

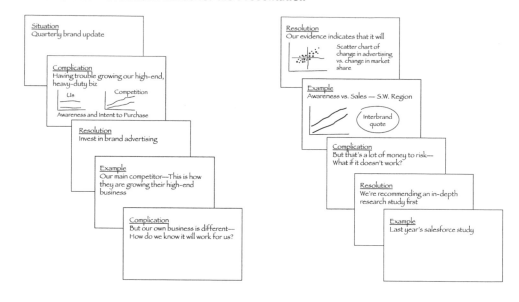

Figure B.9 displays the S.Co.R.E. cards that outline the presentation storyline in Step 6.

Finally, Figure B.10 shows the actual Extreme Presentation version of the presentation, the "after" version from this before and after exercise. It is one slide long, reduced from the original seventy-five slides. It is a conference room style slide, and therefore would be printed out and copies handed to the audience.

FIGURE B.10.   Extreme Presentation Version

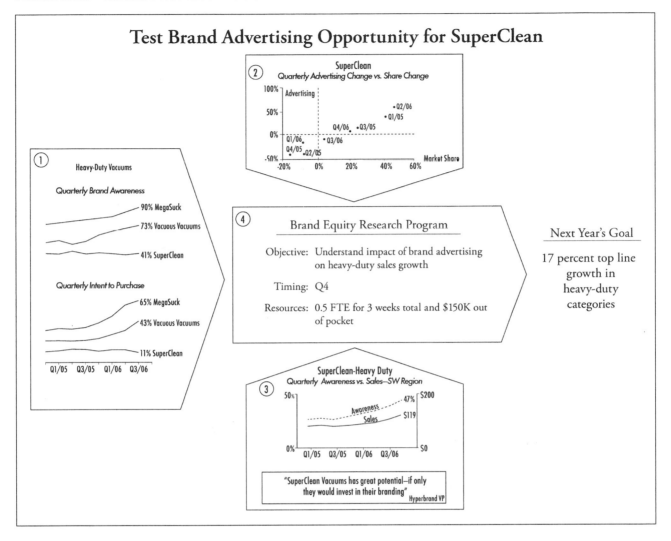

The accompanying spoken part of the presentation would go something like this (you can follow along on Figure B.10):

"Good morning, ladies and gentlemen—we're here for our quarterly brand update. The page in front of you covers our analysis for today. Start on the left side of the page, number 1—as you can see from those two charts on the left, our Heavy Duty business is stagnant: you can see our awareness is roughly flat at 41 percent on the upper chart, and intent-to-purchase is slightly declining, currently at 11 percent.

"This is compared to our main competitors, MegaSuck and Vacuous Vacuums, who have both been showing strong increases in both awareness and intent to purchase over the past several quarters.

"To overcome this gap, we believe that we need to invest in brand advertising for SuperClean in the Heavy Duty Segment, because this is how our competitors are doing it. We recognize that our business model is different from theirs, but overall, we believe that advertising is effective for SuperClean—as you can see at the top of the page—arrow number 2. On the chart we've plotted the change in advertising versus a year ago, on the vertical axis, against the change in market share on the horizontal axis—for several of the recent quarters.

And what you can see is a fairly clear correlation—when we increase advertising, our sales increases, and when we reduce it, the opposite happens. And more specifically, at the bottom of the page—number 3—you can see how—as awareness in our SW region increased over the past year—because of some additional advertising that we did there on heavy-duty vacuums, our sales increased also. And below that we have a quote from Hyperbrand—they singled us out in a recent report—that our brands have great potential.

However, there is still a risk that it may not work, so what we're recommending is a research test—in the middle of the page—number 4. The goal is to test the impact of brand advertising on our heavy duty products, and we want to do this in Q1 of next year. Cost for this study will be half a person for three weeks, and $150K research expense. And the results of this test should show the way to bring us to next year's goal of 17 percent growth. . . ."

There you go—we have taken seventy-five slides and reduced them to a powerful, one-slide presentation.

Thirty-Six Layouts That Pass the Squint Test

Layout Options

Decisions and Alternatives

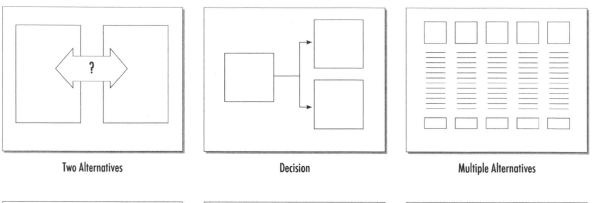

Two Alternatives

Decision

Multiple Alternatives

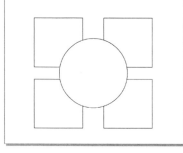

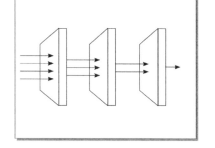

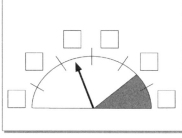

Converging Issues

Screening Alternatives

Avoiding Extreme Alternatives

Processes and Progress

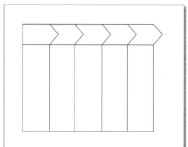

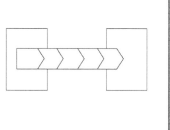

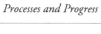

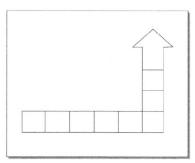

Detailed Process

From-To Process

Course Change

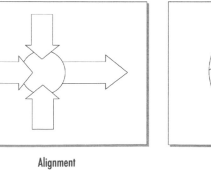

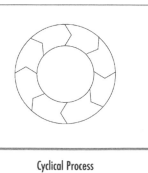

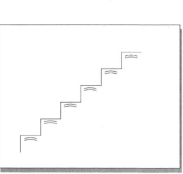

Alignment

Cyclical Process

Improvement Steps

More Processes and Progress

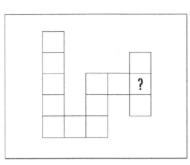

Gameboard—Complex Process

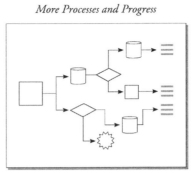

Flowchart/Process Diagram

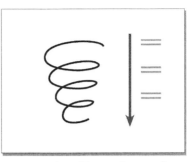

Downward Spiral (Reverse for Upward)

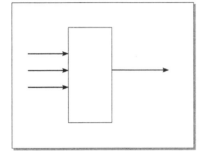

Inputs and Outputs

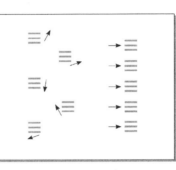

From Chaos to Alignment

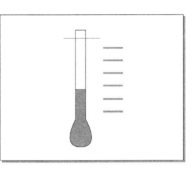

Progress Towards Goal

Problems ("Opportunities")

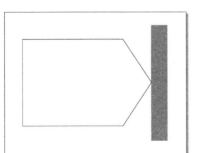

Barrier

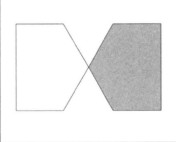

Tension

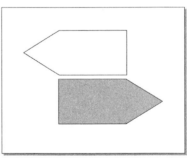

Diverging Approaches or Ideas

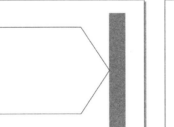

Tip of the Iceberg

Maze—Confusion

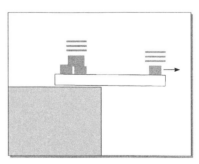

On the Edge

Balance and Miscellaneous

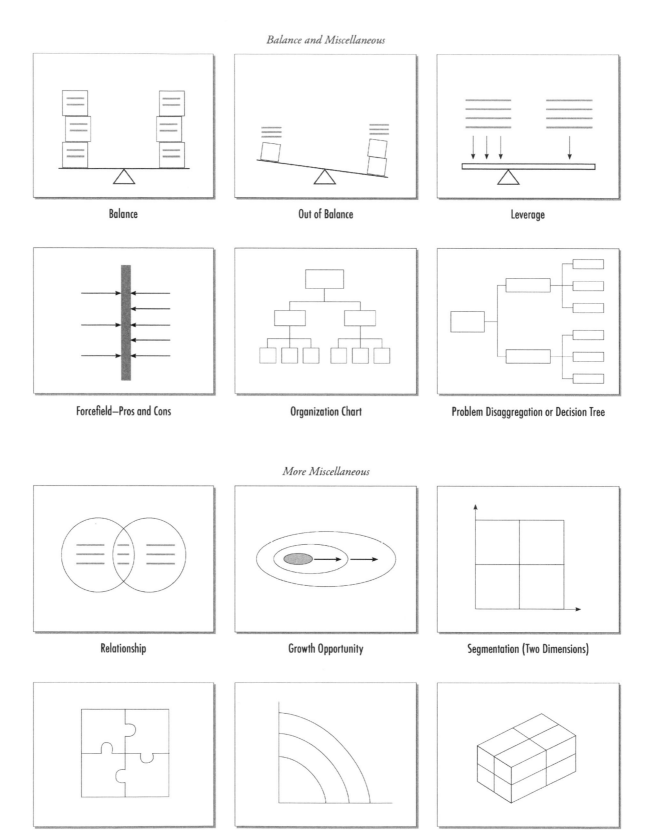

Balance

Out of Balance

Leverage

Forcefield—Pros and Cons

Organization Chart

Problem Disaggregation or Decision Tree

More Miscellaneous

Relationship

Growth Opportunity

Segmentation (Two Dimensions)

Component—Puzzle

Growth Opportunity (Two Dimensions)

Segmentation (Three Dimensions)

Source: Several of these layouts are adapted from G. Zelazny, *Saying It with Charts* and M. Craig, *Thinking Visually*. PowerPoint versions of all these layouts are available at www.ExtremePresentation.com.

Further Reading

Logic

Buzan, Tony. *Use Both Sides of Your Brain*. New York: Dutton, 1989.

De Bono, Edward. *Serious Creativity*. New York: Harper Business, 1992.

Jones, Morgan. *The Thinker's Toolkit*. New York: Three Rivers Press, 1995.

Long, Linda. *The Power of Logic*. Marietta, GA: SCC Publishing, 2006.

Michalko, Michael. *Thinkertoys*. Berkeley, CA: Ten Speed Press, 1991.

Rhetoric/Storytelling

Atkinson, Cliff, *Beyond Bullet Points*. Redmond, WA: Microsoft Press, 2007.

Boettinger, Henry M. *Moving Mountains*. New York: Collier Books, 1969.

Booker, Christopher. *The Seven Basic Plots*. New York: Continuum, 2004.

Kerr, Walter. *The Decline of Pleasure*. New York: Simon & Schuster, 1962.

Robinson, Grady Jim. *"Did I Ever Tell You About the Time…"* New York: McGraw-Hill, 2000.

Silverman, Lori L. *Wake Me Up When the Data Is Over*. Hoboken, NJ: John Wiley & Sons, 2006.

Simmons, Annette. *The Story Factor*. New York: Basic Books, 2001.

Wacker, Mary B., and Lori L. Silverman. *Stories Trainers Tell*. San Francisco, CA: Pfeiffer, 2003.

Graphics

Ballroom Style Presentations

Reynolds, Garr. *Presentation Zen*. Berkeley, CA: New Riders Press, 2008.

Charts and Graphs

Cleveland, William S. *The Elements of Graphing Data*. Monterey, CA: Wadsworth, 1985.

Few, Stephen. *Information Dashboard Design*. Sebastopol, CA: O'Reilly, 2006.

Harris, Robert L. *Information Graphics: A Comprehensive Illustrated Reference*. New York: Oxford University Press, 1999.

Kosslyn, Stephen. *Graph Design for the Eye and Mind*. New York: Oxford University Press, 2006.

Tufte, Edward. *Envisioning Information*. Cheshire, CT: Graphics Press, 1990.

Tufte, Edward. *Visual Explanations*. Cheshire, CT: Graphics Press, 1998.

Tufte, Edward. *The Visual Display of Quantitative Information*. Cheshire, CT: Graphics Press, 2001.

Tufte, Edward. *Beautiful Evidence*. Cheshire, CT: Graphics Press, 2007.

Zelazny, Gene. *Say It with Charts*. New York: McGraw-Hill, 2001.

Diagrams

Craig, Malcolm. *Thinking Visually*. London: Thomson, 2000.

General

Nuts and Bolts of PowerPoint

Bunzell, Tom. *Solving the PowerPoint Predicament*. Indianapolis, IN: Que, 2007.

Delivering Presentations

Hoff, Ron. *I Can See You Naked*. Kansas City, MO: Andrews and McMeel, 1992.

1,000 Good Books

Light Reading

Andersen, Hans Christian
Pictures of Travel in Sweden

Bronte, Charlotte
Jane Eyre

Bronte, Emily
Wuthering Heights

Collins, Wilkie
After Dark
Antonia
Armadale
Basil
The Black Robe
Blind Love
"Blow Up with the Brig"
The Dead Alive
The Dead Secret
The Evil Genius
The Fallen Leaves
The Fatal Cradle
Fatal Fortune
The Frozen Deep
The Haunted Hotel
Heart and Science
Hide and Seek
"I say no"
Jezebel's Daughter
The Law and the Lady
The Legacy of Cain
Man and Wife
Miss or Mrs.?
Miss Bertha and the Yankee
Miss Dulane and My Lord
Miss Jeromette and the Clergyman
Miss Mina and the Groom
Miss Morris and the Stranger
The Moonstone
Mr. Captain and the Nymph
Mr. Cosway and the Landlady
Mr. Lepel and the Housekeeper
Mr. Lismore and the Widow
Mr. Maramduke and the Minister
Mr. Medhurst and the Princess
Mr. Percy and the Prophet
Mrs. Zant and the Ghost
My Lady's Money
My Miscellanies
The New Magdalen
No Name
Poor Miss Finch
The Queen of Hearts
A Rogue's Life from His Birth . . .
The Two Destinies
The Woman in White

Dampier, William
A Voyage Round the World

Daudet, Alphonse
Fromont Jeune
Tartarin

Dickens, Charles
Barnaby Rudge
Nicholas Nickleby
Old Curiosity Shop

Doyle, Sir Author Conan
The Lost World
Sherlock Holmes (series)
White Company

Le Sage, Alain
Gil Blas

MacDonald, George
Lilith

Dumas, Alexandre
The Black Tulip
Three Musketeers
Twenty Years After
The Whites and the Blues

Du Maurier, Daphne
George Trilby

Eliot, George
Adam Bede
Middlemarch
Mill on the Floss
Romola
Silas Marner

Eggleston, Edwards
Brant and Red Jacket
The Circuit Rider
Duffles
The Graysons
The Hoosier School-Boy
The Hoosier Schoolmaster

Fabre, Henri
Selections from Souvenirs
Entymologiques

Gray, Zane
The Call of the Canyon
Desert Gold
The Desert of Wheat
Fighting Caravans
The Last of the Plainsmen
The Last Trail
Nevada
Riders of the Purple Sage

Haggard, H. Rider
Allan and the Holy Flower
Allan and the Ice Gods
Allan's Wife, and Other Tales
Allan Quartermain
Ayesha
Child of the Storm
Colonel Quaritch, VC
Dr. Therne
Joan Haste
King Solomon's Mines
Montezuma's Daughter
The People of the Mist
She
Treasure of the Lake

Hughes, Thomas
Tom Brown's School Days
Tom Brown at Oxford

Hugo, Victor
Les Miserables
Hunchback of Notre Dame
Quatre-vingt-treize

Ibanez, Blasco
Blood and Sand
Four Horsemen of the Apocalypse

Irving, Washington
The Alhambra Tales

Kingsley, Charles
Hereward, the Wake

Park, Mungo
Travels in Africa

Parkman, Francis
Oregon Trail

Poe, Edgar Allen
Tales and Poems

Polo, Marco
Travels

Reade, Charles
The Cloister and the Hearth

Rhodes, Eugene
Best Novels and Stories

Scott, Sir Walter
Ivanhoe
Kenilworth
Rob Roy
The Talisman

Shakespeare, William
Merchant of Venice
Midsummer Night's Dream
Romeo and Juliet

Shelley, Mary
Frankenstein

Sienkiewicz, Henrik
With Fire and Sword
Quo Vadis

Stevenson, Robert Louis
The Master of Ballantrae
Prince Otto
Dr. Jekyll and Mr. Hyde

Swift, Jonathan
Gulliver's Travels

Wallace, Edgar
Sanders of the River
Again Sanders
Bones
Bosambo of the River
Diana of Kara Kara
The Double
Four Just Men
The Girl from Scotland Yard
The Man Who Knew
The People of the River
The Sinister Man

Wells, H.G.
The First Men on the Moon
The Food of the Gods
In the Days of the Comet
The Invisible Man
The Island of Dr. Moreau
The Time Machine
The War of the Worlds

Wister, Owen
The Dragon of Wantley
The Jimmyjohn Boss and Other
Stories
Lady Baltimore
Lin McLean
Members of the Family
The Virginian

Source: From John Senior, *The Death of Christian Culture* (Norfolk, VA: IHS Press). Reproduced with permission.

Heavier Reading

Anderson, Hans Christian
The Fairy Tale of My Life

Austen, Jane
Emma
Lady Susan
Mansfield Park
Northanger Abbey
Persuasion
Pride and Prejudice
Sense and Sensibility
The Watsons

Balzac, Honore de
The Cabinet of Antiquities
Pere Goriot, Ursule Mirouet, and others

Bellamy, Edward
The Blindman's World and Other Stories
The Duke of Stockbridge
Looking Backward
Equality (Sequel to Looking Backward)

Belloc, Hillaire
The Cruise of the "Nona" and many others

Bernanos, Georges
Diary of a Country Priest
A Diary of My Times
The Fearless Heart
Joy
Last Essays

Blackmore, Richard Dodderidge
Cripps, The Carrier
Lorna Doone
A Tale of the South Downs

Borrows, George
The Bible in Spain
Lavengro
Romany Rye (Sequel to Lavengro)

Buchan, John
A Book of Escapes and Hurried Journeys (Collection)
Castle Gay
The Courts of the Morning
The Free Fishers
The Gap in the Curtain
Greenmantle
The House of the Four Winds
Huntingtower
John MacNab
A Lodge in the Wilderness
Midwinter
Mr. Standfast
The Three Hostages
The Thirty-Nine Steps

Butler, Samuel
Erewhon
The Way of All Flesh

Cabell, James Branch
Chivalry
Gallantry

Jurgen
The Silver Stallion

Cable, George Washington
The Cavailier
Old Creole Days
Kincaid's Battery

Cather, Willa
Death Comes for the Archbishop
My Antonia
Shadows on the Rock

Lagelof, Selma
gosta Berling
Jerusalem

Checkov, Anton
Stories and Plays

Chesterton, G.K.
Everlasting Man
Father Brown (series)
A Man Called Thursday

Columbus, Christopher
Four Voyages to the New World

Conrad, Joseph
Almayer's Folley
An Outcast of the Islands
An Arrow of Gold
Lord Jim
Nostromo
The Rescue
A Set of Six
Twixt Land and Sea
Typhoon
Victory

Cook, James
Captain Cook's Explorations

DeMaupassant, Guy
Stories

Dickens, Charles
Bleak House
Martin Chuzzelwitt
Our Mutual Friend

Dostoyevsky, Feodor
Brothers Karamazov
Crime and Punishment

Doughty, Charles
Travels in Arabian Deserts

Fielding, Henry
Jonathan Wilde
Tom Jones

Hakluyt
Voyages to the New World

Hawkins, Anthony Hope
Captain Dieppe
A Change of Air
Double Harness
Half a Hero
A King's Mirror
A Man of Mark
The Prisoner of Zenda
Rupert of Hentzau
Simon Dale

The Secret of the Tower
Tristram of Blent

Hawthorne, Nathaniel
The House of Seven Gables
The Scarlet Letter and others

Hudson, W.H.
Green Mansions
The Purple Land

Irving, Washington
Conquest of Granada
Life of Columbus
Life of George Washington

Jackson, Helen Hunt
Ramona

Loti, Pierre (Louis Marie Julien Viand)
An Iceland Fisherman
India (Without the English)
On Life's By-Ways

Manzoni, Alessandro
The Betrothed

Melville, Herman
Billy Budd
Moby Dick

Moore, Tom
Lalla Rookh

Morris, William
News from Nowhere
The Roots of the Mountains
Sigurd the Volsing and the Fall of the Niblungs

Scott, Robert
Scott's Last Expedition

Shakespeare, William
As You Like It
Hamlet
Henry IV
Henry V
Macbeth
The Sonnets
The Taming of the Shrew
Twelfth Night

Stanley, Sir Henry Morton
How I Found Livingstone

Stendahl
The Abbess of Castro and Other Tales
Armance
The Charterhouse of Parma
Lamiel
Lucien Leuwen
Italian Chronicles
Memoirs of a Tourist
The Red and the Black

Thackeray, William Makepeace
Adventures of Philip
Catherine
Denis Duval
Eastern Sketches
Henry Esmond

The Four Georges
The History of Pendennis
The Irish Sketchbook
Lovel the Widower
Memoirs of Barry Lyndon
The Newcomers
The Paris Sketchbook
Roundabout Papers
The Second Funeral of Na
Sketches and Travels in London
Vanity Fair
The Virginians

Tolstoy, Leo
Anna Karenina
Childhood, Boyhood, Youth
The Cossacks
The Death of Ivan Ilyich and Other Stories
Fables for Children
The Kreutzer Sonata
Master and Man
My Confession
My Religion
Resurrection
Tales of Sevastopol
War and Peace
What Is to Be Done?

Trollope, Anthony
Barchester (series)

Turgenev, Ivan
The Brigadier and Other Stories
Diary of a Superfluous Man and Other Stories
Dream Tales and Prose Poems
Fathers and Sons
A Hunter's Sketches
Knock, Knock, Knock and Other Stories
A Month in the Country
A Nest of Gentlefolk
Rudin
Smoke
Spring Torrents

Undset, Sigrid
The Burning Bush
Catherine of Siena
The Faithful Wife
Gunnar's Daughter
Ida Elizabeth
Jenny
Kristin Lavransdatter
The Master of Hestviken
Sage of Saints
The Wild Orchid

Verga, Giovanni
Cavelleria Rusticana and Other Stories
The House by the Medlar Tree (trans. D.H. Lawrence)
Little Novels of Sicily

Washington, Booker T.
Up from Slavery

References

Abela, Andrew V. (2006). "Achieve Impact Through Persuasive Presentation Design." *Competitive Intelligence, 9*(6), 20–22.

Allen, Mike. (1998). "Comparing the Persuasive Effectiveness of One- and Two-Sided Messages." In Mike Allen and Raymond W. Preiss (Eds.), *Persuasion: Advances Through Meta-Analysis*. Cresskill, NJ: Hampton Press.

Almer, Elizabeth Dreike, Jill R. Hopper, and Steven E. Kaplan. (2003). "A Research Tool to Increase Attention to Experimental Materials: Manipulating Presentation Format." *Journal of Business and Psychology, 17*(3), 405.

Ambler, Tim. (2003). *Marketing and the Bottom Line* (2nd ed.). London: FT Prentice Hall.

Armstrong, Scott. (2008). *Persuasive Advertising: An Evidence-Based Approach for Developing Advertisements*. New York: Palgrave-Macmillan.

Aronson, Elliot. (1999). "The Power of Self-Persuasion." *American Psychologist, 54*(11), 875.

Artz, Nancy, and Alice M. Tybout. (1999). "The Moderating Impact of Quantitative Information on the Relationship Between Source Credibility and Persuasion: A Persuasion Knowledge Model Interpretation." *Marketing Letters, 10*(1), 51–63.

Bacon, Terry. (1996). *Interpersonal and Interactive Skills*. Durango, CO: Self-Management Institute.

Bartsch, Robert A., and Kristi M. Cobern. (2003). "Effectiveness of PowerPoint Presentations in Lectures." *Computers & Education, 41*(1), 77–86.

Benbasat, Izak, and Albert S. Dexter. (1985). "An Experimental Evaluation of Graphical and Color-Enhanced Information Presentation." *Management Science, 31*(11), 1348–64.

Bergen, Lori, Tom Grimes, and Deborah Potter. (2005). "How Attention Partitions Itself During Simultaneous Message Presentations." *Human Communication Research, 31*(3), 311–336.

Boettinger, Henry M. (1969). *Moving Mountains: The Art and Craft of Letting Others See Things Your Way*. New York: Collier Books.

Bohner, Gerd, and Thomas Weinerth. (2001). "Negative Affect Can Increase or Decrease Message Scrutiny: The Affect Interpretation Hypothesis." *Personality and Social Psychology Bulletin, 27*(11), 1417–1428.

Booker, Christopher. (2005). *The Seven Basic Plots: Why We Tell Stories*. London: Continuum.

Bowe, Martin, Dan Jensen, John Feland, and Brian Self. (2000). "When Multimedia Doesn't Work: An Assessment of Visualization Modules for Learning Enhancement in Mechanics." In *Proceedings of the ASEE Annual Conference*. St. Louis, MO: American Society for Engineering Education.

Branigan, Edward. (1992). *Narrative Comprehension and Film*. London: Routledge.

Brinkerhoff, Robert O. (2003). *The Success Case Method*. San Francisco, CA: Berrett-Koehler.

Brinkerhoff, Robert O. (2006). *Telling Training's Story*. San Francisco, CA: Berrett-Koehler.

Broeder, Dale W. (1959). "The University of Chicago Jury Project." *Nebraska Law Review, 38*, 744–760.

Bundschuh, Russell G., and Theodore M. Dezvane (2003). "How to Make After-Sales Service Pay Off." *Mckinsey Quarterly, 4*.

Burrell, N., and R. Koper. (1998). "The Efficacy of Powerful/Powerless Language on Attitudes and Source Credibility." In M. Allen and R. Preiss (Eds.), *Persuasion: Advances Through Meta-Analysis*. Cresskill, NJ: Hampton Press.

Butler, Janet B., and R. David Mautz, Jr. (1996). "Multimedia presentations and learning: A laboratory experiment." *Issues in Accounting Education, 11*(2), 259.

Cahill, Larry, Ralf Babinsky, Hans J. Markowitsch, and James L. McGaugh. (1995). "The Amygdala and Emotional Memory." *Nature, 377*(6547), 295.

Campbell, F.A., B.D. Goldman, M.L. Boccia, and M. Skinner. (2004). "The Effect of Format Modifications and Reading Comprehension on Recall of Informed Consent Information by Low-Income Parents: A Comparison of Print, Video, and Computer-Based Presentations." *Patient Education and Counselling, 53*(2), 205–216.

Chamblee, Robert, and Dennis M. Sandler. (1992). "Business-to-Business Advertising: Which Layout Style Works Best?" *Journal of Advertising Research, 32*(6), 39.

Chaudhuri, A. (2002). "A Study of Emotion and Reason in Products and Services." *Journal of Consumer Behavior, 1*(3), 267–279.

Christ, R.E. (1975). "Review and Analysis of Color Coding Research for Visual Display." *Human Factors, 17*, 542–570.

Cialdini, Robert B. (2001). *Influence: Science and Practice*. Needham Heights, MA: Allyn & Bacon.

Clark, Bruce H., Andrew V. Abela, and T. Ambler. (2006). "An Information Processing Model of Marketing Performance Measurement." *Journal of Marketing Theory and Practice, 14*(3), 191–208.

Cleveland, William S., and Robert McGill. (1984). "Graphical Perception: Theory, Experimentation, and Application to the Development of Graphical Methods." *Journal of the American Statistical Association, 79*(387), 531–554.

Daniels, L. (1999). "Introducing Technology in the Classroom: PowerPoint as a First Step." *Journal of Computing in Higher Education, 10*(42–56).

Dannels, Deanna P. (2003). "Teaching and Learning Design Presentations in Engineering: Contradictions Between Academic and Workplace Activity Systems." *Journal of Business and Technical Communication, 17*(2), 139.

Davenport, T.H. (2006). "Competing on Analytics." *Harvard Business Review, 84*(1), 98–107.

Davis, B.P., and E.S. Knowles. (1999). "A Disrupt-Then-Reframe Technique of Social Influence." *Journal of Personality and Social Psychology, 76*(2), 192–199.

Doumont, Jean-Luc. (2005). "The Cognitive Style of PowerPoint: Slides Are Not All Evil." *Technical Communication, 52*(1), 64.

du Plessis, Eric. (2005). *The Advertised Mind: Ground-Breaking Insights into How Our Brains Respond to Advertising*. London: Kogan Page.

Edell, Julie A., and Richard Staelin. (1983). "The Information Processing of Pictures in Print Advertisements." *Journal of Consumer Research, 10*(1), 45.

Feinberg, S., and M. Murphy. (2000). "Applying Cognitive Load Theory to the Design of Web-Based Instruction." In *Proceedings of the International Professional Communication Conference.* Cambridge, MA: IEEE Professional Communication Society.

Felder, R.M., and J. Spurlin. (2005). "Applications, Reliability and Validity of the Index of Learning Styles." *International Journal of Engineering Education, 21*(1), 103–112.

Fernandez, Karen V., and Dennis L. Rosen. (2000). "The Effectiveness of Information and Color in Yellow Pages Advertising." *Journal of Advertising, 29*(2), 61.

Few, Stephen. (2006). "Beautiful Evidence: A Journey Through the Mind of Edward Tufte." *Business Intelligence Network.* www.b-eye-network.com/view/3226.

Fifield, S., and R. Peifer. (1994). "Enhancing Lecture Presentations in Introductory Biology with Computer-Based Multi-Media." *Journal of College Science Teaching, 23*(4), 235–239.

Finn, Adam. (1988). "Print Ad Recognition Readership Scores: An Information Process." *Journal of Marketing Research, 25*(2), 168.

Fischer, Martin H. (2000). "Do Irrelevant Depth Cues Affect the Comprehension of Bar Graphs?" *Applied Cognitive Psychology, 14*(2), 151–163.

Ford, Gary T., Darlene B. Smith, and John L. Swasy. (1990). "Consumer Skepticism of Advertising Claims: Testing Hypotheses from Economics of Information." *Journal of Consumer Research, 16*(4), 433–441.

Friedrich, James, David Fetherstonhaugh, Sean Casey, and Dennis Gallagher. (1996). "Argument Integration and Attitude Change: Suppression Effects in the Integration of One-Sided Arguments That Vary in Persuasiveness." *Personality and Social Psychology Bulletin, 22*(2), 179–191.

Garcia, M.R. (1991). *Eyes on the News.* St. Petersburg, FL: Poynter Institute.

Gigerenzer, Gerd. (2004). "Dread Risk, September 11, and Fatal Traffic Accidents." *Psychological Science, 15,* 286.

Ginns, Paul. (2005). "Meta-Analysis of the Modality Effect." *Learning and Instruction, 15,* 313–31.

Glick, Jeff. (2004, September 10). "When, How to Tell Stories with Text." *Poynteronline.* www.poynter.org/content/content_view.asp?id=70232&sid=11.

Gold, Jeff, and David Holman. (2001). "Let Me Tell You a Story: An Evaluation of the Use of Storytelling and Argument Analysis in Management Education." *Career Development International, 6*(7), 384–395.

Guadagno, Rosanna E., Jill M. Sundie, Terrilee Asher, and Robert B. Cialdini. (2006). *The Persuasive Power of Computer-Based Multimedia Presentations.* Santa Barbara, CA: University of California (Unpublished manuscript).

Hegarty, M., N. Narayanan, and P. Freitas. (2002). "Understanding Machines from Multimedia and Hypermedia Presentations." In J. Otero, J.A. Leon, and A.C. Graesser (Eds.), *The Psychology of Science Text Comprehension.* Mahwah, NJ: Lawrence Erlbaum Associates.

Hoadley, Ellen D. (1990). "Investigating the Effects of Color." *Communications of the ACM, 33*(2), 120–125.

Hollands, J.G., and Ian Spence. (2001). "The Discrimination of Graphical Elements." *Applied Cognitive Psychology, 15*(4), 413–431.

Holmes, Neville. (2004). "In Defense of PowerPoint." *IEEE Computer, 37*(7), 89–100.

Jackson, Susan, and Alison Esse. (2006). "Making a Difference Through Storytelling at Parcelforce." *Strategic Communication Management, 10*(3), 26.

Jahng, J.J., H. Jain, and K. Ramamurthy. (2002). "Personality Traits and Effectiveness of Presentation of Product Information in e-Business Systems." *European Journal of Information Systems*, *11*(3), 181.

James, W.B., and M.C. Galbraith. (1985). "Perceptual Learning Styles: Implications and Techniques for the Practitioner." *Lifelong Learning*, *8*(4), 59–64.

Jarvenpaa, Sirka L., and Gary W. Dickson. (1988). "Graphics and Managerial Decision Making: Research-Based Guidelines." *Communications of the ACM*, *31*(6), 764–774.

Jensen, M.S., K.J. Wilcox, J.T. Hatch, and C. Sumdahl. (1995). "A Computer-Assisted Instruction Unit on Diffusion and Osmosis with a Conceptual Change Design." *Journal of Computers in Mathematics and Science Teaching*, *15*(1/2), 49–64.

Johnson, Paul M. (1998). *A History of the American People*. New York: HarperCollins.

Johnson, Steve Berlin. (2005, November 22). "How to Cut Through the Info Blitz and Actually Get Some Work Done." *Discover*. http://discovermagazine.com/2005/nov/emerging-technology/.

Kahan, Seth. (2006). "The Power of Storytelling to Jump-Start Collaboration." *The Journal for Quality and Participation*, *29*(1), 23.

Kahneman, Daniel. (2003). "Maps of Bounded Rationality: Psychology for Behavioral Economics." *American Economic Review*, *93*(5), 1449–1475.

Kalyuga, Slava, Paul Chandler, and John Swelliing. (2004). "When Redundant On-Screen Text in Multimedia Technical Instruction Can Interfere with Learning." *Human Factors*, *46*(3), 567–581.

Kapoun, Jim. (2003). "The Use of PowerPoint in the Library Classroom: An Experiment in Learning Outcomes." *Library Philosophy and Practice*, *6*(1).

Kask, S. (2000). "The Impact of Using Computer Presentations (CAP) on Student Learning in the Microeconomics Principles Course." Presented at American Economic Association meeting. Boston, MA.

Kazui, Hiroaki, Etsuro Mori, Mamoru Hashimoto, and Nobutsugu Hirono. (2003). "Enhancement of Declarative Memory by Emotional Arousal and Visual Memory Function in Alzheimer's Disease." *Journal of Neuropsychiatry and Clinical Neurosciences*, *15*(2), 221–226.

Kazui, Hiroaki, Etsuro Mori, Mamoru Hashimoto, Nobutsugu Hirono, Toru Imamura, Satoshi Tanimukai, and Larry Cahill. (2000). "Impact of Emotion on Memory: Controlled Study of the Influence of Emotionally Charged Material on Declarative Memory in Alzheimer's Disease." *British Journal of Psychiatry*, *177*, 343–347.

Kelly, K.J., and R.F. Hoel. (1991). "The Impact of Size, Color, and Copy Quantity on Yellow Pages Advertising Effectiveness." *Journal of Small Business Management*, *29*(4).

King, Wesley, Marie Dent, and Edward Miles. (1991). "The Persuasive Effect of Graphics in Computer-Mediated Communication." *Computers in Human Behavior*, *7*.

Knobloch, Silvia, Matthias Hastall, Dolf Zillmann, and Coy Callison. (2003). "Imagery Effects on the Selective Reading of Internet Newsmagazines." *Communications Research*, *30*(1), 3–29.

Lai, Shu-Ling. (2000a). "Increasing Associative Learning of Abstract Concepts Through Audiovisual Redundancy." *Journal of Educational Computing Research*, *23*(3), 275–289.

Lai, Shu-Ling. (2000b). "Influence of Audio-Visual Presentations on Learning Abstract Concepts." *International Journal of Instructional Media*, *27*(2), 199–206.

LeFevre, J.A., and P. Dixon. (1986). "Do Written Instructions Need Examples?" *Cognition and Instruction*, 3, 1–30.

Lewandowsky, Stephan, and Ian Spence. (1989). "Discriminating Strata in Scatterplots," *Journal of the American Statistical Association*, 84(407), 682–688.

Lohse, Gerald L. (1997). "Consumer Eye Movement Patterns on Yellow Pages Advertising." *Journal of Advertising*, 26(1), 61.

Lowry, Roy B. (1999). "Electronic Presentation of Lectures: Effect on Student Performance." *University Chemistry Education*, 3(1).

Lund, O. (1999). "Knowledge Construction in Typography: The Case of Legibility Research and the Legibility of Sans Serif Typefaces." Thesis submitted for the degree of Doctor of Philosophy. Reading, UK: The University of Reading, Department of Typography and Graphic Communication.

Macdaid, Gerald P. (1997). *CAPT Data Bank*. Gainesville, FL: Center for Applications of Psychological Type, Inc.

Mager, Robert F. (1962). *Preparing Instructional Objectives*. Palo Alto, CA: Fearon.

Mahoney, Michael J., and Bobby G. DeMonbreun. (1977). "Psychology of the Scientist: An Analysis of Problem-Solving Bias." *Cognitive Therapy and Research*, 1(3), 229–238.

Mallon, Bride, and Brian Webb. (2000). "Structure, Causality, Visibility and Interaction: Propositions for Evaluating Engagement in Narrative Multimedia." *International Journal of Human-Computer Studies*, 53, 269–287.

Mantei, Erwin J. (2000). "Using Internet Class Notes and PowerPoint in the Physical Geology Lecture." *Journal of College Science Teaching*, 29(5), 301.

Mayer, Richard E. (2001). *Multi-Media Learning*. Cambridge, UK: Cambridge University Press.

Mayer, Richard E., A. Mathias, and K. Wetzell. (2002). "Fostering Understanding of Multimedia Messages Through Pre-Training: Evidence for a Two-Stage Theory of Mental Model Construction." *Journal of Experimental Psychology: Applied*, 95(4), 833–846.

Mazis, M. (1975). "Antipollution Measures and Psychological Reactance Theory: A Field Experiment." *Journal of Personality and Social Psychology*, 31, 654–660.

McCroskey, James C. (1969). "A Summary of Experimental Research on the Effects of Evidence in Persuasive Communication." *The Quarterly Journal of Speech*, 55, 169–176.

McCroskey, James C., and Walter H. Combs. (1969). "The Effects of the Use of Analogy on Attitude Change and Source Credibility." *Journal of Communication*, 19(4), 333.

McCroskey, James C., and R. Samuel Mehrley. (1969). "The Effects of Disorganization and Nonfluency on Attitude Change and Source Credibility." *Speech Monographs*, 36, 13–21.

McFarland, R.G., G.N. Challagalla, and T.A. Shervani. (2006). "Influence Tactics for Effective Adaptive Selling." *Journal of Marketing*, 70, 103–117.

McLellan, Hilary. (2006, Spring). "Corporate Storytelling Perspectives." *The Journal for Quality and Participation*.

McQuarrie, Edward F., and David Glen Mick. (2003). "Visual and Verbal Rhetorical Figures Under Directed Processing Versus Incidental Exposure to Advertising." *Journal of Consumer Research*, 29(4), 579.

Mehrabian, A. (1981). *Silent Messages: Implicit Communication of Emotions and Attitudes*. Belmont, CA: Wadsworth.

Mehrabian, Albert. (2007). "Silent Messages—A Wealth of Information About Non-Verbal Communication (Body Language)." Personal website. www.kaaj.com/psych/smorder.html.

Meyvis, Tom, and Chris Janiszewski. (2002). "Consumers' Beliefs About Product Benefits: The Effect of Obviously Irrelevant Product Information." *Journal of Consumer Research, 28*(4), 618.

Miller, George A. (1956). "The Magical Number Seven, Plus or Minus Two: Some Limits on Our Capacity for Processing Information." *Psychological Review, 63,* 8109.

Mines, Richard O. (2001). "Do PowerPoint Presentations Really Work?," In *Proceedings of the 2001 ASEE Annual Conference and Exposition: Peppers, Papers, Pueblos, and Professors.* Albuquerque, New Mexico.

Minto, Barbara. (1996). *The Minto Pyramid Principle: Logic in Writing, Thinking, and Problem Solving.* London: Minto International.

Moreno, Roxana. (2006). "Learning in High-Tech and Multimedia Environments." *Current Directions in Psychological Science, 15*(2), 63–67.

Morgan, Susan E., and Tom Reichert. (1999). "The Message Is in the Metaphor: Assessing the Comprehension of Metaphors in Advertisements." *Journal of Advertising, 28*(4), 1.

Mousavi, Seyed Yaghoub, Renae Low, and John Sweller. (1995). "Reducing Cognitive Load by Mixing Auditory and Visual Presentation Modes." *Journal of Educational Psychology, 87*(2), 319–334.

Myers & Briggs Foundation. (2006). "How Frequent Is My Type." Gainesville, FL: Myers & Briggs Foundation. www.myersbriggs.org/my-mbti-personality-type/my-mbti-results/how-frequent-is-my-type.asp.

Myers, Isabel Briggs, Mary H. McCaulley, Naomi L. Quenk, and Allen L. Hammer. (1998). *MBTI Manual: A Guide to the Development and Use of the Myers-Briggs Type Indicator* (3rd. ed.). Palo Alto, CA: Consulting Psychologists Press.

Myers-Levy, Joan, and Sandra A. Peracchio. (1995). "Understanding the Effects of Color: How the Correspondence between Available and Required Resources Affects Attitudes." *Journal of Consumer Research, 22*(2), 121.

Nadolski, Rob J., Paul A. Kirschner, and Jeroen J.G. van Merrienboer. (2005). "Optimizing the Number of Steps in Learning Tasks for Complex Skills." *British Journal of Educational Psychology, 75,* 223-37.

Narayanan, N., and M. Hegarty. (2002). "Multimedia Design for Communication of Dynamic Information." *International Journal of Human-Computer Studies, 57,* 279–315.

Norman, Don. (2004). "In Defense of PowerPoint." www.jnd.org/dn.mss/in_defense_of_p.html.

Norvig, Peter. (2003). "PowerPoint: Shot with Its Own Bullets." *The Lancet, 362*(9381), 343–344.

O'Keefe, Daniel J. (2000). "Guilt and Social Influence." *Communication Yearbook, 23,* 67–101.

Ofir, Chezy, and Itamar Simonson. (2001). "In Search of Negative Customer Feedback: The Effect of Expecting to Evaluate on Satisfaction Evaluations." *Journal of Marketing Research, 38*(2), 170–182.

Ogilvy, David. (1983). *Ogilvy on Advertising.* New York: Random House.

Outing, Steve, and Laura Ruel. (2004). "The Best of Eyetrack III: What We Saw When We Looked Through Their Eyes." St. Petersburg, FL: Poynter Institute. http://poynterextra.org/eyetrack2004/main.htm.

Pearson, M.J., J. Folske, D. Paulson, and C. Burggraf. (1994). "The Relationship Between Student Perceptions of the Multimedia Classroom and Student Learning Styles." Presented at the Annual Meeting of the Eastern Communication Association, Washington, D.C.

Pechmann, Cornelia. (1992). "Predicting When Two-Sided Ads Will Be More Effective Than One-Sided Ads: The Role of Correlational and Correspondent Inferences." *Journal of Marketing Research*, 29(4), 441.

Pennington, Nancy, and Reid Hastie. (1991). "A Cognitive Review of Juror Decision Making: The Story Model." *Cardozo Law Review*, 13, 5001–5039.

Pennington, Nancy, and Reid Hastie. (1992). "Explaining the Evidence: Tests of the Story Model for Juror Decision Making." *Journal of Personality and Social Psychology*, 62(2), 189–206.

Petty, Richard E., and John T. Cacioppo. (1984). "The Effects of Involvement on Response to Argument Quantity and Quality: Central and Peripheral Routes to Persuasion." *Journal of Personality and Social Psychology*, 46(1), 69–81.

Petty, Richard E., John T. Cacioppo, and David Schumann. (1983). "Central and Peripheral Routes to Advertising Effectiveness: The Moderating Role of Involvement." *Journal of Consumer Research*, 10(2), 135–146.

Pittenger, D.J. (2005). "Cautionary Comments Regarding the Myers-Briggs Type Indicator." *Consulting Psychology Journal: Practice and Research*, 57(3), 210–221.

Rackham, Neil. (1988). *SPIN Selling*. New York: McGraw-Hill.

Ranking, E.L. and D.J. Hoaas. (2001). "The Use of PowerPoint and Student Performance." *Atlantic Economic Journal*, 29, 113.

Reinard, John C. (1988). "The Empirical Study of the Persuasive Effects of Evidence: The Status After Fifty Years of Research." *Human Communication Research*, 15, 3–59.

Reinard, John C. (1998). "The Persuasive Effects of Testimonial Assertion Evidence." In M. Allen and R.W. Preiss (Eds.), *Persuasion: Advances Through Meta-Analysis*. Hampton, NJ: Cresskill.

Ricer, Rick E., Andrew T. Filak, and James Short. (2005). "Does a High Tech (Computerized, Animated, PowerPoint) Presentation Increase Retention of Material Compared to a Low Tech (Black on Clear Overheads) Presentation?" *Teaching and Learning in Medicine*, 17(2), 107–111.

Ricks, Thomas E. (2006). *Fiasco: The American Military Adventure in Iraq*. New York: Penguin Press.

Robinson, Grady Jim. (2000). *Did I Ever Tell You About the Time . . .: How to Develop and Deliver a Speech Using Stories That Get Your Message Across*. New York: McGraw-Hill.

Rossiter, John R., and Larry Percy. (1980). "Attitude Change Through Visual Imagery in Advertising." *Journal of Advertising*, 9(2), 10.

Rossiter, John R., and Larry Percy. (1997). *Advertising and Promotion Management*. New York: McGraw-Hill.

"The Science of Stories." (1998). *Harvard Business Review*, 76(3), 42.

Shah, Priti, Richard E. Mayer, and Mary Hegarty. (1999). "Graphs as Aids to Knowledge Construction: Signaling Techniques for Guiding the Process of Graph Comprehension." *Journal of Educational Psychology*, 9(14), 690–702.

Shaw, Gordon, Robert Brown, and Philip Bromiley. (1998). "Strategic Stories: How 3M Is Rewriting Business Planning." *Harvard Business Review, 76*(3), 41–50.

Silverman, Lori. (2003). *Stories Trainers Tell: 55 Ready-to-Use Stories to Make Training Stick.* San Francisco, CA: Pfeiffer.

Silverman, Lori. (2006). *Wake Me Up When the Data Is Over.* Hoboken, NJ: John Wiley & Sons.

Simmons, John. (2006). "Guinness and the Role of Strategic Storytelling." *Journal of Strategic Marketing, 14*(1), 11.

Simpson, Claude L., Lissa Pollacia, Jimmy Speers, T. Hillman Willis, and Rick Tarver. (2003). "An Analysis of Certain Factors Related to the Use of PowerPoint." *Communications of the International Information Management Association, 3*(1), 73–83.

Slusher, Morgan P., and Craig A. Anderson. (1996). "Using Causal Persuasive Arguments to Change Beliefs and Teach New Information: The Mediating Role of Explanation Availability and Evaluation Bias in the Acceptance of Knowledge." *Journal of Educational Psychology, 88*(1), 110.

Slykhuis, David. (2005). "Eye-Tracking Students' Attention to PowerPoint Photographs in a Science Education Setting." *Journal of Science Education & Technology, 14*(5/6), 509–520.

Smart, Graham. (1999). "Storytelling in a Central Bank: The Role of Narrative in the Creation and Use of Specialized Economic Knowledge." *Journal of Business and Technical Communication, 13*(3), 249.

Smith, Faye L., and Joann Keyton. (2001). "Organizational Storytelling." *Management Communication Quarterly, 15*(2), 149.

Snyder, Tom. (2007). *Escaping the Price-Driven Sale.* Sterling, VA: Huthwaite.

So, Stella, and Malcolm Smith. (2003). "The Impact of Presentation Format and Individual Differences on the Communication of Information for Management Decision Making." *Managerial Auditing Journal, 18*(1/2), 59.

Soley, Lawrence C. (1986). "Copy Length and Industrial Advertising Readership." *Industrial Marketing Management, 15*(3), 245.

Sopory, Pradeep, and James Price Dillard. (2002). "The Persuasive Effects of Metaphor: A Meta-Analysis." *Human Communication Research, 28*(3), 382–419.

Spence, Ian, and Stephan Lewandowsky. (1991). "Displaying Proportions and Percentages." *Applied Cognitive Psychology, 5,* 61–77.

Stanton, John L., and Burke Jeffrey. (1998). "Comparative Effectiveness of Executional Elements in TV Advertising: 15- Versus 30-Second Commercials." *Journal of Advertising Research, 38*(6), 7.

Stiff, James B. (1986). "Cognitive Processing of Persuasive message Cues: A Meta-Analytic Review of the Effects of Supporting Information on Attitudes." *Communications Monographs, 53,* 75–89.

Susskind, Joshua E. (2005). "PowerPoint's Power in the Classroom: Enhancing Students' Self-Efficacy and Attitudes." *Computers & Education, 45,* 203–215.

Sutton, R.I., and A. Hargadon. (1996). "Brainstorming Groups in Context: Effectiveness in a Product Design Firm." *Administrative Science Quarterly, 41*(4).

Szabo, Attila, and Nigel Hastings. (2000). "Using IT in the Undergraduate Classroom: Should We Replace the Blackboard with PowerPoint?" *Computers & Education, 35*(3), 175–187.

Tufte, Edward R. (2001). *The Visual Display of Quantitative Information.* Cheshire, CT: Graphics Press.

Tufte, Edward R. (2003a). "PowerPoint Is Evil." *Wired, 11.*

Tufte, Edward R. (2003b). *The Cognitive Style of PowerPoint.* Cheshire, CT: Graphics Press.

Tufte, Edward R. (2006). *Beautiful Evidence.* Cheshire, CT: Graphics Press.

Turner, Mark. (1996). *The Literary Mind.* New York: Oxford University Press.

Tversky, Barbara, Julie Bauer Morrison, and Mireille Betrancourt. (2002). "Animation: Can It Facilitate?" *International Journal of Human-Computer Studies, 57,* 247–262.

Vogel, Doug. (1986). "An Experimental Investigation of the Persuasive Impact of Computer-Generated Presentation Graphics." Dissertation submitted to the graduate school of the University of Minnesota.

Vogel, Doug, and Joline Morrison. (1998). "The Impacts of Presentation Visuals on Persuasion." *Information & Management, 33*(3), 125–135.

Voswinckel, Till. (2005). "Presentation Visualisation: Towards an Imagery-Based Approach of Computer-Generated Presentation Visuals." Dissertation submitted to the Fachhochschule at Furtwangen Hochschule fur Technik Und Wirtschaft, Germany.

Walker, Ian, and Charles Hulme. (1999). "Concrete Words Are Easier to Recall Than Abstract Words: Evidence for a Semantic Contribution to Short-Term Serial Recall." *Journal of Experimental Psychology, 25*(5), 1256–1271.

Weissmuller, Jr., Johnny, and William Reed. (2002). *Tarzan, My Father.* Toronto, Ontario: ECW Press.

Wheildon, Colin. (2005). *Type and Layout.* Hastings, Victoria, Australia: The Worsley Press.

Williams, Kipling D., Martin J. Bourgeois, and Robert T. Croyle. (1993). "The Effects of Stealing Thunder in Criminal and Civil Trials." *Law and Human behavior, 17*(6), 597–609.

Witte, Kim, and Mike Allen. (2000). "A Meta-Analysis of Fear Appeals: Implications for Effective Public Health Campaigns." *Health Education & Behavior, 27*(5), 591–615.

Wolf, S., and D.A. Montgomery. (1977). "Effects of Inadmissible Evidence and Level of Judicial Admonishment to Disregard on the Judgments of Mock Jurors." *Journal of Applied Social Psychology, 7,* 205–219.

Woodside, A.G., T.M. Beretich, and M.A. Lauricella. (1993). "A Meta-Analysis of Effect Sizes Based on Direct Marketing Campaigns." *Journal of Direct Marketing, 7*(2), 19.

Zelazny, Gene. (2001). *Say It with Charts* (4th. ed.). New York: McGraw-Hill.

Zillman, Dolf, Silvia Knobloch, and Hong-ski Yu. (2001). "Effects of Photographs on the Selective Reading of News Reports." *Media Psychology, 3*(4), 301–324.

Index

About the Author

Andrew V. Abela, Ph.D., is an associate professor of marketing at the Catholic University of America in Washington, D.C. His research focus is on the integrity of the marketing process, including effective internal communication and presentation of data, marketing ethics, and measuring marketing returns.

His work has been published in the *Journal of Marketing, Journal of the Academy of Marketing Science, Marketing Management, Journal of Marketing Theory and Practice, European Journal of Marketing, Journal of Brand Management, Journal of Strategic Marketing, Journal of Business Ethics, Business and Society Review,* and the *McKinsey Quarterly.* He was the recipient of the inaugural 2006 Provost's Award for Teaching Excellence at Catholic University.

He provides consulting and training services to major corporations on effective internal communication of complex information using his proprietary Extreme Presentation™ method. Clients include Microsoft, ExxonMobil, Dell, eBay, Kimberly-Clark, Abbott Laboratories, Infinitive Corporation, Motorola, W.W. Grainger, Xerox, and the United States Census Bureau.

Before moving into academia, Dr. Abela was the founding managing director of the Marketing Leadership Council, a for-profit research and executive education think tank of the Corporate Executive Board, serving chief marketing officers at hundreds of leading global firms. He also helped to start up a sister organization, the Market Research Executive Board.

Prior to this he was a management consultant with McKinsey & Co., where he worked with clients on marketing strategy and implementation issues in the United States, Canada, Eastern and Western Europe, and South America, and was actively involved in coaching and training new consultants in problem-solving and presentation skills. He was also a co-founder of McKinsey's Digital Marketing practice. He began his career with Procter & Gamble, where he was brand manager for Clearasil in Canada.

He has an MBA from the Institute for Management Development (IMD) in Lausanne, Switzerland, and a Ph.D. in marketing and ethics from the Darden Business School at the University of Virginia.

Dr. Abela is originally from the island of Malta, and he and his wife Kathleen live with their six children in Great Falls, Virginia.

Pfeiffer Publications Guide

This guide is designed to familiarize you with the various types of Pfeiffer publications. The formats section describes the various types of products that we publish; the methodologies section describes the many different ways that content might be provided within a product. We also provide a list of the topic areas in which we publish.

FORMATS

In addition to its extensive book-publishing program, Pfeiffer offers content in an array of formats, from fieldbooks for the practitioner to complete, ready-to-use training packages that support group learning.

FIELDBOOK Designed to provide information and guidance to practitioners in the midst of action. Most fieldbooks are companions to another, sometimes earlier, work, from which its ideas are derived; the fieldbook makes practical what was theoretical in the original text. Fieldbooks can certainly be read from cover to cover. More likely, though, you'll find yourself bouncing around following a particular theme, or dipping in as the mood, and the situation, dictate.

HANDBOOK A contributed volume of work on a single topic, comprising an eclectic mix of ideas, case studies, and best practices sourced by practitioners and experts in the field.

An editor or team of editors usually is appointed to seek out contributors and to evaluate content for relevance to the topic. Think of a handbook not as a ready-to-eat meal, but as a cookbook of ingredients that enables you to create the most fitting experience for the occasion.

RESOURCE Materials designed to support group learning. They come in many forms: a complete, ready-to-use exercise (such as a game); a comprehensive resource on one topic (such as conflict management) containing a variety of methods and approaches; or a collection of like-minded activities (such as icebreakers) on multiple subjects and situations.

TRAINING PACKAGE An entire, ready-to-use learning program that focuses on a particular topic or skill. All packages comprise a guide for the facilitator/trainer and a workbook for the participants. Some packages are supported with additional media—such as video—or learning aids, instruments, or other devices to help participants understand concepts or practice and develop skills.

- *Facilitator/trainer's guide* Contains an introduction to the program, advice on how to organize and facilitate the learning event, and step-by-step instructor notes. The guide also contains copies of presentation materials—handouts, presentations, and overhead designs, for example—used in the program.

- *Participant's workbook* Contains exercises and reading materials that support the learning goal and serves as a valuable reference and support guide for participants in the weeks and months that follow the learning event. Typically, each participant will require his or her own workbook.

ELECTRONIC CD-ROMs and web-based products transform static Pfeiffer content into dynamic, interactive experiences. Designed to take advantage of the searchability, automation, and ease-of-use that technology provides, our e-products bring convenience and immediate accessibility to your workspace.

METHODOLOGIES

CASE STUDY A presentation, in narrative form, of an actual event that has occurred inside an organization. Case studies are not prescriptive, nor are they used to prove a point; they are designed to develop critical analysis and decision-making skills. A case study has a specific time frame, specifies a sequence of events, is narrative in structure, and contains a plot structure—an issue (what should be/have been done?). Use case studies when the goal is to enable participants to apply previously learned theories to the circumstances in the case, decide what is pertinent, identify the real issues, decide what should have been done, and develop a plan of action.

ENERGIZER A short activity that develops readiness for the next session or learning event. Energizers are most commonly used after a break or lunch to stimulate or refocus the group. Many involve some form of physical activity, so they are a useful way to counter post-lunch lethargy. Other uses include transitioning from one topic to another, where "mental" distancing is important.

EXPERIENTIAL LEARNING ACTIVITY (ELA) A facilitator-led intervention that moves participants through the learning cycle from experience to application (also known as a Structured Experience). ELAs are carefully thought-out designs in which there is a definite learning purpose and intended outcome. Each step—everything that participants do during the activity—facilitates the accomplishment of the stated goal. Each ELA includes complete instructions for facilitating the intervention and a clear statement of goals, suggested group size and timing, materials required, an explanation of the process, and, where appropriate, possible variations to the activity. (For more detail on Experiential Learning Activities, see the Introduction to the *Reference Guide to Handbooks and Annuals*, 1999 edition, Pfeiffer, San Francisco.)

GAME A group activity that has the purpose of fostering team spirit and togetherness in addition to the achievement of a pre-stated goal. Usually contrived—undertaking a desert expedition, for example—this type of learning method offers an engaging means for participants to demonstrate and practice business and interpersonal skills. Games are effective for team building and personal development mainly because the goal is subordinate to the process—the means through which participants reach decisions, collaborate, communicate, and generate trust and understanding. Games often engage teams in "friendly" competition.

ICEBREAKER A (usually) short activity designed to help participants overcome initial anxiety in a training session and/or to acquaint the participants with one another. An icebreaker can be a fun activity or can be tied to specific topics or training goals. While a useful tool in itself, the icebreaker comes into its own in situations where tension or resistance exists within a group.

INSTRUMENT A device used to assess, appraise, evaluate, describe, classify, and summarize various aspects of human behavior. The term used to describe an instrument depends primarily on its format and purpose. These terms include survey, questionnaire, inventory, diagnostic, survey, and poll. Some uses of instruments include providing instrumental feedback to group members, studying here-and-now processes or functioning within a group, manipulating group composition, and evaluating outcomes of training and other interventions.

Instruments are popular in the training and HR field because, in general, more growth can occur if an individual is provided with a method for focusing specifically on his or her own behavior. Instruments also are used to obtain information that will serve as a basis for change and to assist in workforce planning efforts.

Paper-and-pencil tests still dominate the instrument landscape with a typical package comprising a facilitator's guide, which offers advice on administering the instrument and interpreting the collected data, and an initial set of instruments. Additional instruments are available separately. Pfeiffer, though, is investing heavily in e-instruments. Electronic instrumentation provides effortless distribution and, for larger groups particularly, offers advantages over paper-and-pencil tests in the time it takes to analyze data and provide feedback.

LECTURETTE A short talk that provides an explanation of a principle, model, or process that is pertinent to the participants' current learning needs. A lecturette is intended to establish a common language bond between the trainer and the participants by providing a mutual frame of reference. Use a lecturette as an introduction to a group activity or event, as an interjection during an event, or as a handout.

MODEL A graphic depiction of a system or process and the relationship among its elements. Models provide a frame of reference and something more tangible, and more easily remembered, than a verbal explanation. They also give participants something to "go on," enabling them to track their own progress as they experience the dynamics, processes, and relationships being depicted in the model.

ROLE PLAY A technique in which people assume a role in a situation/scenario: a customer service rep in an angry-customer exchange, for example. The way in which the role is approached is then discussed and feedback is offered. The role play is often repeated using a different approach and/or incorporating changes made based on feedback received. In other words, role playing is a spontaneous interaction involving realistic behavior under artificial (and safe) conditions.

SIMULATION A methodology for understanding the interrelationships among components of a system or process. Simulations differ from games in that they test or use a model that depicts or mirrors some aspect of reality in form, if not necessarily in content. Learning occurs by studying the effects of change on one or more factors of the model. Simulations are commonly used to test hypotheses about what happens in a system—often referred to as "what if?" analysis—or to examine best-case/worst-case scenarios.

THEORY A presentation of an idea from a conjectural perspective. Theories are useful because they encourage us to examine behavior and phenomena through a different lens.

TOPICS

The twin goals of providing effective and practical solutions for workforce training and organization development and meeting the educational needs of training and human resource professionals shape Pfeiffer's publishing program. Core topics include the following:

Leadership & Management

Communication & Presentation

Coaching & Mentoring

Training & Development

E-Learning

Teams & Collaboration

OD & Strategic Planning

Human Resources

Consulting

What will you find on pfeiffer.com?

• The best in workplace performance solutions for training and HR professionals

• Downloadable training tools, exercises, and content

• Web-exclusive offers

• Training tips, articles, and news

• Seamless on-line ordering

• Author guidelines, information on becoming a Pfeiffer Affiliate, and much more

Discover more at www.pfeiffer.com